MILLIONAIRES' ROW: THE LEGACY

Kathy Keller and A. J. Billman

Copyright © 2021 by **Kathy Keller**

All rights reserved. No part of this publication may be reproduced, distributed or transmitted in any form or by any means, without prior written permission.

Kathy Keller
655 Tree Side Lane
Ponte Vedra, Florida 32081
www.KathyKeller.com

Publisher's Note: This is a work of fiction. Names, characters, places, and incidents are a product of the author's imagination. Locales and public names are sometimes used for atmospheric purposes. Any resemblance to actual people, living or dead, or to businesses, companies, events, institutions, or locales is completely coincidental.

Millionaires' Row: The Legacy – 1st ed.
ISBN 978-1-7370503-3-9

See how the Douglas story begins in book one:

MILLIONAIRES' ROW

"Sometimes life brings you full circle to a place you have been before just to show you how much you have grown."

—UNATTRIBUTED

CONTENTS

The Homecoming 1
Hiding in Plain Sight 8
Consequences 16
A Secret Unburied 24
Shattered 33
Estrangement 36
An Unwelcome Rival 39
The Challenge Begins 45
A Seed Is Planted 50
A New Age, A New Vision 54
A Game of Strategy 67
Face of a Movement 72
An Ultimatum 81
Carry On 83
Ambivalence 87
An Unlikely Alliance 91
Another Reality 100
A Wedding 106
The 14th Amendment 110
Sunday Brunch 114
Waiting To Be Noticed 118
Reckoning with the Past 129
Moving Ahead 141
Irons in the Fire 146
In a New Light 151
Chess vs. Checkers 164

A New Suffragette	174
The Streetcar War	178
Up Against a Wall	181
A Win or a Loss?	185
Going Home	189
The Tour	198
Challenging the Status Quo	210
Shared Goals	214
A New Path Forward	218
The End Game	235
A Matter of Diplomacy	238
Wall of Silence	246
The Visit	252
Sucker-Punched	255
A New Chapter	258
The Campaign	264
A New Generation	271
Financial Panic	281
Blindsided	286
Circling the Wagons	296
Saving a Legacy	312
A New Attorney in Town	319
The Enemy We Can't See	328
The End of a Chapter	333
Lost	335
Driving Miss Lizzie	338
Just a Matter of Business	344
A Clean Slate	348
The Tapestry of Life	352
More Than Friendship	358

Full Circle 363
Afterword 366

CHAPTER ONE

The Homecoming

Spring 1902

Twelve-year-old Morgan Douglas bounded down the stairs to stand beside his father. Ian Douglas cocked a brow at his son's appearance. The boy's tie was askew and his sandy blond hair had not been combed.

Anticipating his father's comments, Morgan gave him a sheepish but unapologetic smile. "She's just gonna redo everything anyway," he said. "C'mon, Mama," he yelled. "We'll be late to the station. Mary Katherine will think we're not coming."

Upstairs in her bedroom, Eleanor Douglas sighed. What was she to do with that boy? Any attempt to instill manners in her son seemed to roll off his back like water from a duck. She gave her toilette a last critical look in the floor-length mirror and nodded with satisfaction, proud that at the age of 42, her petite form was still slender and firm—her waist a whittled 23 inches.

The maid affixed a hat atop her mistress' upswept blonde hair with a decorative hatpin, then handed her soft leather gloves. With a final straightening of her fitted waist jacket, Eleanor pulled on her gloves and strolled confidently out of the room.

When she appeared at the top of the stairs, both father and son looked up in admiration as she regally descended the wide, sweeping staircase—the queen of Rossburg society. Upon reaching the bottom of the stairs, she regarded her son with a disapproving lift of her brow and proceeded to straighten his tie and comb through his hair with her fingers.

Morgan looked up at his father. "See, I told you," he murmured under his breath.

This was the routine before departing anywhere, whether Morgan presented a disheveled appearance or not. Thus, with the practicality of a young boy, Morgan had quickly come to the conclusion that he didn't need to expend the extra energy himself.

Ian was hard pressed to hold back a chuckle. When Eleanor next turned her attention to him, straightening his tie, he caught the smirk on his son's face and sent the boy a quelling glare.

"You look beautiful, my dear," said Ian to his wife.

Eleanor smiled. The look in her husband's silver-blue eyes brought a warm glow to her cheeks. "You look quite dashing yourself, sir."

At 42, her husband carried his years well, she thought. They had not bowed his tall, broad-shouldered frame, thickened his waist or, beyond a few character lines, aged his handsome face. The touch of gray at the edges of his light brown hair, she had decided, only served to make him look more distinguished.

"Oh, for gosh sakes," snorted Morgan impatiently, "we're never gonna get to the station if we don't hurry. Do you think Mary Katherine will look the same, Mama? She has been gone a year on the Grand Tour. Maybe we won't recognize her."

"I'm sure we will, dear." Eleanor turned to Ian. "Have the invitations gone out for the homecoming ball?"

"Yes, Mother. Everything is taken care of."

Eleanor passed a last scrutinizing eye over her men and smiled with pride. "No woman could have two more handsome escorts than I," she said, linking arms with them.

When they stepped through the door onto the veranda, Morgan spied the shiny motorcar parked in the driveway. He pulled away from his mother and raced toward it. "Papa, can I steer the motorcar? Please, Papa. You said I could."

"The word is *may* I," interjected Eleanor. "And no, you may not. You are still a child. Besides, that contraption seats only two. We are taking the carriage," she said, her decision final. "You shouldn't put such notions in his head, Father. It will be a long time before I allow Morgan to drive that thing."

Morgan groaned loud and long and turned to appeal to his father. "Papa…"

"Listen to your mother, son."

"I am not a child," grumbled Morgan, slowly following his parents to the horse-drawn carriage that awaited them.

They made good time across town, and, in spite of Morgan's fears, they arrived at the train station with time to spare. As they waited on the platform for the train to come in, Ian experienced déjà vu.

It was 23 years ago that he had stood on this same platform, eagerly and nervously awaiting Eleanor's arrival home from her Grand Tour. He was her father's sawmill foreman then and had been sent to meet her train. He could still see the look of disappointment on her face when she saw that it was he and not her father who had come to welcome her home.

Ian moved closer to her and took her hand; she looked up and smiled at him. It had not been an easy journey for them. There had been trials and tribulations along the way—most of them of their own making—but he was so glad that they had persevered.

The shrill whistle roused Ian from his musings as the train came into view and chugged to a stop at the platform. Morgan fidgeted, and Ian and Eleanor eagerly searched for their daughter among the passengers that were disembarking.

"There she is," shouted Morgan, waving to his sister as she stepped down from the middle car.

A fashionably dressed, young woman with saucy blonde curls beneath a broad-brim hat waved back excitedly. Despite Eleanor's assurance to Morgan that his sister would look the same, a father's discerning eye saw a striking difference. Ian's chest swelled with pride. His little princess was 20 years old and all grown up, and she was as beautiful as her mother. The cygnet that had left a year ago had returned a swan.

Mary Katherine pointed out her trunks that had been set outside the baggage car to the porter, then hurried over to her family.

"Mama, Papa," she cried, enthusiastically hugging them, "I have missed you. And you, too, Morgie," she added, tousling her little brother's hair.

Morgan took great affront. "I'm taller than you. And don't call me 'Morgie' anymore. I'm not a child."

"Goodness, you have sprouted up, haven't you," said Mary Katherine, giving him a big hug.

Morgan made a face and self-consciously disengaged himself from his sister's arms. "See, Mama, even Mary Katherine thinks I've grown up."

"Yes, dear," replied Eleanor. "Mary Katherine, are skirts that short in Europe?" she asked, noting that the hem of her daughter's skirt didn't brush the ground.

"Oh, Mama, I have so much to tell you. You should see what they are wearing—or not wearing—in Paris," said Mary Katherine.

As she whispered in her mother's ear, Eleanor's eyes widened in disbelief. "Oh, dear," she murmured. She prided herself on being a leader of fashion in Rossburg, but she wasn't sure that she was ready to go without a corset.

"Times are changing, Mama," said Mary Katherine, her blue eyes twinkling with excitement. "Emily says that one day women will have the right to vote."

"Who is Emily?" asked Eleanor.

"Emily Stoddert. I met her in England on the Grand Tour. Her family lives in New York City. But imagine this, Emily is to have her own brownstone and has invited me to visit."

Eleanor was aghast. "Mary Katherine, I don't believe that it is proper for a young woman to live alone."

Mary Katherine laughed. "Oh, Mama, you are so conventional." She linked arms with her parents as they moved toward the carriage. "And Mama, Papa, I wish to be called Mary Kate. I am a woman of modern conventions now, and Mary Katherine sounds so old-fashioned."

Eleanor's brow rose higher, and she looked at her husband not quite sure what to make of this young woman who claimed to be their daughter.

Ian met her eye with amusement. "Times are changin', Mother."

"Well, let us hope not too much," replied Eleanor uneasily. While she tried to be open to new ideas, she was still the product of a more conservative generation.

* * * * *

Maven O'Brien Stanton stood at the window staring out at the street, tapping the envelope against her fingertips.

"There you are," said Parker Stanton, entering the room. "Why so pensive?"

Maven turned to her husband. "This came in the morning mail. 'Tis an invitation to a homecoming ball for Mary Katherine."

Parker went to her and put his arms around her. "I know how difficult these events are for you and Eleanor. If I weren't Ian's partner and friend, we could beg off. But as it is, I don't see any way around this without inviting questions."

Maven sighed and rested her head against his shoulder. "I know."

"Why don't you and Eleanor let the secret come out? It is hurting both of you."

Maven shook her head. "No...not after all these years. This is best for everyone."

"You're a proud and stubborn woman, my dear. That is why I love you so much." Parker lowered his head and kissed her tenderly.

"Aren't you a little old for that?" teased a young man from the doorway.

Parker reluctantly broke away and laughed. "Not when you have the right woman. Of course, it took me some time to convince your mother that I was the right man. And may I say that we take great umbrage at your use of the word 'old.' Your mother is just 40 years old and the same beautiful woman I married ten years ago. She doesn't have a gray hair on her head."

"That's because you have them all," quipped Patrick. "According to the actuaries, the life span for your generation is—"

"Have a care, young man. Twenty years can pass in the blink of an eye. Your son will be holding this same conversation with you before you know it."

"Never-you-mind, dear," said Maven to her husband, "your silver hair gives you an air of authority. Now off with ye."

She gave him a playful push and turned her attention to her tall, handsome son. Nearly 21 years old, Patrick O'Brien resembled her from his auburn hair to his personality. But the eyes and steady gaze that looked back at her were very much his father's, she thought with a tug on her heart. "I am so pleased to have you home from Philadelphia, Patrick, if only for a short time," she said.

Patrick smiled. "I dare say that you will have me underfoot more than you may want."

Maven's face lit up. "Ye be comin' back to Rossburg—to stay?"

Patrick nodded. "Parker has offered me a partnership in his firm. And I found that I have missed you and this town more than I realized. I have to return to Philadelphia for a few weeks to tie up some loose ends."

"I would have told you earlier," said Parker, "but Patrick wanted to surprise you. He's accompanying me to the office today."

"I'll wait outside for you, Parker. Mother, don't keep me waiting now," said Patrick with a playful wink.

Maven's cheeks turned red. "Patrick O'Brien! Such things as ye be thinkin'! I not be knowin' where ye've left your manners," she shouted after him. As Parker chuckled with amusement, she rounded on her husband in annoyance. "And ye not be helpin'."

"Me thinks ye doth protest too much."

Maven gave a huff of exasperation. "Oh, off with ye now before Patrick gets more notions in his head."

"Nothing wrong with a boy knowing that his mother is loved," said Parker. He bent down and kissed her on the cheek. "Patrick and I will be home early for dinner."

As he crossed the room to leave, Maven called out to him. "Parker…thank you."

"For what?"

"For embracin' and guidin' Patrick the way ye have, for helpin' him into law school and now bringin' him into your firm. After Tommy died, he was so lost until ye stepped in."

"Patrick was a good boy, and he is growing into a fine man. I suspect that his mother had a good deal to do with that." Parker hesitated. "Maven, think about what I said. Secrets come out sooner or later and never in a good way."

CHAPTER TWO

Hiding in Plain Sight

The Douglas mansion on Grandview Place was easily seen from miles around this night as lights shone from every room in the house. It was the only residence in Rossburg equipped with electricity, and this new power was a source of curiosity. The windows and doors in the ballroom were thrown open to the gentle May breeze, and the scent of spring flowers filled the room as music from a string quartet sounded in the background.

Eleanor was resplendent as she stood next to her husband to receive their guests. Her fitted gown of a copper color lame was covered with layers of sheer silk. The décolletage dipped fashionably low without crossing the bounds of propriety, and the bodice was sleeveless with straps fashioned from artificial flowers falling off her bare shoulders. The design may have been simplistic, but the gown was exquisite for the material chosen. Henri of New York had outdone himself for his favorite customer.

Ian had difficulty keeping his eyes off his wife. When there finally came a break in the receiving line, he leaned down and remarked in a low voice: "Ye be lookin' like an angel this night, Ellie, a vision to be sure."

Eleanor smiled up at him. His Scottish accent used to be a great source of annoyance to her—a reminder of his humbler origins when she didn't want to be reminded of them. But now, it was just another side of him that she had come to love. She self-consciously averted her eyes, then, a bright pink tinting her cheeks. His term of endearment was not lost on her. 'Ellie' was a name he reserved for their more intimate moments.

Ian was amused by her flustration. She had come a long way in their relationship. But even after all these years, she still had difficulty overcoming her shy reserve when it came to acts of intimacy. It had taken him years to realize that it had nothing to do with the way she felt about him but stemmed from over-instruction on proper bedroom etiquette for polite society. And he learned to respect her need for modesty.

"Ahem. Are we interrupting something?"

"Parker, as usual, your timin' is off," said Ian with a laugh.

Eleanor felt the heat of a blush fan across her face again and quickly moved to compose herself. "Mr. and Mrs. Stanton, welcome. I am happy that you could attend," she said, once again the consummate hostess.

"Thank you, Mrs. Douglas. It was nice of you to invite us," replied Maven. "You know my son Patrick."

Eleanor turned her eyes to the tall, young man. "It is nice to see you Patrick. I understand that you just graduated from law school at the University of Pennsylvania. I believe a welcome home is due you as well."

"Thank you, Mrs. Douglas."

"Will you be returning to Philadelphia to practice law?" she inquired.

"No, ma'am. I have accepted a partnership in my stepfather's law firm. I shall be making my home in Rossburg."

Eleanor's smile wavered, and she glanced at Maven. "I see…well, congratulations. I hope you will enjoy the evening."

"Thank you, Mrs. Douglas."

"Maven, 'tis nice to see ye this evenin'," Ian greeted her. He gave her a warm smile and took her hand. "Ye be lookin' well." Her silk-figured gown hung in graceful folds on her tall, slender frame, the white and gold colors presenting a striking contrast to her dark auburn hair and the earth tones in her complexion. Ian inclined his head toward Parker. "Life with this scoundrel must be agreein' with ye," he joked.

"That's what I keep telling her," Parker was quick to respond.

"This can't be Patrick," said Ian, reaching out to take the young man's hand in a firm handshake. "I would scarce recognize ye, except for your likeness to your mother. I hear that ye will be a partner in the Stanton Law Firm. Perhaps now I shall get some competent advice."

"Yes, sir—I mean no, sir," stammered Patrick. "That is I still have much to learn, sir, from Parker."

Ian chuckled. "Ye be learnin' from the best, son," he said on a more serious note.

With the initial awkwardness of the greeting behind her, Maven relaxed and allowed Parker to lead her onto the dance floor.

Patrick wandered off and was immediately drawn to a group of young people. At the center was a vivacious blonde expounding on the injustice of women not being allowed the rights of men. The girls nodded their heads in agreement, while the young men rolled their eyes in boredom and forbearance.

"They have the right to own property and businesses and to work in some jobs also held by men. What other rights would you have them enjoy?" inquired one young gentleman in the group.

"Why the right to vote, of course," replied the pretty blonde.

As the men broke into polite laughter, Patrick was moved to comment: "The minds of women do not grasp the complexities of affairs of state. If given the right to meddle in such things, they will most assuredly bring chaos to an ordered society."

The young woman wheeled about, her blue eyes flashing. "This is the 20th century. What cave did you just crawl out of—" She stopped and looked at him in surprise. "Patrick? Patrick O'Brien?"

Patrick's eyes narrowed as he regarded her more closely. "Mary Katherine?" He broke into a grin. "Still creating trouble I see. Just as opinionated and wrong-headed as usual."

She gave a huff of indignation. "It is Mary Kate now, and you are just as annoyingly impractical and unreasonable as always," she retorted.

They looked at each other and burst out laughing then, feeling the easy familiarity of their childhood friendship.

"You are all grown-up—at least in one respect," noted Patrick. "The last time I saw you, you had pigtails. What are your plans now, besides spending your father's money?"

"Oh, just to shop and wait for a rich husband to come along," she replied airily.

Patrick smiled. "Okay, I guess I deserved that."

"When did you become so cynical?" asked Mary Kate.

"I guess it comes with the profession. Seriously, what are you going to do now? You're not like the other girls here. I can't imagine you settling down. You are too curious and full of life—and you're smart."

"So you finally admit it. Can I get that in writing?"

"Not on your life."

"I've been away at school so much over the years that Mama and Papa want me to stay at home now. I suppose I'll attend Dickinson Seminary for a time." Mary Kate shrugged. "After that, we'll see."

"Mary Kate how about a dance?" asked a young man in the group.

He was muscular in build and above average in height and spoke with a faint German accent. He was neither handsome nor unattractive but nondescript with wide-set brown eyes and brown hair that was receding from a high forehead. But his family possessed wealth and that was all the attraction that was necessary.

"Oh, Horace, perhaps the next dance," said Mary Kate. "I have promised this one to Mr. O'Brien."

The young man passed a dismissive eye over Patrick. "Of course," he replied with stiff formality.

"I don't think Horace was too pleased," noted Patrick as Mary Kate led him to the dance floor.

"Horace Biederman is okay but boring. His father bought the train line from Peter Jeffries. Unlike you, he doesn't engage in lively debate. In fact, his conversation is usually one-sided, if you know what I mean."

"You mean it isn't all about you," teased Patrick.

She made a face at him. "You haven't changed a bit, Patrick O'Brien. Now dance with me before Horace thinks me a liar—if you know how."

"Is that a challenge I hear?" he questioned archly. There was a twinkle in his eye as he swung her into a waltz with a grace and rhythm that took her breath away. "We have dances in Philadelphia, too," he said with smug satisfaction at the look of surprise on her face.

From their places, Eleanor and Maven watched the attractive, young couple with growing concern. From his vantage point across the room, Ian smiled with approval. The lad not only had good sense, he had good taste as well.

Ian looked around for his son. Free from his mother's watchful eye for the moment, Morgan was happily indulging himself with an array of refreshments. Ian smiled, amused.

He furrowed his brow as he further considered his son. Eleanor coddled the boy too much, he thought. His own boyhood experiences had been a far cry from the luxury that surrounded his son. He was just a few years older than Morgan when he had been tasked with providing for his younger sister, mother and crippled father. Ian quickly shrugged off the memories. Perhaps he was being too judgmental. After all, wasn't it a father's responsibility to ensure that his children enjoyed a better childhood than he had experienced?

Parker snatched two flutes of champagne from the passing silver tray and walked over to Ian. "Nice ball," he said, handing the host a glass. "Remember the first ball that you and Eleanor gave?"

"Like it was yesterday," replied Ian. "'Tis hard to believe it was that long ago. The guests refused to eat, drink or dance. It was a disaster. Eleanor thought I had sealed her fate as a social outcast forever and would nae talk to me for days."

"Well, you did leverage the attendance of the elites," Parker reminded him.

Ian smiled and took a sip of his champagne. "Aye, but we made them pay."

Parker nodded. "You said you were going to forge a new society, and you did. But I wonder if much has changed, except the names of the players."

Ian fell silent for a moment. "I fear that ye may be right." He set his half empty glass on a table. "I've never been partial to this stuff. Let's slip into the study and get a real man's drink."

"Eleanor might have something to say about that."

"I doubt that she'll notice," said Ian, as she floated by in the arms of another dance partner.

Parker chuckled. "Maybe you should dance with her."

"Dancin' was not a priority to a boy growin' up in the Basin."

Parker looked at his longtime friend in surprise and burst out laughing. "You don't know how to dance, do you? My God, I've known you for over 20 years and never guessed. So there *is* something the great Ian Douglas cannot do."

Ian glared at Parker. "There are some things I choose not to do. Dancing be one of them," he corrected firmly. "'Tis one of the understandin's that Eleanor and I have come to. Now, let's get that drink," he said, changing the subject.

In the study, Ian poured two tumblers of Scotch and handed one to Parker. "Have a seat."

Parker took a seat on the leather settee, while Ian seated himself in the armchair. Both men fell silent as they savored the first sip of the fine malt whiskey.

"It's nice having the kids home again," said Parker at length. "They seem to have grown up when our backs were turned."

Ian gave a light laugh. "Mary Katherine insists upon being called Mary Kate now. She thinks it sounds less old-fashioned." He looked at Parker. "You have done well by Patrick," he said on a more serious note. "I would not have wanted for him to end up in the sawmill."

"Like his father Tommy?"

"Let's not to go there," warned Ian.

Parker was unfazed. "Admit it, Ian. You are a hypocrite."

"It is no crime to want people you care about to have a better life."

"It is when all you judge them by is their station in life. Isn't that what you used to accuse Eleanor of doing to you?"

For once, Ian had no response. He took another sip of his Scotch and changed the topic. "When are ye goin' to convince Maven to move to the hill?"

"She's happy where she is."

Ian sighed. "With Maven it is always about the roots. At least you got her to move off Evergreen to Park Place. What has she been up to? I hardly see her anymore. Come to think of it, I have nae seen much of her this evenin'."

"A couple of the ladies admired her gown tonight, so she is discussing the design of some dresses with them. You know Maven. She never misses an opportunity to bring business to her dress shop."

Ian shook his head. That was so typically Maven. "Do ye think she'll ever give up the shop?"

"Not likely," said Parker.

"It is nice to see that some things stay the same," remarked Ian. He lapsed into silence for a moment. "I'm glad that she was able to find happiness with you, Parker. Maven deserves that."

"Tommy's death was not your fault, Ian. Maven doesn't blame you. It has been over 14 years. It is time for you to stop blaming yourself."

"They were bad times with the labor unrest, Parker. Tommy was on the front lines—for me."

"He knew the risks. He chose to support you."

Ian turned a level eye on Parker. "I should have had Tommy's back. He always had mine. If it had been me that day, he would have been there."

"You didn't know the lengths to which Franklin Jeffries would go to destroy you."

"I should have calculated that." Ian looked away, his thoughts private. "What was it all for, Parker?" he asked at length. "The lumber tracts are playing out...most of the mills are closed now."

"Times change, Ian. Let the past go for your sake as well as for Maven's. Come now, let's go and enjoy the party. Tonight is about Mary Kate."

Ian nodded and threw back the rest of his drink.

CHAPTER THREE

Consequences

Eleanor sat at one end of the table directing with formal precision the event that was dinner.

"Mary Kath—Mary Kate," she amended, catching the glare from her daughter, "I saw Mrs. Benway today. She said that Clarence would be calling." Eleanor ignored the face that Mary Kate made. "And, Father, didn't you say that Mr. Biederman's son Horace is also quite keen to press his suit?"

Ian smiled and winked at Mary Kate. "Yes, Mother, but, if you recall, the Biedermans are German."

"Yes, well, they still seem a presentable family."

"Mama, I am not interested in Clarence or Horace."

"That's because she is sweet on Patrick O'Brien," interjected Morgan.

"Hush up you little runt, or I will stuff a potato in your mouth."

"Mary Katherine! You will do no such thing. But you have been seeing a good deal of the O'Brien boy. I think it best that you see others as well."

"I like the young man," said Ian. "I do nae see the harm if she wants to spend time with Patrick, Mother."

Mary Kate jumped up from the table and kissed her father on the cheek. "Thank you, Papa. I won't be late."

"Where are you going?" asked Eleanor in surprise.

"Out for a walk…with Patrick."

"But we haven't finished dinner," sputtered Eleanor as Mary Kate rushed out of the room. She looked at her husband. "Ian, do something."

"What do ye want me to do?"

"Insist that she see other young men."

"Mary Kate says that Clarence Benway looks like a frog and has two left feet, and Horace Biederman is boring," volunteered Morgan.

His mother turned a stern eye on him. "Never-you-mind, Morgan James Douglas. This is none of your concern. You may be excused."

"What about dessert?" protested Morgan.

"You may take it in your room. I believe you have homework to finish."

When the boy petulantly left the room, Ian regarded his wife with curiosity. "What is troublin' ye, Eleanor? Ever since the ball ye've been disturbed about somethin'."

"I worry about Mary Katherine. I swear that girl would marry a garbage collector just to spite me."

"Patrick O'Brien be hardly a garbage collector. He graduated top in his class from a prestigious law school, and Parker is makin' him a partner in his firm." Ian looked at his wife closely. "What do you have against this young man? Is your objection to him that he is Maven's son?"

"Is that why you are championing him?" she shot back.

As a dark shadow crossed her husband's features, she realized the can of worms she was opening. When he spoke, she could hear the edge in his voice. "I thought we had laid that matter to rest a long time ago, Eleanor."

She forced a smile. "I'm sorry, darling. Of course, we did. Forgive me."

* * * * *

At the tinkle of the bell, Maven looked up and caught her breath. A feeling of ill ease washed over her as Eleanor Douglas walked into the dress shop. She wasn't surprised to see her. Maven knew this visit was coming. She had tried to prepare herself for it. But how does one prepare for an impending maelstrom?

"Mrs. Douglas…how might I help ye?" asked Maven hesitantly.

"Mrs. Stanton, is there someplace where we might talk privately?"

"My assistant be out on an errand. We are alone."

"Then I will get to the point," said Eleanor. "I am sure that you are aware that our children have been seeing a good deal of each other."

"Aye. I've been tryin' to discourage it."

"As have I, but it seems to no avail. Mrs. Stanton, I have sent Mary Katherine away to school for over half her life to protect against this very thing from happening. Now that she is home, I would like for her to stay."

"Ye want me to convince Patrick to leave Rossburg," said Maven, her voice flat.

"With your husband's connections, your son could join a top firm in Philadelphia, which would do more for his career than joining your husband's law firm and staying here." When Maven didn't say anything, Eleanor continued. "Mrs. Stanton, our children cannot be allowed to develop an intimate relationship. You have had the chance to know your child. I haven't. I am asking you for that chance now."

Maven looked at Eleanor, tears welling up in her eyes. "Be there no other way?"

"There is, but I am sure you will agree that it serves no one to avail ourselves of it. I'm sorry," said Eleanor, her voice softening. "I know how it feels to have to send your child away."

At this moment, Patrick entered the store and came to an abrupt stop. He was catapulted back to a time over 14 years ago when Mrs. Douglas came to the shop, similarly distressing his mother.

As Maven quickly dashed away a tear, Patrick moved protectively to her side.

"Mrs. Douglas, may I be of some assistance?" he asked.

Eleanor smiled, the distress plain on her face as well. "No...thank you. Your mother and I have finished our business." She turned and left the shop.

Patrick looked at his mother quizzically. "What did she want?"

"She is concerned that you and Mary Katherine are becomin' too involved—as am I."

"We've been over this before, Mother," he said in a firm tone. "Mary Kate and I enjoy each other's company. We enjoy talking and debating ideas. I don't understand why that should be such a matter of concern to you and Mrs. Douglas."

"You and Mary Katherine are young, Patrick. Young people don't always know their own minds or use the best judgment. Mrs. Douglas and I feel that ye should be gettin' to know other young men and women as well."

"I am 21 years old, Mother. I have just graduated from law school. Grant me that I know my own mind. I am not some lovesick schoolboy. Now, I don't wish to discuss the matter again. I am here to tell you that Parker will be late for supper tonight. And I am taking Mary Kate to the Carleton House for dinner.

Across town, William Asherton, President of the Lumbermen's Bank of Rossburg looked over the ledgers with increasing concern as the accountant stood quietly by.

"You are certain about this?" asked Asherton.

"Yes, sir."

"Bring me the files on those accounts. Then call Mr. Stanton and tell him that I need to see him. It may be nothing. But I'm not taking any chances."

"Yes, sir."

An hour later, Asherton walked into the Stanton Law Office and was ushered into Parker's inner office.

Parker came forward to greet his visitor with a handshake. "Have a seat, William. What can I do for you? My assistant said you sounded disturbed."

Asherton settled himself in the leather armchair, while Stanton took his seat behind the ornate mahogany desk.

"My accountant brought something to my attention that may or may not be coincidental," said Asherton. He pulled out three files from his case and laid them on the desk. "These are loans that the bank holds on Allied Machine Company, Penmark Wagons, and the Rossburg Hotel. Last week, within days of each other, all three loans were paid off. I don't know what it means and, as I said, it may be nothing, but I thought you and Mr. Douglas should be aware of this."

Parker looked thoughtful for a moment. "You say this occurred last week."

Asherton nodded.

"Thank you for coming in, William. I'll pass this along to Mr. Douglas. Should any more transactions of this kind occur again, please contact me immediately."

After Asherton departed, Parker considered the matter for several minutes, when a thought suddenly came to him. He grabbed his hat and coat and the files. "I'm going out for a little while," he said as he passed by his secretary's desk.

The secretary looked up. "What about your two o'clock appointment, Mr. Stanton?"

"Reschedule it," Stanton shouted back.

When Parker burst into Ian's office at the mill yards, Ian cocked a brow in surprise. "Who lit the fire that is burnin' under ye?"

"Asherton was just in my office with a curious matter. It seems that Crandle, Hockings, and Jacobs all paid off the loans on their companies last week," he said, setting the files on Ian's desk.

Ian opened the files and scanned them, then leaned back in his chair his manner contemplative.

"Are you thinking what I'm thinking?" asked Parker, pulling a chair up to Ian's desk and sitting down.

"That somebody is buyin' votes on the Board of Trade?"

Parker nodded. "It is no coincidence that a vote is coming up on the Board of Trade on whether to allow J. J. Widman to build a store in town. Who do you think it is?"

Ian's mind sorted through possibilities. "Benway is nae happy about the competition, but he nae be in a position to pay off other companies' loans. There be a faction on the Board that is opposed to outside businesses comin' into Rossburg, but, with the lumber industry in decline, the city needs more industry to provide jobs."

"Do you think it is an outsider trying to come in?"

"Hard to say," replied Ian. "Do the payoffs on the loans correspond with a withdrawal of that size from any of our account holders?"

"Asherton didn't say. I'll find out. I find it doubtful, though, if someone is trying to cover his tracks. And we're not the only bank in town."

"Can ye put someone inside the Rossburg National Bank who can get access to those accounts?" asked Ian.

"Possibly, if there is a position open. But it's not likely. Jobs are pretty scarce," said Parker.

"Did ye nae say that ye need another person in your office?"

Parker grinned. "I guess I could always use an extra pair of hands."

"Find out who is unhappy at the Rossburg National Bank that has the kind of access we need and offer a higher salary," instructed Ian. "That will leave an opening at the bank that we can slip our man into."

Stanton nodded. "I'll put Nick on it."

Ian opened the drawer, pulled out a box of cigars, and offered one to Stanton.

Parker laughed. "Eleanor won't let you smoke them at home, I'm guessing."

"Women do nae appreciate the smell of a good cigar," said Ian with a rueful smile. "She says it smothers the fragrance of the fresh flowers sittin' around the house."

They clipped the heads of their cigars and lit up.

"Patrick and Mary Kate seem to be getting pretty close," said Parker off-handedly.

"Aye. Clarence Benway and Horace Biederman have shown great interest, but Mary Kate seems to have taken quite a shine to Patrick. He's a fine, young man. Truth is I would nae object to a match between them," replied Ian.

"There was a day when that didn't appeal to you," Stanton reminded him.

Ian looked at his old friend and partner. "We had this conversation before, Parker. Stop tryin' to be my conscience," he warned. "Things change. Life changes."

"Have you considered how difficult this would make things for Eleanor and Maven?"

"The past is past."

"It doesn't eliminate it, Ian."

"C'mon, Parker, that matter was laid to rest a long time ago. Maybe a marriage between Mary Kate and Patrick be what we need to bring the families together."

"Still, it is hard for Eleanor and Maven to be friends."

"I'll nae interfere between Mary Kate and Patrick," said Ian on a note of finality.

Silence fell between them then, each man private with his thoughts.

"What can be done to convince the Board of Trade members to allow more industry?" asked Parker at length, moving to a less contentious topic. "Rossburg is dying."

Ian thought for a moment. "Their chief objection is competition, particularly when it comes from the outside. No one can argue though against bringin' patronage from the outside," he said with a crafty smile.

"How are you going to do that? Do you have a plan?"

"Maybe. I have to think it through a little more."

"Whatever it is, count me in," said Parker. He had learned a long time ago to trust his partner's instincts.

Later that evening, from their table at the Carleton House, the Biedermans became increasingly disturbed as they watched Mary Kate and Patrick in animated conversation across the room.

"George, I thought you had talked to Mr. Douglas on Horace's behalf," said Mrs. Biederman.

"I did. I told him that Horace was interested in courting his daughter."

"What did he say?"

"He wasn't opposed to it."

"Well, I happen to know that Mrs. Douglas does not favor Mr. O'Brien," his wife reported.

Horace shrugged, unconcerned. "It is a passing fancy, Mother. They were childhood friends or some such thing. O'Brien is unworldly. Outside of Philadelphia, he knows only Rossburg. Mary Kate will soon tire of him."

The Biedermans looked at their son, not as convinced.

"I don't think I need tell you, Horace, how much a marriage between you and the daughter of Ian Douglas would elevate our standing and our fortunes. In spite of the fact that my railroad controls a large share of the commerce in this town, we are still treated as outsiders. Perhaps you should press your case a little harder," his father advised him curtly.

CHAPTER FOUR

A Secret Unburied

Ian frowned as he studied the figures. The number of logs in the boom would not last the season. Twenty-three years ago, the boom had been too small to hold an adequate amount of lumber. Now, there was not enough lumber to fill it. He stood up and walked over to the window. Resting an arm against the casement, he looked out over the mill yards, conscious that an era was ending.

His foreman poked his head in the door. "Mr. Douglas, a Mr. Biederman is here to see you."

Ian turned. "Biederman? What does he want?"

The foreman shrugged. "Says he wants to talk to you."

"Show him up."

When George Biederman entered the office, he looked about him in surprise at the crude accoutrements of the richest, most powerful man in Rossburg. Ian was amused. He had much the same reaction when admitted to the office for the first time. Then, it had been Cyrus Morgan's office. Though Ian had rebuilt the mill after the riots and updated over the years, he had taken a page from his father-in-law's book and kept the workplace simple. He found that it helped him to connect better with the workers.

He stepped forward and extended his hand. "George, what brings ye here today?"

The stocky German returned a hearty handshake. "Thank you for seeing me, Ian. I know you to be a busy man."

Ian motioned Biederman to a chair and took his seat behind his desk. "What can I do for ye?" he asked curiously.

"I've come about the matter of our children. My son is most desirous of pursuing a courtship with your daughter."

Ian shrugged. "Ye know that I nae be opposed to Horace approachin' Mary Kate on the subject."

"I'm glad to hear you say that," said Biederman.

"Then what is the problem, George?"

Biederman, never known for his tact, declared bluntly, "Your daughter is the problem."

Ian cocked a brow in surprise. "Oh? How so? I have nae heard that Horace has made his intentions known to Mary Kate."

"Well, it has not been from lack of trying," said Biederman with a snort of annoyance. "Your daughter appears to be distracted by the O'Brien boy. And when young people don't know what is in their best interests, it behooves their parents to step in."

Ian leaned back in his chair, just slightly amused. "Ye nae be suggestin' an arranged marriage, are ye, George? 'Tis nae the old country, and we be at the start of a new, more modern age I've been told."

"Bah," scoffed Biederman. "Practicality is never out of fashion. The fact is, we're not getting any younger, Ian. We need grandchildren of good stock to pick up the banner and carry it forward. A marriage between your daughter and Horace would forge a powerful empire."

"And how does your son feel about an arranged marriage with Mary Kate?" asked Ian.

"He understands his role in preserving the family legacy."

"I see. I'm sorry, George. Horace will have to press his own suit. If Mary Kate is agreeable to it, I'll nae object. Otherwise, I'll nae have a hand in it."

Biederman looked at Ian, clearly taken aback. "You can't possibly mean to leave the future of your empire up to the romantic whims of a young woman. Think of what is at stake here."

"I know the harm of a forced marriage, George. Mary Kate's happiness be more important to me than an empire built on her sorrow."

A hard glint came into Biederman's eyes. "Let me put this another way, Ian. The old lumber tracts near the river are played out. You are forced to go farther west to find adequate timber. You need my train to transport your lumber from those tracts to the boom. Do I make myself clear?"

Ian leaned forward in his chair. "My daughter is not for sale at any cost. Do I make *myself* clear?"

Biederman bristled and stood up. "You will regret this, Douglas."

Ian leveled cold steel-blue eyes on him. "I fought a battle before with a man tougher than you, George, and I won. I would advise ye to think long and hard before engagin' me in a war."

Biederman stomped out of the room and returned to his office in a sour mood.

His son sauntered in. "How did it go with Mr. Douglas? Is Mary Kate in the bag?"

"No. Douglas made it quite clear that she is not even a chip on the bargaining table."

"Did you threaten to deny him transportation of his lumber?"

Biederman nodded. "It didn't make any difference. He knows the lumbering boom is over, and he has plenty of other business interests that don't require the use of my trains."

"Too bad. Mary Kate is most appealing. I wouldn't have minded having her in my bed."

Biederman looked at his son in annoyance. "Douglas didn't say you couldn't court her, Horace. He just said that you would have to approach her yourself. You will have to be the one to convince her of the merits of a marriage with you."

"Well, how do I do that?" asked Horace.

"How the hell do I know? Figure it out. You know the girl. Meanwhile, find out who was acquainted with Douglas in the old days. I want to know how he came to prominence. Hire a detective…check the newspapers over the last 20 years. I want to know everything about the man, Horace. Everything! I don't care how small the detail. I want to know if he spits on the sidewalk."

*****

Eleanor stared at Ian as though he had lost his mind. "You are shutting down the mill yards?"

"Just the sawmill, Eleanor. The finishin' part of the company will continue to do millwork."

"But why?"

"The lumber is playin' out. We have to look farther afield for new lumber tracts, and 'tis becomin' too expensive to transport the timber back. Most of the other mills have already shut down."

"What about the construction business?"

"I have nae decided yet. The town has lost population. Homes are nae bein' built at the same rate. Times are changin', Eleanor. Rossburg will have to look to other enterprises, or it will become a ghost town."

"Rossburg has only known lumbering. What else is there?"

"'Tis what I been tryin' to get the Board of Trade to consider."

Eleanor dropped onto the settee. She didn't want times to be changing. She was quite happy to keep things as they were.

Ian saw the dejection on his wife's face. "We nae be destitute. I still have the bank, the utilities, and the millworks."

Eleanor looked up at him. "There is something that you aren't telling me. You didn't just come to this decision, Ian. I know you. The sawmill is important to you…for more than just profit. It was the cornerstone of your empire."

Ian hesitated. "I'll not wager Mary Kate's happiness," he said in a low voice.

"What are you talking about?"

"Biederman is refusin' to ship my lumber from the western tracts unless I force Mary Kate to marry his son. I will nae do to her what I did to you."

Eleanor was shocked by the revelation. "At least I was attracted to you, and, however much I resented your high-handed methods, there was a love to build on. But I don't believe that to be the case with Mary Katherine and Horace. Oh, I knew I didn't like that man. How like Franklin Jeffries George is. I shall drop Mrs. Biederman from my social registry."

"Do nae antagonize them more, my dear. If Mary Kate and Patrick are serious about each other, I think the quicker they declare themselves, the sooner Mary Kate will be off the bargainin' table. I'll have a talk with Parker."

Eleanor stood up and put a hand on her husband's arm. "No, Ian. I don't think that is a good idea."

Ian looked at her quizzically. "Why?"

"Well…you would be guilty of the same charge that you make of George Biederman," she said, casting about for an explanation.

"I'm hardly forcing our daughter into a marriage with Patrick O'Brien, Eleanor," he said, somewhat affronted. "I'm just nudging the matter to a quicker conclusion."

"You still would be interfering. Let it play out as it will. Please, Ian."

There was a measure of entreaty in her eyes and voice that perplexed him, but he couldn't deny her talent for handling delicate situations. She had saved his life once. "Very well," he conceded, "if you think it is best."

Three weeks before Christmas, the matter did play out, thanks to Horace's more ardent pursuit of Mary Kate.

In a gathering in the parlor of the Douglas mansion, Maven sat in one chair. Parker stood behind her, his hand on her shoulder. Eleanor sat in another chair to the right of Maven, a small table between them. Mary Kate and Patrick sat on the settee, and Ian stood beside the fireplace, his arm draped across the mantle. There was an indefinable tenseness in the room coupled with an air of excitement and expectation on the part of Ian, Mary Kate and Patrick.

"I would guess that we all know why we are here," said Ian with a pleased smile.

Patrick grasped Mary Kate's hand. "With your permission, sir, I would like to marry your daughter."

They looked so happy. Maven closed her eyes and bit her lip to hold back tears. Parker squeezed her shoulder for support.

Taking a deep breath to gather her strength, Eleanor was the first to speak. "You are a fine man, Patrick, and I know that you will make a good husband. But Mr. Douglas and I cannot give you permission to marry our daughter. I am very sorry."

The young couple and Ian looked at her stunned.

"Mama, why are you doing this?" cried Mary Kate.

Ian started toward his wife. "Eleanor, for the love of God—"

"Maven and I have to concur with Eleanor," said Parker, stepping forward.

Ian looked from Eleanor to Parker in utter disbelief. And the young couple stared at everyone, hurt and confused, as the unexpected drama unfolded.

"Mother, why are you objecting?" asked Patrick.

Tears brimmed in Maven's eyes as she looked from Patrick to Ian. "Please forgive me," she said, the plea wrenched from her soul. "Ian...Patrick is your son."

The dead silence that followed was thunderous. It seemed to stretch forever until Mary Kate jumped up from the settee and ran sobbing from the room.

"My God," said Ian, staggered.

Patrick stood up. He stared incredulously at Maven, then at Ian. Father and son regarded each other for a long moment before Patrick walked angrily out of the parlor.

Ian looked as though a knife had been plunged into him. "Did Tommy know?"

Maven stared down at her hands in her lap and nodded.

The rift that had developed between him and his childhood friend years ago suddenly made sense to Ian. "Why did ye nae tell me?" he asked in a ragged voice.

"You had already married Eleanor when I found out that I was with child. Tommy guessed the truth and asked me to marry him. He raised Patrick as his own, and we never spoke of the matter again."

Ian turned to Parker, his tone laced with anger. "When did you know?"

"Eleanor told me when she asked for my help in convincing you to send Mary Katherine away to school just before the mill riots."

Ian looked at Eleanor. "And you—when did you know?"

"I knew the minute I saw Patrick at that first lawn party we had for the company workers all those years ago," she said. "He has your eyes, your expressions…and a woman knows these things," she added quietly. "When I asked Mrs. Stanton about it, there was no denying it, and we decided it was best for everyone to keep the secret." Eleanor lifted pain-filled eyes to her husband. "It wasn't done to hurt you, Ian, though I see now that it has afflicted us all."

Ian stared at her, having difficulty absorbing everything. It was too overwhelming, and he turned and left the parlor without another word. A few minutes later, Eleanor, Maven and Parker heard the front door slam.

Ian raced the car down the street as fast as he could push it to go. His thoughts were in such turmoil that he hadn't stopped to grab his overcoat when he fled the house, but he was numb to the cold air that whipped through his hair and tore at his clothes. He didn't know where he was going. In the past, he would have sought out Maven for solace and wisdom in times of crisis, but, in the end, she had betrayed him as well. He had no idea how long he had been driving when he stopped the car alongside a farmer's field and got out. In unbridled fury, he pounded his fists on the hood and kicked the side of the car until he was spent and emotionally numb.

Maven found Patrick at the house throwing his clothes into a suitcase.

"How is Mary Kate?" he asked without looking up.

"She is upset. She has locked herself in her room," replied Maven. "Where might ye be goin'?"

"Back to Philadelphia." His tone was angry and determined, his manner implacable.

"Patrick, we need to talk about this. Please do not leave this way."

Patrick turned and looked at his mother, stone-faced. "The time for discussion was 21 years ago before you gave yourself to a man who intended to marry another woman—" He felt the crack of Maven's hand across his cheek.

"Do not ye dare to judge me or your father," she said, her eyes sparking with anger. "Ye have no idea about life yet."

"Oh, I think I just got a pretty good dose of it today. Now, I understand why there was tension whenever Mrs. Douglas came into the shop, or when you encountered each other on the street. I always sensed her ambivalence toward us but could never figure out why. Tell me, Mother, did you love Tommy O'Brien, or was it always Ian Douglas?"

"There are different types of love, Patrick. I loved them both in different ways."

"Did Papa—Tommy—know about me?"

"Yes, and it made no difference to him. He loved ye just the same."

"At least in that you were honest."

Maven took a deep breath, struggling to conceal her hurt. "Patrick, please try to understand. Ian, Tommy, and I grew up together. We always shared a special bond. As we became older, I thought that meant that the kind of love I had developed for Ian was the same love that he felt for me, but, too late, I realized that I was wrong. We were not in the same place. Tommy understood that."

"I'm sorry, Mother. I can't stay here." He closed his suitcase and picked it up. "I'll let Parker know where I am."

As he walked out the door, tears trickled down Maven's face, and she wondered if her debt for a mistake made in youth would ever be paid in full.

* * * * *

Horace rushed into his father's office. "Mary Kate is gone."

George Biederman looked up in annoyance at the interruption. "What are you talking about?"

"I went to the Douglas mansion to invite her out for dinner, like you told me to. Her brother said she left town four days ago."

Biederman looked at his son in surprise. "Where did she go?"

"Her brother said she went to New York and doesn't know when she'll be back."

"Where is O'Brien? Did he go with her?" asked Biederman in alarm.

Horace shook his head. "O'Brien returned to Philadelphia. Nobody knows any more than that."

Biederman leaned back in his chair, his mouth curving up in a pleased smile. "Find out where she is in New York."

"Then what?"

"Take yourself there and do whatever the hell you have to do to get her to agree to marry you."

Horace's manner was smug. "I told you she would tire of O'Brien."

CHAPTER FIVE

Shattered

Parker opened the door to the study that was Ian's sanctuary and quietly entered. Ian was staring out the window, a bottle of whiskey in one hand and a glass half full in the other.

"It has been three days, Ian. Eleanor said you hardly leave this room. She is worried about you."

Ian continued to stare out the window. "All those times Tommy brought Patrick to the mill, and I never guessed. Someone should have told me, Parker," he said, his tone low and flat.

"What would you have done?" challenged Parker. "Patrick knew only Tommy as his father, and Tommy was a good father. Later, Patrick had me to help guide him through life. You had your own family with Eleanor. Would you have upended the life of a young boy too emotionally ill-equipped to deal with such a truth...thrown your own family into turmoil...subjected Maven to more scandal? You had already put Maven and Eleanor through enough hell with the murder trial. If Mary Kate and Patrick hadn't been drawn to one another, no one would have been the wiser."

Parker paused for a minute to give Ian a chance to think about everything he had said.

"Look, Ian, there is no good way to deal with a situation like this," he continued. "Eleanor and Maven agreed on an action that they thought would cause the least amount of hurt to all involved. Keeping this secret has not been easy for either of them. You have to respect that."

Ian turned around. The depth of his pain and sorrow was etched on his face. "Mary Kate left the next mornin' for New York. She would nae speak to Eleanor or me."

"I know. Patrick went back to Philadelphia. It tore Maven apart," said Parker. "They just need time to sort things out."

"I have lost a son I did nae know I had and a daughter I was becoming reacquainted with. How do I reconcile that, Parker?"

"They'll come back when they are ready. In the meantime, I think it best if we keep this information among ourselves."

Ian emptied his glass in one swig. "Get out, Parker. Leave me be."

"Eleanor needs you, Ian. Morgan is wondering why his family is in turmoil. And business decisions have to be made. You need to pull yourself together."

Later that afternoon, Eleanor looked up in surprise when Ian entered her bedroom. He was clean-shaven and attired in a burgundy velvet smoking jacket. But he still looked haggard, and his eyes were filled with pain. She rose from the vanity.

Ian didn't know what he was going to say when he finally faced her, and words were slow in coming. "I-I'm sorry, Eleanor," he said in a halting voice.

Eleanor went to him and put her arms around him. "I'm sorry, too, Ian."

He dropped his head to her shoulder. And they held each other and cried.

When their sorrow was spent, Eleanor looked up at him. "It is Maven who has suffered the most, I believe. You need to make your peace with her," she said.

Ian nodded. "I love ye, Eleanor. I do nae know what I would do if I lost ye. I am so sorry for everythin' I have put ye through."

Eleanor raised a hand to caress his cheek. "None of us are blameless, Ian. And my feelings for you have not changed."

She saw relief flood his face, and another question came into his eyes. In answer, she took his hand and led him to her bed. As the shadows lengthened into evening and the evening folded into night, she held him and yielded to his needs until he fell into a slumber untortured by guilt or grief.

CHAPTER SIX

Estrangement

It all seemed a blur to her. Mary Kate had spent Christmas away from her family before, but this time was different. She was in New York City during the most festive time of the year, and she felt alone and miserable. She wanted to be with her family, but her anger and resentment at the situation they had created ran deep. She didn't think she could ever go home again. She wasn't even sure if she could ever forgive them.

"C'mon, Mary Kate, it is New Year's Eve. You're so glum you are ruining the party," complained her friend Emily Stoddert. "Buck up."

Mary Kate accepted a flute of champagne and raised her glass. "Salute," she said, forcing a smile.

The townhouse was full of people she didn't know. They were mostly Emily's friends and a few strays Emily had picked up—artists, musicians, writers who railed against the dehumanization of the industrial age and adopted a bohemian style of dress. Mary Kate wondered what her prim and proper mother would think about this odd collection of guests.

"You look as though you could use a friend," remarked a male voice.

Mary Kate looked up to see an attractive, young man trim in build and close to six feet in height. He was clean-shaven, and his dark hair was neatly trimmed. He obviously wasn't one of Emily's friends. The fashion and fit of his suit bespoke money, and he had that polished, ivy-league look about him that Mary Kate so disdained. But he didn't seem to press the advantage.

"You must be Mary Kate Douglas, Emily's new roommate," he continued.

"It's probably more accurate to say I'm just another stray that Emily took pity on," replied Mary Kate.

He chuckled. "Well, stray or not, I am happy to make your acquaintance, Miss Douglas."

"Who are you?"

"I am Andrew Stoddert, Emily's older brother. The parents send me around periodically to make sure she stays out of trouble. They'll be happy to know that you appear to be a stable influence."

Mary Kate laughed. "I guess that depends on your definition of stable."

"Hmmm. Emily did say that she had dragged you into the suffragette movement. I guess that would make you a radical of sorts," he noted.

"Where do you stand on the subject of woman's suffrage, Mr. Stoddert?"

"Call me Drew. Are you putting me on the spot, Miss—may I call you Mary Kate?"

"That depends, Drew."

"On what?"

"On your answer."

Andrew Stoddert grinned. "Well, as it so happens, I support your position. I believe that women should have the right to vote. They are an important part of the community and deserve to have a say. I don't think that societies always do admirably by their women and children, particularly when they are controlled by old, white men who are too busy protecting their own self-interests."

Mary Kate blinked in surprise. "How enlightened you are, sir—if you believe what you say."

He looked at her, his manner taking on a more serious air. "I never say anything I don't mean. My profession requires that I be painfully honest."

"Then you may call me Mary Kate," she said.

He extended his hand. "They are starting a cake dance. Shall we?" When she hesitated, he said: "This is the 20th century now. Doctors are recommending that people be more physically exercised to ward off the stress of this new age of industry."

Mary Kate took his hand. "And how do you know that?" she asked, her tone skeptical.

"I'm a doctor," he replied, leading her artfully into the dance.

CHAPTER SEVEN

An Unwelcome Rival

Ian brought the motorcar to a stop in front of Maven's dress shop. It had taken him a month to work up the courage to come. He knew she would be preparing to close for the day. He got out of the car and stepped onto the boardwalk. Outside the door, he hesitated for a moment before opening it.

"I be closin' now," said Maven, coming from the back room. She stopped short when she saw Ian.

He noted her uneasiness and smiled. "Eleanor knows that I am here. She suggested I come—a month ago to be exact."

"What do ye want, Ian?" she asked guardedly.

"To make peace with ye. Now that all is known, I can see how much ye suffered. I am nae proud of myself in those days—"

"We were young, Ian. We both made mistakes. Unfortunately, we couldn't realize then the impact our decisions would have later. Because of our children, the mistakes we made will never remain in the past, and we will have to accept that. All we can hope is that Mary Kate and Patrick will one day forgive us, so that we are able to forgive ourselves."

Ian nodded. She offered no excuses or explanations for the decisions she had made, but he didn't expect her to. "How is Patrick?" he asked.

"Still angry. He has joined a law firm in Philadelphia."

Ian looked away for a moment. "I do nae know which is more difficult to bear—not knowin' the truth all these years or that I might never have learned about Patrick at all." It wasn't an indictment, just an expression of the deep pain and confusion he felt. "Should I try to see him?"

"I think it best if you wait for him to take the first step. What about Mary Kate?"

"She be much the same as Patrick—angry, confused, resentful. She is stayin' in New York City with a young woman she became friends with on her Grand Tour. I had the family checked out. They appear to be above reproach and well-connected." Ian gave a sad smile of resignation. "Mary Kate dinnae answer our letters. She wrote once to say that she is never coming back to Rossburg. She contacts Parker when she needs money. I hired a detective agency to keep an eye on her."

"I'm sorry," said Maven.

He looked at her. "Have we lost our children, Maven?"

Maven sighed. "I do not know, Ian."

* * * * *

Horace strode smugly into his father's office. "I found her."

"Who?" asked George Biederman, distracted by the paperwork on his desk.

"Mary Kate. I got the address from her brother."

Biederman looked up at his son. "It's about time."

"She's living with a friend in a townhouse on Fifth Avenue in New York City. I'm leaving on the train tomorrow morning. But what do I tell her? I should have a reason to be there. I can't have her thinking I am chasing after her. I do have my pride, Father."

"Tell her you are there to negotiate a deal with a supplier for rail. That should impress her. And let her think that her parents are pushing the match." As his son turned to leave, Biederman called out to him. "Horace, don't screw this up."

Horace's mouth twisted into a grimace as he pulled the door closed behind him. He was getting damned tired of the Old Man treating him as though he was less than competent.

"I'll show him," Horace muttered to himself. By the time he was done wooing Mary Kate Douglas, she would be begging him to marry her.

He immediately set about making arrangements for his trip. He debated whether to contact her and let her know that he was coming to New York and decided against it. If he had learned anything from his father, it was that the element of surprise usually gave one the advantage.

*****

It was late in the day when Andrew walked into the parlor of his sister's brownstone.

"Who died?" he joked. "There are flowers everywhere."

"They're for Mary Kate," said Emily. "They began arriving this morning."

"Oh? From whom?" asked Andrew, curious.

"Horace Biederman. He is someone she knew in Rossburg."

Andrew looked around him. "Where is Mary Kate?"

"Out—with Horace Biederman."

"The man is here in the city?"

Emily nodded. "It seems that he is here for a few days on business and decided to look her up. I think it is more the case that he tracked her down."

"There's a difference?" questioned Andrew.

"Most definitely. One looks someone up when he wants to say 'hello.' One tracks someone down when he has a purpose. Trust me, Drew, this guy has a purpose."

"Has Mary Kate ever mentioned him? Is he why she left Rossburg?"

"I don't know. She has never talked about him." Emily regarded her brother closely. "Why are you so interested?"

"No reason," said Andrew, trying to affect a more casual air. "What's this Horace Biederman like?"

Emily shrugged. "He's the buttoned up type, self-important. You probably wouldn't like him."

Andrew picked up Horace's card from the table. "Does Mary Kate appear to like him?"

"I don't know. It's hard to tell. She was certainly surprised when she opened the door to find him standing on the doorstep yesterday." Emily's brow knit in suspicion. "Why are you here, Drew?"

"Just thought I would check on you. You know how Mother worries. I had the evening off and figured I would treat you girls to dinner. But it seems I am too late."

"I'm still available," said Emily.

"Oh…yes…so you are."

"I'll get my hat and coat."

Andrew sighed, trying not to show his disappointment. Spending the evening with his sister wasn't exactly what he had in mind. He let the card flutter to the table. How much of a problem was Horace Biederman going to be? he wondered.

At Delmonico's, Mary Kate listened with half an ear, trying to hide her boredom, as Horace talked about his favorite subject—himself—and of his family's wealth, position, and importance in the Rossburg community. He took no notice that Mary Kate hardly spoke. It was enough that she nodded and smiled a few times, appearing to show interest.

Finally, the evening ended, and he escorted Mary Kate back to the brownstone. She thanked him and bid him a hasty good night. As he was promising to call on her the next day, she closed the door on him and let out a long groan. Horace, on the other hand, returned to his hotel in a jocular mood. He called his father and proudly reported a most promising beginning with Mary Kate.

After that, flowers began to arrive once or twice a month, usually heralding visits from Horace, until Mary Kate began to regard the deliveries as a dreaded event. Andrew allowed six months of this nonsense before deciding it was time to run interference.

He made it a point to show up at the brownstone when a visit from Horace seemed imminent and even went so far sometimes as to "happen" into the restaurant where Horace and Mary Kate were dining. Mary Kate always looked relieved to see him and usually invited him to join them, which he did much to Horace's annoyance.

Another time, Horace arrived at the brownstone with high expectations for an evening at the theater, only to find that Emily Stoddert and her brother would be accompanying them. Dr. Stoddert had earlier arrived with the same invitation. So, it made perfect sense that they all attend together, Mary Kate had explained.

It hadn't made perfect sense to Horace. From the first meeting, he and Andrew had promptly concluded that they didn't like each other. Horace found the doctor arrogant and irritating. He always managed to turn the conversation to topics that Horace had no interest in and proved to have little knowledge of, including the field of business in which Horace claimed to have an expertise. Andrew thought Horace a narcissist and an empty suit.

"Why do you put up with this guy?" he asked Mary Kate one day, with more than a hint of exasperation in his tone.

"His parents are friends with mine. I can't be totally rude," she said.

"You do know this to be a courtship, Mary Kate."

"Of course, I do. Horace tried before...but I was interested in someone else at the time," she added quietly. "Now that circumstances have changed, I suppose he sees this as another opportunity to press his case. I've tried to let him know that I'm not interested, but he doesn't seem to take the hint."

Andrew snorted. "That's not surprising. He hears only his own voice." He wanted to ask who the other man was and what circumstances had changed, but he knew that he had already traversed farther into her life than he had a right to do.

Mary Kate looked at him quizzically. "Horace seems to have made quite an impression on you, Drew. I've never seen you so out of sorts."

"Don't mind Drew," chimed in Emily, glancing at him in amusement. "He is just being a big brother."

"Oh. Well, don't worry. Sooner or later, Horace will tire of this and move on," Mary Kate assured him.

Andrew wasn't so convinced. Horace had held on this long. Mary Kate was undeniably a big catch. She was rich and beautiful when many men of their class had to settle for just rich.

"I've decided to take some classes at the university," Mary Kate suddenly announced.

"What prompted this decision?" asked Emily in surprise.

"The women's movement isn't enough," replied Mary Kate. "I need something more to do."

Andrew found he rather liked the idea and voiced his support. It would keep her out of trouble and hopefully away from home the next time Horace Biederman called.

CHAPTER EIGHT

The Challenge Begins

Rossburg was built on the industry of lumber, gentlemen, and that era has come to an end. We need industry in this town," said Ian, speaking before members of the Board of Trade. "And it will come only from the outside. I, therefore, speak in favor of allowin' J.J. Widman to build a store here."

"There are those of us who stand to suffer too much from the competition," said Benway with rising emotion.

"I remember when members made the same argument against you," Ian pointed out.

"These are tough times, Douglas. We can consider this at another time when the economy is better."

"It is not going to get better if we don't attract industry that will employ our people. I stand with Ian," said Stanley Dunbar. "If men don't have jobs, they don't have money. If they don't have money, they can't shop in your store anyway, Benway. Where's the sense in that? Competition is good for the community."

"That's easy for you to say, Stanley. "You own the grain store. Nobody is trying to take away customers from you. The rest of us don't have enough business to share with outsiders."

Murmurs went around the room, the membership divided on the measure. The president banged the gavel on the table. "We have debated this long enough. We will take the vote now. I make a motion that Widman be given the permit to build a department store on Third Street."

"I second that motion," called out Dunbar.

"A show of hands then. All in favor...all against."

The motion was voted down by a large majority.

"If members are so determined to keep businesses from comin' into Rossburg," said Ian, "I would like to suggest that the Board of Trade support local business development that will draw patronage from outside the town."

"What are you proposing?" asked one of the members.

"That a fund be set up to provide start-up capital in the form of a loan to any resident of Rossburg who wishes to begin a new business. The applicant would have to present a business plan and demonstrate profitability and may not currently be a member of the association."

The members looked at each other. A couple nodded, a few shrugged.

"How do we fund it?" asked Crandle.

"Each member will contribute $1000 a year until the fund is self-sustainin'. I will suggest to the mayor and the city council that your contributions be an allowable deduction from city taxes. When the business that has received the loan is determined to be stable, the owner shall begin to repay the capital that was borrowed over a mutually agreed upon period of time interest free."

There was a murmur in the room as members discussed the idea among themselves. After a few minutes, Benway stood up. "I don't see the harm in that. I'll make that motion."

When another member stood up to second the motion, Parker and Ian looked at each other and smiled. There was more than one way to skin a cat.

The president took the vote. "Ayes have it," he announced. "Motion is carried. Jacobs, I'll charge you with putting together a committee to draw up the criteria. Any other business?"

Crandle raised his hand. "I want to make a motion that George Biederman be given membership in the association."

"Biederman is an outsider," Dunbar shouted out.

"He bought an existing industry. He didn't bring in one from the outside to compete with us."

"But he's German," protested another. "You can't trust Germans."

"I agree with Crandle," said Jacobs. "I'll second his motion."

Again, the president took the vote. "The motion has passed," he said. "George Biederman will be granted membership in the Board of Trade."

When the meeting was adjourned, Ian followed Parker to his office.

"I guess we know who was buying votes," said Stanton. He took out a bottle, poured two drinks and handed one to Ian. "Maybe you should have let well enough alone and kept Cyrus Morgan's rules intact. It would seem that your success in making the Board of Trade more inclusive is coming back to bite you."

"It needed new blood, and it was the only way to break the stranglehold the old guard had on the city."

"And, now, the new guard wants to assert that same stranglehold. Rather ironic, isn't it? Funny thing about power."

Ian ignored the subtle innuendo and took a sip of his whiskey. "Have you had a report from your contact in the Rossburg National Bank?"

Parker nodded. "The money came from the outside, and three loans held by Rossburg National were also paid off around the same time as the loans at your bank. All the loan holders are members of the Board of Trade who—"

"Voted for Biederman for membership today," finished Ian. "Biederman was buyin' votes."

"Yep." Stanton furrowed his brow in puzzlement. "I don't get it though. Biederman never came near the two-thirds majority needed for membership before. And this time, he passes the vote with three to spare. We know he most likely bought six of the votes, but what about the others? Not all members carry loans…how many could he afford to pay off anyway?"

"I would guess Biederman used leverage," said Ian. "Many of the members need his railroad to conduct business."

"Why didn't he use it before?"

"He thought he had an ace in the hole."

"What?"

"Not what...who."

Briefly, Ian told Parker about Biederman approaching him on the subject of an arranged marriage between Mary Kate and Horace and of Biederman's threat when Ian refused.

"That's why you shut down the sawmill?"

Ian nodded.

Parker shook his head in disgust. "What's so damned important about being a member of the Board of Trade anyway that he would go to such lengths?"

"Biederman is ambitious. He wants standin' in the community. Rossburg society isn't partial to Germans," said Ian.

"I don't see how membership in the association is going to make that much of a difference for him."

Ian quaffed the rest of his drink. "Gettin' into the association is just the first step, Parker. I think his long-term plan is to gain control of it. He will look for weaknesses to exploit in the members he can't leverage."

Parker looked at Ian in alarm. "Then, he'll pretty much control Rossburg. Christ, Ian, this has a familiar ring. I think Biederman has studied your play."

"If that be the case, I have the advantage," said Ian. "I know what his moves will be."

"That can cut both ways," Parker warned him.

"Maybe. See if your operative can find out the details of the payoff instruments."

"I'll get to it right away."

Ian fell silent for a moment. "I'm travelin' to New York next week on business. I hope to see Mary Kate."

Parker sighed and refilled their glasses. "I'm sorry, Ian. I thought the kids would have come home by now. Maven has tried talking with Patrick, but I guess they just need more time. What have you told Morgan?"

"Just that Mary Kate has decided to go to school in New York. Morgan is too busy findin' trouble to take any more notice of the situation."

"Morgan isn't doing well in school I take it," said Parker with a chuckle. "He's young. He'll come around. He's in that devil-may-care stage."

"Eleanor blames herself for not havin' a closer relationship with Mary Kate. She is determined not to make the same mistake with Morgan and is too lax with the boy. I've tried to talk her into sendin' him to boardin' school where he'll have a firmer hand, but she will nae hear of it. No irony there," laughed Ian. He gulped the rest of his drink and stood to leave. "Let me know when you have some information."

CHAPTER NINE

A Seed Is Planted

Maven studied the work of her two apprentices. "Very good, Lydia. Tilda, these stitches should be looser."

The bell tinkled at the opening of the door, and Maven looked up to see a young girl walk uncertainly into the dress shop. Her clothes were that of the lower class, and she had the look of one in sore need.

"May I help ye?" asked Maven approaching her.

"I need a job, miss." The girl kept her head lowered, and there was desperation in her voice.

Maven's heart went out to her. "I'm sorry, but both of my positions are filled."

The girl raised large, blue eyes to her. "Please, miss," she pleaded, "I have nowhere else to turn. I've been everywhere. The factories are full. I'll be forced to the streets if I do not find somethin'."

"Be there no charitable organization that can be of help to ye?" asked Maven.

The girl shook her head. "They have no help to spare, they say. I ain't afraid of hard work. I can clean your shop for food. I'll do whatever you need me to do."

"What be your name, lass?"

"Annie, miss."

"Have ye any skills, Annie?"

Annie shook her head miserably. "I ain't had much schoolin'. I can read and write a little and do some numbers."

"How old are ye?"

"Fourteen, miss."

"Have ye no family?"

"I grew up in an orphanage. They just turned me out cause they ain't got enough room. They said I was old enough to make my own way now."

Maven regarded the young girl thoughtfully.

"Perhaps I can use someone to clean the shop. Ye may stay in the room in the back. But I have one condition, Annie. Ye must go to school durin' the day. I will take care of gettin' you enrolled."

The girl's face lit up. "Oh, thank ye, miss. You won't be sorry. I'll work real hard."

At dinner that night, Maven recounted the story of Annie to her husband.

"Are you certain that was wise to allow her to stay in the shop?" questioned Parker. "She could be a con artist."

"I do not think so," said Maven. "I know that look from growin' up in the Basin. There be a need for a place for girls like her. If they are on their own, the factories don't pay enough for them to live. The charities are overextended. The girls have no skills and little education. They have no choice but to turn to the streets for income to keep body and soul together. Somethin' needs to be done."

Parker could see that his wife was clearly disturbed, and he knew her well enough to know that an idea was germinating in her mind. "What do you want to do?"

"I want to provide a way for these girls to get an education and to learn a skill that will give them dignified and gainful employment."

"You are talking about a school?"

"Aye, I suppose I am."

"What about the Muncy Normal School and the Dickinson Seminary?"

"Those are preparatory schools. These girls be needin' a school with a different approach."

"You may be right, Maven, but starting a school can be pretty costly. You will need capital for a building, equipment, teachers, lodging, food, and perhaps a small stipend for your students for personal items. The young women you are talking about likely won't be able to pay any tuition. You would have no revenue to sustain you."

Maven was undeterred. "Did ye not tell me that the Board of Trade has set up a fund for loaning start-up capital to new businesses?"

"Yes, but current members are not eligible."

"I am not a member," she pointed out to him. "You are. I am a separate business entity."

He laughed. "We are married. I don't think they would see you as a separate entity."

"Be there particular mention of family members bein' excluded?" questioned Maven.

Parker thought for a moment. "Come to think of it, I don't believe there is," he replied in surprise. "Anyway, the members would take a dim view of a business that cannot show any real source of revenue."

"What about the money from the sale of my house on Evergreen?"

"It will take all of that, if not more, just to open the school. It would leave you with no operating capital."

"Perhaps some families might be able to pay somethin'."

"I have another suggestion," said Parker. "Why don't you let me be your investor? I have plenty of money."

Maven adamantly shook her head. "It is important that I do this on me own."

"Why? You never take any money from me, Maven. You even made Patrick work his way through law school. You are my wife. Let me do this for you."

"Ye be a good and generous man, Mr. Stanton, and I thank ye kindly for the offer. But the answer is still 'no.' Now, what must I do to apply for the Board of Trade loan?"

Parker was surprised at her determination to proceed in spite of the obstacles. "Well, you will have to put together a business plan before you can make application. After that, assuming that you are able to proceed, you will need legal expertise—someone to pull permits, apply for licenses, negotiate contracts. If you won't take my money, at least allow me to donate my services."

Maven smiled. "I believe I can accept that. How soon do we start?"

Parker hesitated. "Maven, I will do all that I can to make your case to the Board of Trade, but I have to warn you this loan is a long shot. Your revenue stream is speculative—and you are a woman."

"What does bein' a woman have to do with anythin'?"

"The association members are men, and men tend to think they make better businessmen."

"That's ridiculous. I have run a successful business in this community for over 14 years."

"I doubt they would consider that a good test. The dress shop is specific to one segment of the community—a segment they consider to be of less importance in the scheme of things."

Maven immediately grasped his meaning. "And me school is not only for young women, but for young women with little means and even less standin'."

"I'm sorry, darling. Are you sure you want to go ahead with this?"

"Yes," she said, her voice full of resolve. "I have to try."

Parker nodded, keeping his doubts to himself. "First, we have to come up with a business plan, then I'll start the paperwork on the application and get the ball rolling."

CHAPTER TEN

A New Age, A New Vision

Ian had just finished shaving and was splashing water over his face when Eleanor entered his bedroom.

"Have you seen this notice in the paper?" she asked.

Ian toweled himself dry and turned to her. He didn't have to see the paper. He knew the notice to which she was referring.

"I heard about Jeffries," he replied. "I was goin' to tell you."

"Poor Peter. He died alone in that asylum. I guess I should thank you. If it hadn't been for you, I would have married him."

"There was a time when you did nae thank me," Ian reminded her lightly.

Eleanor gave him a rueful smile. "I was a foolish woman then—and you were impossibly arrogant."

"All that matters is that we both came to our senses when we did."

"Yes, but it is unfortunate that we wasted so much time and energy being angry with each other," she replied, regretful. "Are you certain that you don't want me to go with you to New York? Mary Kate may not see you, you know. I fear that she has inherited the willfulness of her father."

Ian shook his head. "I have other business to attend. And I seem to recall that her mother can be pretty stubborn as well."

Eleanor sighed. "Then I fear the poor girl is condemned."

"Mary Kate will come around."

"What of Patrick?" asked Eleanor.

"Parker said that it is much the same with him. But Mary Kate and Patrick will find someone else and move on."

"It has been six months, Ian. Pray that they don't waste too much more time, or they may find their opportunities gone."

Ian pulled up his suspenders and slipped on his vest. "Has Morgan left for school yet? I need to have a talk with him. The school principal has brought another complaint."

"That old fuddy duddy is always complaining about something. He picks on the boy."

"Perhaps with good reason. The boy skips school, is disruptive in class, and his grades are below standard," said Ian, putting on his coat. "Morgan needs a firmer hand, Eleanor. Nothin' will change until we force it to. Perhaps spendin' a summer working in the finishin' mill will make him think more seriously about his future."

"No, Ian, I'll talk with him. I promise." She smoothed Ian's coat across his shoulders and kissed him on the cheek. "Have a safe trip, darling."

As Ian made his way to the train station, his son was making his way toward trouble once again. Looking over his shoulder, Morgan furtively walked to a more secluded side of the school where his friend impatiently awaited him.

"Did you get them?" asked Billy Hooper.

Morgan grinned and pulled out two cigars that he had filched from his father's humidor.

"Do you think he'll notice that they're gone?"

"Naw. Besides, Papa is on his way to New York for a few days." Morgan took out the cutter and cut off the heads of the cigars, as he had seen his father do, before handing one to Billy. With an inexperienced flourish, he struck a match and lit the cigars. "Suck on it... harder," he instructed.

The boys inhaled deeply and began to cough. They gave it another try, the aroma of the cigar enveloping them.

"I don't feel so well," said Billy.

"You just have to get used to it," Morgan counseled him. "Try it again."

"I don't think so." Holding his stomach, Billy suddenly leaned over to retch.

Morgan was about to berate his friend on his lack of stamina when he, too, was seized with overwhelming nausea and sank to his knees to throw up. The boys leaned weakly against the wall, groaning and holding their stomachs, the cigars lying forgotten on the ground.

"Mr. Douglas and Mr. Hooper," said a sharp voice.

The boys looked up through a green haze to see their teacher Mr. Lutz staring down at them.

"Oh, bloody hell," moaned Morgan, employing one of his father's more colorful expressions.

"Are you adding swearing to your list of accomplishments now, Mr. Douglas? I am sure your parents will be happy to hear that you are learning something, though I doubt they will applaud your choice of subjects." Mr. Lutz yanked the boys to their feet. "I believe you know the way to the principal's office."

Billy looked at his teacher in alarm. "You're not going to tell my parents, are you?"

"That's the process, Mr. Hooper."

Billy continued to plead with Mr. Lutz as the teacher marched the boys to the principal's office. The panic that had initially seized Morgan subsided when he remembered that his father was out of town and his mother could be counted on to smooth things over with anyone who mattered. Thus, it was that he arrived at the principal's office in a much better frame of mind than Billy, much to the annoyance of his teacher.

* * * * *

Ian arrived in New York the next morning.

"The Mercantile Bank of New York on 35th and Fifth Avenue," he said to the cab driver and climbed inside the carriage.

Traffic was heavy; the trip across town was slow. At one point, four carriages became hopelessly entangled, blocking the street. Shouting ensued and two of the occupants nearly engaged in fisticuffs before the police arrived.

"Let me out here," said Ian. "I'll walk the last two blocks." He paid the driver and got out. When he arrived at the bank, he was immediately ushered into the president's office.

John Rinker enthusiastically greeted him. "Ian, it is good see you. It has been awhile."

The two men shook hands and Rinker motioned Ian to a chair.

"Sorry I'm late, John. I encountered quite a traffic jam."

Rinker shook his head. "It gets worse every day. The motorcars don't help." He opened a wood box and extended it to Ian.

Ian helped himself to a cigar and sniffed it appreciatively. "Cuban…mighty fine. Business must be good." He snipped off the head, took out a match and lit it. Taking a few puffs, he settled back into the chair to enjoy the aroma.

"What brings you to New York this time?" asked Rinker, taking his seat behind the desk.

"I have a couple of projects in the works that I want to keep quiet for awhile, John. So, I am seekin' outside funds. If I sell assets, it may raise suspicion."

The bank president smiled. "Reminds me of the old days. Franklin Jeffries is dead. Who are you embattled with this time?"

"A man by the name of George Biederman. He bought Jeffries' railroad from Jeffries' son durin' the '93 Panic. Apparently, Rossburg is nae big enough for the two of us."

Rinker gave a sigh of disgust. "There are always those who aren't content with the lion's share. They have to have it all. To bad they don't realize that once one gets it all, someone else appears to try to take it away. Do you ever get tired of fighting, Ian?"

"Sometimes."

"Well, I'm getting damned tired of it. I had hoped this no-holds-barred, bare knuckles capitalism would die with Cornelius Vanderbilt, but Rockefeller, Carnegie, and J.P. Morgan are just as bad—if not worse. It won't be long before every major industry in the country is in the hands of a few. How much wealth is enough for these people?"

"It's not about the wealth, John. It's about the the game and winnin'. The money be the icin' on the cake. And the advantage goes to those who can see what is comin' around the bend."

"What are you looking to invest in, Ian?"

"I want to expand my electric company. The company currently supplies power to most of the commercial sites and a few residents, and I just renewed a five-year contract with the city for streetlights. Thanks to the Niagara Falls Power Project and Edison's expanded electrical grid, electricity is becomin' cheap enough for the public to afford. I want to extend lines throughout the city and into rural areas, and I have to retool to change over to the AC current. An expansion of my phone company is already underway. I made sure that the right of ways I acquired would apply to electric lines as well. It would be helpful if I could string both lines at the same time."

"That's pretty ambitious."

"Just lookin' around the bend, John. Technology is progress. There be no turnin' it back."

"Why do you need to keep the project a secret? Is there another electric company in Rossburg?"

"Aye. But it services only the trolley system. It offers no competition at this point."

"What's the problem then?" asked the bank president.

"I sold the gas company to a local group of investors a few years back. Biederman is one of them. They're resistant to any efforts to replace gas with electricity," explained Ian. "They resurrect Rockefeller's campaign of fear whenever they feel threatened. None of the dangers they cite are true, of course, but it is difficult to unring a bell. I don't want to give them the chance to ring it this time. As it is, a sizable number of people are already convinced that electricity will make their watches run backwards."

Rinker shook his head. "Fear and superstition can be pretty hard to fight."

"As more and more people come to see that it is a safer, cleaner way to light their homes, they'll come around," said Ian with an air of confidence. "It is like anythin' else that is new or different."

"You mentioned another investment. What other bend are you looking around?"

"I want to start a motorcar company."

At this, the bank president raised a brow. "That's pretty speculative, Ian, even for you. The industry is still in its infancy."

"Motorcars are becomin' very popular, John. So popular, in fact, two brothers opened a garage in Rossburg to service them. They also sell new and used cars but can nae get their hands on enough of them. They approached me with an investment idea of buildin' our own motorcars. It would be a partnership, but I would have controllin' shares. The brothers would be responsible for the product. I would supply the capital."

"I don't know, Ian. There are a lot of companies out there building cars in every state. There are car manufacturing companies near you in Reading and York. What would be your competitive edge?"

"A better car," replied Ian. "I've seen the design, John, and the brothers are soon to build a prototype of a two-seater. It is sleek. They tell me the engine will be quieter than current motors, and the car will get up to a speed of 50. Next, the brothers intend to design a car large enough to transport a family."

"There are already models called limousines being built across the country that seat four, Ian."

"But there are not many, John. They are not affordable to enough people, and they are not closed to the elements. They have only a top cover. Our family cars will be enclosed."

Rinker didn't look entirely convinced. "I don't know. It would be a long time before you would see a sizeable return—if any at all—on that investment. Still, you have never been wrong about other ventures. What about the Association of Licensed Automobile Manufacturers? The five-member board has to unanimously agree to license your cars."

"As long as we agree to pay the royalty, I do nae think there will be a problem."

"How much do you need?"

"Five hundred thousand should be enough."

"Is your bank sound?"

"Aye. I keep double the required cash reserves and more in collateral," replied Ian.

"What about your personal worth? As I understand it, the lumber industry is in decline there."

"Aye, but my millworks and utility companies are profitable, and I own a good bit of real estate."

"Any stock on margin?"

"Not on margin. I learned that lesson in the Panic of 1893."

"Then I think we can do business," said Rinker. "You have always shown yourself to be a man of your word. Besides, I guess I owe you for paying off Ben Thompson's debts."

"Caroline Thompson was a friend of my wife. And I felt responsible since I vouched for Ben when you asked me for a reference."

"Ben did all right. He had some sound investments until he got the idea that he could run with the big dogs. It all began to fall apart when he hooked up with Charles Morse. I hated to call in the loan, but I had to do it before he lost any more money. This is a state bank. I can't sustain those kinds of loses."

"How is Mrs. Thompson doing since Ben died?"

Rinker smiled. "She has forgiven me. I'm courting her now."

Ian looked at him in surprise. "I thought you were a confirmed bachelor."

"I was until I met Caroline. There is something about the woman that screams out for someone to take care of her. She told me all about the past and why she and Ben left Rossburg. Nasty business that."

"When is the weddin'?" asked Ian.

"I don't know. After being left with no resources when Ben died, she won't marry me until she can support herself. I know an editor at the *New York Times* and helped her to get a job there, so hopefully the wedding won't be too far off. Caroline is a proud woman."

Ian smiled. "I know a couple of women like that."

"When are you returning to Rossburg?"

"Day after tomorrow. I have some other business in the city. John, what do you know about Ogden Stoddert and his family?"

"The Stodderts? They are an interesting family."

"How so?"

"Stoddert's money comes from a transatlantic shipping company. Ogden is an affable, easy-going fellow but smart. Nothing gets by him. He managed to survive J. P. Morgan's take over of the industry last year. He could be a high flier if he chose to be. He was invited to be a member of J. P.'s Metropolitan Club, but I guess he prefers to keep his enemy at arm's length. The family is more civic minded. I see them at charity events, particularly those benefiting Bellevue hospital. His wife is a benefactor. Why do you ask?"

"My daughter is makin' her home with Emily Stoddert."

Rinker laughed. "Mrs. Stoddert and her daughter can be quite a handful. They consider themselves to be free thinkers. Ogden indulges them and is a bit amused by it all, I think. He once told me that he gave up trying to control the women in his family; it made for a more peaceful house that way."

"I understand the son is a doctor," said Ian.

Rinker nodded. "Andrew is quite respected. Got his training in England, not at one of these diploma mills in America. He could have a thriving practice on Madison Avenue treating the elite, but Andrew prefers to work in the city hospital. He's an expert on respiratory diseases. Helped to open the Bellevue Chest Service last year during an outbreak of tuberculosis and is one of the founders of the National Tuberculosis Association. He's wealthy in his own right, you know. He invested in this new technology—x-rays and radiation."

Ian stubbed out his cigar and stood. "Thank you, John, for the loan, the cigar, and the information. I wish you and Caroline well."

Ian emerged from the bank and decided to walk the six blocks to the Granger Detective Agency. It was a pleasant June day, and the street traffic was still heavily congested.

It had been a long time since he had been to New York. The changes were astounding. There were signs of progress everywhere. Buildings so high that they were dubbed skyscrapers were being constructed at an astonishing rate. And papers were full of news of the construction of an underground electric train system. The first line was expected to open in 1905. What others viewed as noise and chaos of a modern world, Ian saw as endless possibilities in a bright, new age. And he marveled at his good fortune to live in such a time.

When Ian arrived at the Granger Detective Agency, he noted the rich appointments of the principal's office. The detective clearly concerned himself with mostly—if not exclusively—wealthy clientele. Parker's New York contact had referred Granger. The man curried favor with the elite and derived power by keeping their secrets. Ian knew the type without even meeting him and was reluctant to retain the man's services, but Mary Kate had entered a different world here. The elites in New York were not the same as the elites in Rossburg.

"Mr. Douglas, a pleasure to meet you, sir," greeted Granger with a hearty handshake. "Sorry to bring you all the way to New York, but I don't like to discuss personal matters over the telephone you understand. Please have a seat."

"I had other business to attend to in New York, Mr. Granger. 'Twas not an imposition. What did ye want to see me about?" asked Ian, settling himself in a chair. After meeting the man, Ian still didn't care much for him. For all of Granger's upper class affectations and expensive suit of clothes, there was something slimy about him.

The burly detective took his seat behind his desk and assumed a serious air. "I've had my best man watching out for your daughter. The latest reports are concerning, Mr. Douglas. You should know that she is borrowing trouble."

"How so, Mr. Granger?"

"She has become involved in a dangerous movement, and it isn't likely to end well."

Ian looked at the detective in surprise, his ill ease increasing. "What movement?"

"That movement that has been agitating for women's right to vote."

Ian relaxed. "If ye be talkin' about the suffragette movement, tis been around since before the Civil War, Mr. Granger. I hardly consider these women a dangerous group. They'll hold a few meetin's, and the issue will peter out until next time. 'Tis nothin' new."

"I'm afraid they mean business this time, Mr. Douglas. The movement is gaining traction here in the city and in upstate New York, and I understand it is spreading in Philadelphia, Washington, D.C., Virginia, and other places around the country. With the telegraph and now the telephone available to them, it is becoming easier for these women to organize on a national level." Granger snorted. "Matters of importance should be left to the decision of men. Women are too emotional for rational thought."

"What is your point, Mr. Granger?"

"Heretofore, the police have indulged these radical women. I am getting reports from some sources in the department that it will no longer be the case. The numbers of these women are growing, and they are becoming more outspoken to the point that they are ruffling too many feathers."

"How is my daughter involved?" questioned Ian.

"Miss Douglas has been in attendance at many of these meetings and has even spoken at a few. You need to persuade her to turn her energies to other pursuits—perhaps that of finding a husband to keep her in line—or she will most likely get hurt, Mr. Douglas. The police are putting out the word that they will no longer deal gently with these women. They need to nip this insurrection in the bud."

"I would nae call it an insurrection, but thank you for your report, Mr. Granger. I will have a talk with my daughter," said Ian.

Ian left the detective agency more disturbed than he had let on to the detective. He had planned to see Mary Kate the next day, but his concern was such that he immediately took a cab to the brownstone on Fifth Avenue.

There wasn't much he had feared in his life, but he felt nervous now about facing his daughter for the first time in six months. When the driver pulled up to the address, he sat for a minute to collect himself before stepping out of the conveyance. He paused again in front of the brownstone, then walked up the steps, and knocked on the door. A pretty, vivacious young woman with brunette hair and lively brown eyes answered the door.

Ian removed his hat and smiled. "I am Ian Douglas, Mary Kate's father," he said. "I understand her to be stayin' here."

The girl looked at the tall, stately gentlemen in surprise. "Mr. Douglas...I-I am pleased to meet you. I am Emily Stoddert. Forgive my manners, sir. Please come in."

Ian followed the young woman into a bright, sun-lit parlor.

"Mary Kate didn't say that you were coming for a visit."

"I did nae tell her that I would be in New York. I thought if I gave her notice, she might nae be here," replied Ian with a wry smile.

"Oh...well, Mary Kate is in her room. I'll tell her that you are here," said Emily. "Please make yourself comfortable, Mr. Douglas. I'll just be a minute." She went out into the foyer and rushed up the stairs to the second floor, not certain what to make of this. She knew that her friend was estranged from her family, but she didn't know the circumstances.

Ian remained standing, too nervous to sit.

A few minutes later, the front door opened, and a young man called out as he entered the parlor: "Emily, tell Mary Kate that I'm here—" He stopped short when he saw Ian. "I'm sorry. I didn't know Emily had a guest. I'm Andrew Stoddert, Emily's brother," he said.

The young man had a pleasant smile and an easygoing, forthright manner. Rinker's assessment appeared accurate, thought Ian. There was nothing pretentious about him.

When Ian introduced himself, Andrew was as surprised as his sister. "I'm happy to make your acquaintance, Mr. Douglas," he said extending his hand. "Mary Kate didn't mention that you were coming for a visit."

Ian shook Andrew's hand. "She did nae know. I take it that ye be here to see my daughter as well."

"Yes, sir. I persuaded Mary Kate to a dinner and an evening at the theater. She is a stubborn woman."

Ian smiled. "She takes after her mother that way. I understand ye to be a doctor."

"Yes, sir."

Emily appeared then, looking somewhat discomfited. "I'm sorry, Mr. Douglas. Mary Kate is-uh-not feeling well."

Ian smiled. "In other words she is refusin' to see me. You make a terrible liar, Miss Stoddert."

Emily gave up the pretense. "I'm sorry, Mr. Douglas. I tried to convince her to come downstairs, but—"

"'Tis quite all right. I suppose I should have expected that. I'll be stayin' at the Endicott Hotel until the day after tomorrow in case she changes her mind."

"I'll see you out, Mr. Douglas," said Andrew.

At the door, Ian turned to the young man. "Would you walk with me, Dr. Stoddert?"

"Of course."

As they walked down the steps to the sidewalk, Andrew glanced quizzically at Ian. "Do you wish to speak with me about something, sir?"

"Aye. I've had a detective keepin' an eye on Mary Kate while she has been here."

"I see," said Andrew, not quite sure how he was supposed to take that disclosure. "Are you saying that you object to me seeing your daughter, Mr. Douglas? If that is the case, I can assure you that—"

"No, that is not it, Doctor. I understand that Mary Kate is involved in the suffragette movement."

Andrew relaxed, visibly relieved. "Yes, sir—my sister, as well."

"How committed is my daughter?"

"Well, I'm sure you know that Mary Kate is a very passionate woman when it comes to things she cares about. She believes deeply in this cause."

"I was afraid of that," said Ian. "Where do you stand on the matter?"

"I support them, sir. This is a different age. Women should have a right to chart their own destiny."

"Hard issues are hard won, Doctor."

"Things of importance usually are, Mr. Douglas."

"Perhaps, but information has come to me that the police intend to deal harshly with any woman active in the movement. They consider it to be a subversive activity. I do nae wish for Mary Kate or your sister to be harmed."

"I understand your concern, sir. I will look after them."

Ian nodded. He paused for a moment. "Tell me, Dr. Stoddert, do ye have special feelin's for my daughter?"

The question took Andrew by surprise, but he met Ian's eye unflinchingly. "Yes, sir, I do—if only I can make her see that."

Ian smiled. "I wish ye luck, Doctor."

CHAPTER ELEVEN

A Game of Strategy

Parker settled into the leather wing chair in Ian's study. "I'm glad you are back, Ian. Eleanor said Mary Kate refused to see you in New York. I'm sorry to hear that."

Ian shrugged, more hurt than he wanted to admit. "As ye said, 'twill take time. I sense that another matter has brought ye here though. What is it?"

An expression of concern crossed Parker's face. "Since Harry Sims died, Biederman is making a move to take over the Rossburg Passenger Railway Company."

Ian was pensive as he poured drinks, handed one to Parker, and sat down on the leather sofa. "How overextended is he?"

According to my investigator, he isn't, and we were right about him paying off the loans of Crandle, Hockings, Jacobs, and the other three members for their votes for his membership on the Board—and for future votes. My operative encountered Crandle at the Crystal Palace and bought him a few drinks, and he spilled the beans. "I think you were right, Ian. Biederman is aiming to take over the association. Crandle told my operative that he is planning to bring up his son for membership."

"Horace is ineligible. He does nae own his own company," said Ian.

"You're right. I had forgotten about that provision."

The same thought suddenly occurred to both men at the same time.

"That's why Biederman wants the Passenger Railway Company," said Parker.

"To give Horace ownership of a company for membership eligibility," continued Ian. "There be nothin' in the bylaws to say that Horace has to be the one to purchase the company. Biederman can sign ownership over to him."

"That is something that will have to change," remarked Parker. "Why don't you bid on the trolley company yourself?"

Ian shook his head. "Biederman would find another way to get Horace into the association. And the trolley company nae be doin' well as it is."

"That's because Sims was too cheap to extend the rails. Don't forget that the 1863 charter signed by Governor Curtain gave the company carte blanche to lay trolley tracks on any street in the city. That still stands."

"With Biederman, one has to choose his battles," said Ian. "This nae be one I want to fight with him. Besides, I hear Jasper Tomlin is interested in acquirin' the company. Let him fight it out with Biederman."

"You could apply to the state and start your own passenger railway," suggested Parker.

"As you pointed out, the Passenger Railway Company has the monopoly on all the streets. Besides, I do nae believe the trolley is the future for mass transportation. 'Tis restricted to those areas where there is track."

Parker looked at his friend questioningly. "What then is the future?"

Ian smiled. "The motorcar."

Parker looked doubtful. "They are becoming more popular, but that's a pretty big leap."

"Have a little faith, Parker."

Stanton glanced at Ian. "You are up to something. And don't deny it. We've been friends far too long."

Ian smiled and explained his plans to expand the electric company and to start the city's first motorcar manufacturing company.

"Geez, Ian, that is a lot of capital. You won't see much of a return on either investment for a long time. What if Biederman acquires the trolley system and expands the electric company that comes with it to compete against you?"

"You forget he's part of the consortium that bought the gas company from me, Parker. Rather than expandin' electrification to the city and county, he'll be doin' everythin' he can to prevent it. Hopefully, he'll be too busy with his other concerns to notice my business."

Again, Parker looked doubtful. "He has made it his business to know your business. Once you start running lines, he's going to notice."

"Not if I run them simultaneously with the phone lines. It'll buy me some time," said Ian.

"He'll notice when you start retooling and building another power station."

"It won't matter once I get the subscriptions and have the lines run. As far as the Sun Motorcar Company goes, he'll probably see that as a fool's errand instead of an opportunity."

Parker shook his head. "I hope you know what you're doing."

"I'm not just talkin' about people motorin' about. Think about it, Parker. Transportation of goods by trains is limited to rails as well, rails that are expensive to maintain. And several of the lines have already shut down because there isn't enough freight to fill all the railcars. Crop yields are down, and Rockefeller built a pipeline system to transport his oil to his refineries. There needs to be a larger kind of motor carrier that can move goods easier and cheaper throughout the country."

"That's pretty far off, Ian—probably beyond our lifetime. You would need a system of roads and fueling stations in place."

"This is the age of industry, Parker. It is a short step from imagination to reality these days. But the foundation must be laid now."

"I hope you are right."

"Progress has never been made from inactivity. Speakin' of progress, how go Maven's plans for the school?"

Parker sighed. "I hardly see her. She has been running all over town looking for space, talking to retired teachers about lending their instruction, scrounging for supplies. She persuaded Mrs. Curtis' company to donate some reconditioned sewing machines and typewriters. There are already a number of young women in the city ready to sign up, and Maven plans to send advertisements to the papers in Harrisburg and other surrounding towns."

Ian laughed. "When Maven has an idea in her head, there be no gettin' it out. How goes the application for the loan from the Board of Trade?"

"The committee keeps dragging its feet," replied Parker. "Since I found the loophole in the requirements—or rather Maven did—that doesn't specifically exclude the family of board members, they're arguing that it is implied. If they reject Maven's application on those grounds, they know I'll take it to court. Neither of us want that, so the committee is looking for other reasons to refuse it."

Ian snorted. "I wonder if the application and argument had been made by a male family member, would it be seein' the same objections?"

"I warned Maven that being a woman opening a technical school for young women to compete against men for better jobs could be a bit of a problem," said Parker. "It might give them other notions as well don't you know?" He laughed humorlessly. "I am sure the committee is busy revising its eligibility requirements."

Ian shook his head in disgust. "Some things never change no matter the technological progress. If Maven is really serious about this, why do ye nae be an investor?"

"You know Maven. She wants to do this on her own," replied Parker. But until she gets some paying students to cover the costs of those who can't afford to pay, she has no stream of revenue. The proceeds from the sale of the house that she had with Tommy won't carry her very far. If she doesn't get the money from the Board of Trade, I don't see how she can move forward with the school."

"I can secure a loan for her at the bank," said Ian.

"You know how she feels about bank loans. She won't take it."

"She has nae changed over the years either, has she?"

Parker's mouth twisted in a wry smile. "Not much. I had to fight her tooth and nail to get her to allow a telephone in the house. She still won't use it. She claims it is a threat to her privacy. Imagine what she'll say to electricity and a motorcar. Is Morgan out of the dog house yet?"

Ian laughed. "Sin is its own punishment. The boy can nae so much as look at a cigar without turnin' green. He has also learned that his father notices when expensive cigars go missin' and that his mother is comin' to the end of her rope with him. When the truth of the incident came out, Eleanor agreed that Morgan should be made to work the summer. I compromised on it bein' at the bank instead of at the finishin' mill. Next time, he will nae be so lucky."

CHAPTER TWELVE

Face of a Movement

Eleanor looked up and smiled as Mary Kate was escorted to her table in Delmonico's. Mary Kate didn't return the smile.

"Thank you for coming," said Eleanor, masking her disappointment. "I wasn't certain that you would."

"I almost didn't," Mary Kate replied candidly as she took the seat that the waiter held out for her. "Why are you here, Mama? If you came to talk me into coming home, you wasted a trip."

"Your father and I were very concerned about the tuberculosis epidemic. It will happen again. You would be safer in Rossburg."

"I told you then that Emily's brother is a doctor and has educated us on the precautions to take during outbreaks. And they are becoming fewer."

"Still, we worry about you. The holidays are almost upon us. At least come home for Christmas."

Mary Kate remained stubbornly obstinate. "No, I can't, Mama."

Eleanor sighed, at a loss as to how to connect with her daughter. "Your father was very hurt that you refused to see him when he was here. Don't you think you have punished him enough? He has suffered as much as you have."

"Perhaps he should have thought of that when he made one woman pregnant and married another."

Eleanor blanched at her daughter's blunt assessment. "That's not fair. You don't know the circumstances."

"I don't care what the circumstances were. What if Patrick and I had shared intimacies?"

Eleanor looked at her daughter in alarm. "Mary Kate, tell me you didn't—"

"Don't worry, Mama. At least in that regard I am your daughter." She paused. "Patrick is getting married, you know." Her voice dropped, and a shadow of pain crossed her features. "I saw it on the society page in the paper—the daughter of a partner in his law firm. It promises to be quite the society wedding in Philadelphia."

"Yes, I know." Eleanor reached out and took her daughter's hand to console her, but Mary Kate pulled it away.

"Apparently, Patrick was able to move on," she said, her tone bitter. "But I still love him, Mama. And every day I am haunted by what might have passed between us before the truth came out. How do I get past that?"

Eleanor was stricken by the hurt in her daughter's eyes and the anger in her voice. "I am very sorry for your pain, Mary Kate. But you have to let go of this, or it will destroy you. Until you make peace with it and your father, you will never be able to move on."

"Has Patrick made peace with Papa?"

"No," Eleanor admitted.

The waiter came to the table to take their order.

"I'm not staying for lunch," said Mary Kate. "I'm afraid you made the trip for nothing, Mama."

When she stood up to leave, Eleanor pleaded with her: "Mary Kate, please—"

"I'm sorry, Mama. I'm not ready to forgive any of this. If you want to do something to help, tell Horace to stop pestering me."

Eleanor looked up at her daughter. "Horace Biederman has visited you here?"

"You don't have to look so surprised. I know you gave him my address. Horace has given me to know that you and Papa are encouraging his courtship."

"Mary Kate, I didn't—"

"But it's not going to work. I don't love him, and I am not going to marry him no matter how hard you, Papa, and Horace try to convince me. Goodbye, Mama." She turned and quickly wove her way through the restaurant to the door.

Eleanor sighed and a heavy sadness fell over her. Not in the mood for lunch now either, she started to gather her things to leave, when a woman approached her.

"Hello, Eleanor."

The woman was older, a little heavier, and her brown hair was flecked with gray, but Eleanor had no trouble recognizing her childhood friend. "Caroline! What a wonderful surprise. I can't believe—this is really quite amazing. I was thinking about you just the other day. Please, sit down."

Caroline took the chair that Mary Kate had vacated. "I was having lunch when I looked over and saw you. I knew it was you. You've hardly changed at all, Eleanor."

"Thank you. Neither have you, Caroline."

Her old friend smiled. "You are too kind. I saw your daughter. She looks like you."

Eleanor gave a short laugh. "I doubt that she would consider that a compliment. Mary Kate is living here in New York now. I was hoping to persuade her to come home with me. But the young these days seem to have minds of their own," she said with a heavy sigh. "But tell me about you, Caroline. What are you doing in New York?"

"Ben and I came here when we left Rossburg. We figured we would find anonymity here until everything was worked out. It was a few years before I was able to obtain a divorce from Peter," explained Caroline. "I've wanted to write you many times over the years, but I didn't know how you would receive my letters."

Eleanor smiled. "I never judged you, Caroline. In fact, the last time we talked, you made me reconsider a lot of things. I have always taken your side. And now, I think the whole affair is well in the past. You know that Peter died recently."

"Yes, I heard. Ben passed as well—three years ago."

"I'm sorry."

"I thought of returning to Rossburg then, but my parents were still unforgiving of the scandal. Now they are gone, and there seemed to be no point to it."

Caroline paused and looked away for a moment. "It was a very difficult time for me when Ben died, Eleanor. It came to light that he had made some bad investments, and I was left with rather large debts. I had neither money nor a skill. I was about to be turned out of my house. I didn't know what to do or where to turn. Your husband helped me. I don't know where I would be today if it hadn't been for his kindness. I owe him so much."

Eleanor's eyes widened in surprise. "Ian never told me."

"I was so ashamed I asked him not to say anything to you. He has connections with the bank that held Ben's debts. He heard about my problem and covered all of Ben's loans. I expect one day to repay Mr. Douglas. I have a job writing for the women's section in the *New York Times*. Mr. Rinker, the bank president, helped me to secure an interview with an editor at the paper." Caroline smiled shyly. "Mr. Rinker and I are courting now."

Eleanor was amazed. "I am very happy everything has turned out well for you, Caroline."

"I was going to write and tell you all of this one day. Where are you staying?"

"At the Waldorf-Astoria. I leave tomorrow."

"My house is not so grand as the Waldorf-Astoria, but please come and stay with me, Eleanor. We have so much to catch up on."

"I would like that very much, Caroline. Thank you." Eleanor's brow furrowed then with another thought. "Caroline, what do you know of this suffragette movement? My daughter seems to have gotten herself involved in it."

"I know."

"You know?"

"Yes. I met Mary Kate a few months ago at one of the rallies that the newspaper had sent me to cover. She was one of the speakers." Caroline smiled. "When I saw her and heard her name, I knew she had to be your daughter. Her resemblance to you is striking. I approached her and explained that I was an old friend of yours. Since then, our paths have crossed a few more times."

Caroline hesitated. "I must confess that I am not here by happenstance, Eleanor. I saw Mary Kate yesterday, and she told me that she was meeting you at the restaurant today. I-I was hoping to see you again. I have greatly missed your friendship. We used to have such good times together."

Eleanor smiled. "Yes, we did. I have missed you as well, and we shall not lose touch again," she vowed.

"I was hoping you would feel that way," replied Caroline. "Now, to your question about the movement. Many women support it but are limited in what they can do. They must practice discretion so as not to compromise their husbands' careers or their own jobs. High society women, on the other hand, generally oppose it."

"Why?" asked Eleanor. "I should think them to be more progressive."

"One would think so, but they fear it will diminish the power they hold by virtue of their status," replied Caroline. "Other women believe it unseemly to question their husband's authority. And, then, there are those women who believe the propaganda that suffragettes are masculine, abnormal females. These women actually fear they will grow beards if given the vote."

"You're joking," said Eleanor, astounded by the ignorance.

Caroline shook her head. "I wish I were. Working class women do what they can for the cause, but it is mostly members of the literary elite—like your daughter—who are carrying the movement forward," she explained. "It is thanks to them that the momentum is building.

These young women are highly educated, articulate, and are from families of means. It is more difficult for opponents to paint them as crackpots, and pressure is being put on the police to stop their activities by whatever means."

"Dear God, what has Mary Kate gotten herself into? How much danger is she in?" asked Eleanor, concerned.

Caroline hesitated. "Mary Kate and Emily Stoddert are fast becoming the local faces of the movement."

"What is that to mean?"

"Besides speaking at rallies, Mary Kate and Emily are lending their images to posters and promotional materials," said Caroline. "Their youth and beauty help to counteract the myths and fears being disseminated by the movement's detractors."

Eleanor became alarmed. "Then, Mary Kate will become a target. Ian has no influence here."

"Mary Kate's connection to the Stoddert family will afford her some protection," Caroline assured her. "But I have advised her and Emily to be especially careful and to perhaps pull back a little."

This didn't help to dispel Eleanor's concern. "In Mary Kate's case, that's like telling a child she can't go near the water. It draws her all the more. Do you support this movement, Caroline?"

"Yes, I have to say that I do. Times have changed, Eleanor. Young women today are much more independent-minded. They are demanding the right to direct their own lives, and it cuts across all classes. The daughters of affluent families are refusing to exchange their voices for privilege. They are not willing to be bargaining chips in arranged marriages anymore. And more and more women are joining the workforce demanding the same protections and opportunities as their male co-workers."

"What difference does the vote make for women when it is men who write the laws?" questioned Eleanor.

"The vote is the first step to opening the door for women to have a say in the laws that are written."

Eleanor was skeptical. "Women have been fighting for suffrage for decades. While I applaud the courage of these women, I fear that they are putting themselves—my daughter included—in danger to no avail."

"It is different this time," replied Caroline. "In this modern age, women have ways to organize that they didn't have before."

Mary Kate arrived home from the luncheon with her mother in a heavy mood and was starting up the stairs to her room, when Andrew and Emily came out of the parlor.

"There you are," said Andrew. "I came to ask you and Em to dinner tonight, but, as it turns out, Em has plans. So I guess it comes down to you and me."

"I wouldn't be very good company, Drew," she responded dully.

Andrew concealed his disappointment. "Em said you met your mother for lunch. I take it that things did not go well."

"I don't want to talk about it."

"Locking yourself up in your room and moping for the rest of the day isn't going to help. Come on, Mary Kate. You girls don't keep enough food in the house to feed a mouse. And an evening out will take your mind off whatever is troubling you."

As Mary Kate continued to hesitate, Andrew shot a glance at his sister, silently pleading for her support. He had to seize his moments when Horace Biederman wasn't around.

"He's right," said Emily, taking her brother's cue. "And it isn't often that Drew offers to pick up the tab. If I were you, I wouldn't pass up his invitation. It could be ages—if ever—before he makes the offer again."

Mary Kate sighed. "All right, you win. Pick me up at six o'clock. But I can't promise you that my mood will be much improved," she warned. "You might want to reconsider."

"I'll take my chances," said Andrew.

When Mary Kate disappeared up the stairs, Emily took her brother aside. "Don't push her too hard." She handed him a crumpled page of newspaper. "Mary Kate was reading this a couple of days ago when her spirits took a nosedive. I think this notice may explain a few things."

It was a society engagement announcement in a Philadelphia paper. Andrew wasn't sure what it had to do with Mary Kate until his attention was drawn to the fact that the groom-to-be was a native of Rossburg, Pennsylvania.

He folded up the paper and put it in his pocket. "Thanks, Em, I owe you."

As he headed for the door, Emily called out to him. "Don't think I won't collect."

Andrew turned and smiled. "Let's see where this goes first."

At dinner that evening, Mary Kate was reserved throughout much of the meal, seemingly unimpressed with the posh, rooftop restaurant above Madison Square Garden.

"How long is your mother in the city?" asked Andrew, casting about for conversation.

Mary Kate shrugged, moving the food around on her plate with a fork. "She didn't say; I didn't ask. She came to talk me into returning home."

"Did she succeed?"

"No. We seem to be at an impasse on the subject."

"I suppose that is not surprising. Your father said that you and your mother are much alike—both stubborn," remarked Andrew lightly.

Mary Kate looked at him. "You talked with my father?"

"Yes, I met him when he came to the brownstone in June. He seemed to be a nice man. I liked him."

"You don't know him," she responded with a sharp edge to her tone. Mary Kate forced a smile then. "Let's not talk about my family. May I have another glass of wine?" she asked, holding out her goblet.

Andrew signaled to the waiter, who immediately came forward and refilled their glasses.

"It might help you to talk about it," Andrew prodded gently.

"Talk about what?"

"You have been living with my sister for a year now. You won't talk about your family or your home. You refused to see your father when he came to visit, and I take it that things did not go well with your mother this afternoon. What are you running from, Mary Kate?"

The question took her by surprise, and her manner took an abrupt turn. "I'm sorry, Drew. This was a bad idea. Please take me home now."

Andrew studied her for a long moment before signaling the waiter for the check.

They rode home in the cab in awkward silence, punctuated by the clip clop of the horse's hooves on the pavement. Andrew knew he had pushed her enough for one evening. He wondered if he would get another chance with her. When they arrived at the brownstone, he handed her down. She started up the steps, but he put a hand on her arm.

"You have to deal with whatever is bedeviling you, Mary Kate. You will become a lonely, embittered woman if you don't, forever stuck in the same place."

"I'm sorry if I ruined your evening, Drew." She pulled her arm free and hurried up the steps.

As she disappeared inside the residence, he frowned. She had firmly shut him out. He took out the newspaper item that had sent her into such a tailspin and tried to fit the pieces of the story together. Obviously, she had had a prior relationship with this Patrick O'Brien that her parents had disapproved of, and they had put an end to the romance. That he could deal with. More difficult for him was that, after all of this time, Mary Kate was still unable or unwilling to put the matter behind her, blinding her to any other possibilities. How could he get her to notice him?

CHAPTER THIRTEEN

An Ultimatum

Horace sat uncomfortably before his father to deliver his most recent report on his pursuit of Mary Kate. These conferences were becoming more frequent, as his father grew impatient for results. And once again, Horace was forced to report little progress.

"There's this doctor who keeps getting in the way," said Horace in his defense. "He's the brother of the girl Mary Kate is living with, and he interferes every chance he gets. I send her flowers every other week and take her to the best restaurants and entertainment in the city. What more can I do?"

"You can quit harassing her," said Ian, walking purposefully into the room. "She is not interested, Horace." He shut the door on the assistant who followed after him and pulled the blinds in the office.

Both father and son stared at Ian in disbelief.

"What are you doing here?" sputtered the elder Biederman.

"I'm putting an end to Horace's courtship of my daughter," replied Ian in no uncertain terms. "Had I known of it sooner, I would have been here then."

"You said you had no objections to Horace pressing his suit."

"I also said it was Mary Kate's decision. My daughter made it quite clear to my wife during her recent visit to New York that she does not welcome Horace's interest in her."

George Biederman forced a smile. "Ian, be practical. What do flighty, young women know?"

"My daughter knows that she doesn't want to spend her life with Horace, and that is good enough for me."

"She didn't say that to me—exactly," Horace finished weakly as Ian turned an icy glare on him.

"Move on, Horace, you don't really love her. Any rich girl will do for you," he said.

George Biederman's manner became smug. "You should appreciate that I allow my son to consider a courtship with your daughter, Douglas. Not many fathers of our class would, in light of the fact that you were once charged with murder and created quite a scandal involving a Mrs. O'Brien."

Ian's features hardened. "The murderer was found, and I was exonerated of the charge. As for Mrs. O'Brien and me, we are childhood friends. The rumors were groundless, but they caused her and my wife a great deal of pain. So be careful, Biederman. If you stir that pot again, you won't have only me to deal with."

"Are you threatening me, Douglas?"

Ian leveled a hard gaze on the man. "No, I'm warning you, George. Mrs. O'Brien is now Mrs. Stanton. If you do anything to hurt her, Parker will bring down upon your head every major legal authority from here to Philadelphia to New York—everywhere your trains go. He is well connected and can be very creative when it comes to litigation."

Ian turned and left the office then, leaving father and son speechless.

CHAPTER FOURTEEN

Carry On

Mary Kate stood nervously in the hall of Bellevue Hospital. It seemed a very long time since the nurse had gone in search of Dr. Stoddert. She was beginning to think that he didn't want to see her, when he appeared from the ward wearing a white lab coat.

"Mary Kate, the nurse said you were here," said Andrew, surprised. After their last dinner date, he had decided to give her some space. Concern suddenly shadowed his face. "You are not ill, are you?"

"No, Drew. You haven't been by for quite some time, and we missed you at your parents' Christmas festivities. I—Emily has been wondering where you have been," she quickly amended.

"Oh. Over the holidays, I always cover for the doctors who have kids," he explained. "The family knows that. And since Christmas, an outbreak of the flu has kept me busy at the hospital. Does Em need something? She's usually happy to have me keep my distance."

"No, Emily is fine. I—we haven't had a chance to thank you for the brooch timepieces you sent us for Christmas," said Mary Kate, searching for conversation. "They are lovely. See, I wear mine now." She lifted one side of her wrap to show the watch.

Drew laughed. "I see that. Emily has lost so many timepieces I figured if the watch were pinned to her blouse or jacket it wouldn't be so easy for her to lose. As it is undetermined how many of Em's bad habits have rubbed off on you, I thought it best to give you one too."

"Well, I shan't lose mine," Mary Kate assured him.

"Between you and me, I think Emily misplaces the watches on purpose so that she has an excuse to be late," joked Andrew. "They are probably all in a drawer somewhere."

Mary Kate giggled. "It wouldn't surprise me."

"But you didn't have to come all this way to thank me, Mary Kate."

Mary Kate shifted uncertainly. "Actually, Drew, I came because—well, I was hoping that you might ask me to dinner," she finally got out.

"Why? Is Horace in the city again?"

Mary Kate laughed. "No. As a matter of fact, he hasn't visited for quite some time. I think he got the message. The truth is I feel guilty for the way I behaved the last time we went to dinner, and I miss our discussions. I promise to be a much more pleasant companion this time around…I'll pay," she added as a further enticement.

Andrew smiled. "Well, my wits could do with a bit of sharpening. How does tomorrow night sound?"

"I'll be ready," she replied.

As she moved to the entrance to leave, Andrew called out to her. "Mary Kate, wait…I've had a change of mind."

Mary Kate's face fell, and she turned back to him. "Drew, I know that I—"

"Make it dinner this evening—seven o'clock," he said.

She smiled broadly. "It's a date, Doctor."

True to her word, Mary Kate was of a much better temperament and a much more engaging dinner partner this time. Her eyes shone and her personality crackled as she told Andrew about the convention that she and Emily were going to be attending in England with a group of suffragettes. She was more animated than he had ever seen her. And Andrew sat back captivated, content to allow her to carry the evening.

"And what did Mother have to say about Emily going to England?" he asked curiously.

"Not only has Mrs. Stoddert given her consent, she has decided to accompany us as well," Mary Kate informed him.

Andrew laughed. "Father must be happy about that."

"Emily says your father is very supportive. He is quite forward thinking." Mary Kate fell silent for a moment. "He reminds me of my father in that way," she said in a low, quiet tone.

Andrew signaled to the waiter who immediately came forward to refill their wine glasses. "So, when do you leave?" he asked, getting her back on track. He wasn't about to let this evening go flat.

Mary Kate recovered her excitement. "We sail March 30th and return the end of April."

"Six weeks—that soon? What about your studies?"

Mary Kate sighed. "Honestly, Drew, I don't think I am cut out for books. They bore me. I need to be more active."

Andrew thought for a moment. "Why don't you consider volunteering at the hospital when you come back from England?"

Mary Kate looked at him in surprise. "What would I do? I have no training."

"You could work in the women's ward reading to patients, running errands for the nurses, doing simple chores."

Her eyes lit up as she considered the suggestion. "Yes, I think I would like to try that."

The more he thought about it, the more Andrew liked the idea as well. It would be nice, not to mention beneficial, having her near him.

They finished their dinner, and he saw her home. When he walked her up the steps of the townhouse, Andrew was loath to say goodnight. But the night air was cold, and he could see that Mary Kate was shivering. "I shall miss you while you are in England," he said, opening the door for her. "Who else am I going to argue issues with?"

"I'm sure you will not lack for distractions," she replied with an impish smile. "But for what it is worth, I shall miss you, too. It was a lovely evening, Drew. Thank you. I quite enjoyed it." She kissed him on the cheek and entered the house in high spirits.

Andrew sighed. It was going to be a damnably long month without her.

CHAPTER FIFTEEN

Ambivalence

In Philadelphia, Patrick O'Brien picked up a newspaper from the corner newsstand on his way to his law office. As he leafed through it, the picture of a group of determined-looking ladies embarking on a trip to England for a suffragette convention caught his eye. He had to smile. Mary Kate was standing front and center. His mood suddenly fell flat. It was moments like this that stirred a well of anger inside of him just when he thought he had laid the past to rest.

When he entered the building, he stopped at the receptionist's desk. "Any messages, Miss Warner?"

"Just one from your fiancée reminding you of your luncheon date, sir."

"Oh...right," replied Patrick, his tone lacking enthusiasm. He wasn't in the mood to talk about wedding plans now.

He went into his office. He had three hours to collect himself, and he threw himself into the one thing that helped him to restore a sense of equilibrium in such times—his work. He was so successful in his goal that he arrived at the restaurant a half hour late.

His fiancée waved to him, and Patrick quickly made his way to her table. "Sorry, Abby, I was going through a deposition and lost track of the time," he said, sliding into a chair.

Abigail smiled. "No matter. You are here now."

Patrick felt a measure of contrition. Abigail was generous that way. She was never critical, never demanding.

He summoned the waiter. The waiter came quickly. Patrick was a frequent diner, and the waiter knew that this patron didn't like to dilly-dally. Patrick placed the luncheon order, and the waiter immediately dispatched it to the kitchen.

The order arrived promptly, even by Patrick's standards. As they ate, Abigail launched into an account of the wedding plans. Patrick listened with half an ear, his mind on another matter. Even so, he noticed as her face lit up with excitement as she presented the details.

She was two years his junior. Her features were plain but not unattractive. He liked the way her eyes crinkled and her cheeks dimpled when she smiled and the way her lips curled up when she was amused. And he liked her keen sense of humor that did not dip into silliness. Her hair was brown and straight, dressed in a more severe style with no waves or curled tendrils to soften the effect, and, while the material of her dress was expensive and expertly tailored to her tall, slim figure, the style was conservative as well.

Her personality was on the whole demure and calm, reflective of a mature woman of intelligence, good sense, and even temperament. She was the opposite of the blonde, blue-eyed, vivacious Mary Kate, whose curly hair always seemed to be at odds with her comb and pins and whose passionate nature and vision conflicted at times with the world around her. Perhaps that was why he had chosen Abigail Tanner. She was nothing like Mary Kate.

"Patrick, you are a million miles away. You have scarcely heard a word I've said," said Abigail with a resigned smile. She recognized that faraway look in his eyes. It appeared whenever she began to talk about the wedding. "I need your input."

Patrick mentally shook himself. "Abby, the wedding is a year away. You will more than likely change your mind a dozen times before then." He paused with another thought. "Abby, where do you stand on the suffragette movement?"

Abigail looked at him in surprise. The question had come out of nowhere. "Why do you ask?"

Patrick shrugged. "No reason. In regards to the wedding, you have impeccable taste, my dear. I am sure you will make the right choices."

On the outside, Abigail's manner was calm and collected. Inside, she felt disturbed and uncertain. Patrick had not been himself lately. He seemed distant, disengaged, uninterested in the wedding plans—more so than usual—and he spent too many hours at the office, in spite of the fact that her father had given him time off to prepare for the grand event. It was to be the society wedding of the year, and she was becoming increasingly worried that he might be absent from it—if not in body, then in spirit. He had never been overly demonstrative toward her, but from the moment he had looked her way, he had captured her heart. And imbued with the principles of her class, she had not asked for anything more in return.

"You are not getting cold feet, are you?" she teased, trying to keep her voice light.

Patrick looked into her large, brown eyes. They were her most attractive feature. That and her dimples were the first things that he had noticed about her. He smiled and patted her hand reassuringly. "A difficult case has come up."

"But Father has given you the time off."

"This is your wedding, Abigail. I want you to do whatever makes you happy."

"No, Patrick, this is *our* wedding—yours and mine," she reminded him quietly but firmly.

"If it were my wedding, we would be getting married by a justice of the peace at the town hall, my dear. Weddings are for women. They should be planned by women." He stood up. "I have to return to the office now."

"You are impossible, Patrick O'Brien. I don't know why I agreed to marry you in the first place."

"Yes, you do," he replied with a smile and a wink.

Abigail's heart melted. When he allowed his mischievous side to show, she found it easier to discount her fears that he didn't love her and that she was just a steppingstone to him in his career.

CHAPTER SIXTEEN

An Unlikely Alliance

Ian had closed down the sawmill when all the logs were used up from the millpond and moved his office closer to the finishing mill. It had been a difficult chapter to close in his life, but he knew it was time to move on and embrace a new reality. The lumber era was dead in Rossburg.

He was studying reports, trying to figure out his next move regarding the millworks, when Parker suddenly burst into his office in a high state of agitation.

"What the devil has you by the tail?" he asked in surprise.

Stanton threw a letter on the desk. "The Board of Trade refused Maven's grant request for start-up capital."

"We both knew it was a long shot. What reason did they come up with?"

"They awarded it to someone else—Horace Biederman. Apparently, the fact that his father is a member of board isn't an issue."

"I didn't know Horace had applied. How the bloody hell is he eligible?" questioned Ian.

"George sneaked the application in at the last minute. It seems that Horace is the new owner of the Rossburg Passenger Railway Company. The sale was publically announced this morning. I told you that you should have fought for it," said Parker.

Ian furrowed his brow in bewilderment. "One of the criteria for the loan is that the applicant be startin' a new business. 'Tis in the motion that was passed. Horace is takin' over ownership of a business that already exists. He nae be eligible."

"Yeah, I made that argument," responded Parker, disgusted. "The committee maintains that new ownership and new license is technically a new business."

"The hairs they split keep gettin' thinner," remarked Ian satirically. "How much is the association puttin' up?"

"One third. The Rossburg National Bank is loaning the rest."

Ian leaned back in his chair as he considered the matter. "So George gets control of the electric company and the trolley system by way of Horace without any financial risk to himself. Smart move. His next step will be to get Horace into the association. That will give him another vote."

"We could start a competing trolley company," suggested Parker.

Ian shook his head. "What good would that do? You know the Rossburg Passenger Railway Company was given a state charter that gave it a monopoly on the streets."

"That was in 1868. We can get the legislation changed," argued Parker. "I have contacts in Harrisburg. We can work quietly behind the scenes and present Biederman with a fait accompli, like we did when we got the boom rate increased in 1879. The lumber barons didn't know what had hit them."

Ian smiled. "That was a moment of sweet revenge," he admitted. "I'll think about it. But it doesn't solve Maven's problem."

Parker ran a hand threw his hair. "Geez, Ian, what am I going to tell her? She has her heart set on this school. She has been working night and day to bring it all together."

"She is goin' to have to swallow some of her pride and take a loan from the bank if she won't accept money from you," replied Ian matter-of-factly.

"You tell her that."

Ian laughed. "Marriage has turned you into a coward, my friend."

"Oh, and I suppose Eleanor holds no sway over you." Parker looked at his watch and groaned. "I have to go. Maven wants me to meet her at this building she found for the school. Any advice?"

"Flowers, a nice piece of jewelry, and a couple glasses of champagne before you tell her."

Parker gave him a wry smile. "This is Maven, Ian. She would know in an instant something was up."

Reluctantly, Stanton made his way to the site, practicing several different speeches along the way and finding none to suit. Maven waved to him, and his heart dropped. He could see the excitement on her face. As he crossed the street to her, he was beginning to wish he had taken Ian's advice to, at least, ply her with champagne before their visit to the site.

"What do ye think?" she asked, when he had reached her. "It would make a perfect school, and the location is handy to the streetcar."

Parker looked at the run-down, two-story building. "It will need a good bit of work," he said, hoping to dim her enthusiasm. "How much is the owner asking for it?"

"Given the condition of the buildin', I was able to negotiate a price well within me budget," she replied.

"*You* negotiated—I thought that was my job."

"It is, dear, but ye be so busy I didna want to bother ye. When I researched the property, I found out that the city has been threatenin' the owner with fines if he does not make repairs to it. I simply pointed out to Mr. Harrison that it would cost him more to make the repairs than he could sell the property for. It was not difficult to show him that my offer was the better option. I was thinkin' that the Rossburg Tech School for Boys might make it a class project. I've spoken with the school's administrator, and he is quite enthusiastic about the idea. I would need to pay only for supplies."

Parker regarded his wife with wonder. He always knew she was capable and smart, but, still, she never ceased to amaze him. "What made you think to research the property?"

"'Tis a very good attorney I be married to," she said with a twinkle in her eye.

"Well, your plan is sound," he conceded. He paused, hating to have to burst her bubble. "Maven, I have to tell you something."

"What is it, dear?"

"The Board of Trade awarded the loan to someone else. I'm sorry, darling."

Maven's face fell, and the light faded from her eyes. "Oh. I guess it shouldn't come as a surprise. Ye warned me that my application would not be met with much favor."

"All does not have to be lost," said Parker. "Ian's bank will make you the loan, or you can take the money from me."

Maven shook her head. "No, it was a silly idea. Heavens, I have my hands full with the dress shop."

"It was not a silly idea. You will save a lot of young women from the factories and the street." He took her firmly by the shoulders. "If you believe strongly in this school, Maven, you will set aside your pride and consider these other two options."

"I'll think about it," she said, forcing a smile.

All that night, Maven grappled with the problem. It had been important to her to maintain her independence and achieve the dream of this school on her own. But was that more important than the realization of the goal? Could she sacrifice a chance to make young women's lives better for the sake of her pride?

The next morning, she was about to enter her dress shop, when a carriage pulled up and the driver approached her with a note. Maven read it with surprise, and, after a long moment of deliberation, she nodded to the driver. "Aye, I'll be there," she responded.

As the note requested, Maven made her way to the Carleton House at noon and was immediately shown to a table. Eleanor Douglas looked up and smiled. "Thank you for coming, Mrs. Stanton."

"Your invitation was rather unexpected," confessed Maven, both wary and curious as she sat down. "Ye mentioned a business proposition."

"Yes. Ian told me that the Board of Trade has denied your application for the loan to start a training school for women. To get to the point, Mrs. Stanton, I wish to invest in your school."

Maven looked at Eleanor in astonishment. "I-I not be knowin' what to say, Mrs. Douglas. I am not sure that—"

"You would have full authority over the school. I would be merely a benefactor. It is not a loan, Mrs. Stanton. If the school fails, I lose my investment as well. You have nothing to lose."

"Why are ye doin' this?" asked Maven.

"My success derives from my husband's success. I wish to have an achievement of my own," replied Eleanor. "Ian said the business plan you submitted to the association was sound, and I support your goals."

"Mrs. Douglas, please do not be takin' this the wrong way, but does your husband have any involvement in your support of this endeavor?"

Eleanor smiled. "No, Mrs. Stanton, he does not. I am perfectly capable of making my own decisions, and I have my own money. When Ian and I reconciled, he set up a generous fund for me as a goodwill gesture, so that I might have the option to leave the marriage if I so chose. It is not likely to happen. My funds are quite substantial now."

When Maven still appeared wary, Eleanor went on to further explain her position. "Mrs. Stanton, I know first hand that, no matter the class, if a woman has no funds of her own, she has no independence, no options. I wish to provide women with a chance to achieve the financial independence they need to be able to chart their own course, and your school is the perfect vehicle for it. Women can't wait for laws to change. They have to go around them."

Maven was speechless. "Mrs. Douglas, again, I not be knowin' what to say. It is my thinkin' as well, but I should hate for ye to lose your money if I've miscalculated—and I'm not sure how well we would work together."

"I understand, Mrs. Stanton. I have had the same consideration. But I see the value of this project and believe in it enough to set aside our past history and take the risk. The question is, do you?"

Maven was momentarily taken aback. Parker had asked her much the same thing when she had refused his financial backing. And she became conscious of the fact that she quite possibly held the lives of many young women in her hands.

She looked at Eleanor. "Aye, Mrs. Douglas, I do believe in the school enough to take the risk. Still, I am reluctant to chance anyone's money but me own."

"Perhaps we don't have to chance either one of our investments," said Eleanor as a thought suddenly came to her.

Maven furrowed her brow in bewilderment. "I do not understand."

"I can raise the funds we need through fundraising. I have the contacts needed for raising that kind of capitalization, and I dare say I am rather good at it. You can use the contributions for business operations, which will enable us to hold our personal funds in reserve."

The idea was sound, and Maven quickly weighed the pros and cons—and risks—of entering into a partnership with the most unlikely woman in Rossburg. She still had reservations, but, when forced to pit her pride against her conscience, she could see no way to refuse.

"I accept your proposition, Mrs. Douglas."

"If we are to be in business together, please call me Eleanor. And may I call you Maven?"

"Yes, of course."

Over lunch, the two women continued to solidify their plans. Maven found that Eleanor brought a unique perspective to the project and made several good recommendations. Eleanor found Maven to be an astute businesswoman.

Over the next few months, Ian and Parker watched with total amazement and admiration as the two women worked hand in hand to make the school a reality, seeking little counsel and no resources from their spouses. On several occasions, Ian arrived home to find Eleanor hosting tea parties, adeptly drawing in the ladies with seemingly idle chitchat that ended with them making generous contributions to the project. Maven, for her part, concentrated on the renovation of the building, lined up instructors, and twisted merchants' arms for donations of supplies.

* * * * *

Parker entered the Rossburg Men's Club and spied Ian sitting in the corner. "You must find yourself alone this evening as well," he remarked.

"I hardly see Eleanor anymore since she started this project," replied Ian with a snort of irritation. "When she is at home, she's hosting hen parties. By the time she shows the women to the door, they are fallin' all over themselves to give her money for this school. I've never seen anything like it. I ought to hire her."

Parker laughed and sat down. "You still haven't learned that Eleanor is a woman of many talents. Between the shop and the school, Maven is a ghost herself. I hate to see what will happen when the school finally opens. Have you given any more thought to starting a new trolley company?"

"Aye. But I think the specter of competition will be more of a threat to Biederman."

"What do you mean?"

"I want you to work quietly behind the scenes in Harrisburg to break the Rossburg Passenger Railroad Company's charter and monopoly of the streets."

Parker's face lit up. "Now, you're talking. I know a judge that might be helpful."

"When you are successful, make sure Biederman hears about it."

"He'll appeal it, you know."

"I'm countin' on it," said Ian. "The more money he has to commit to that streetcar company the better."

"It is Horace's company," pointed out Stanton. "The Board of Trade requires that he have his own source of money in order to receive the startup loan. How can Biederman advance the company money?"

"He'll arrange for it to look like an outside investor. Tell your investigator to keep a sharp lookout for it."

"Then what?"

"Go through the motions to set up a new trolley company," replied Ian. "List it under a sham corporation."

Parker laughed heartily. "By this time, Biederman should be getting plenty paranoid. Do you want him to know that it is you?"

"Let him dig for it."

"You already have an electric company to support a new trolley system. Biederman will suspect that it is you, but he won't know for sure. That should set him on his ear," chuckled Parker.

"George will want to hedge his bets in case the appeal doesn't come down on his side," conjectured Ian.

"What do you mean?"

"I'm betting he will instruct Horace to expand the trolley lines all over the city if he fears that he may lose the monopoly on the streets. That should put quite a dent in his coffers—and give the city a much-needed expansion of its transportation system."

"What if the appeal goes Biederman's way?"

"All that matters is that he thinks it won't," said Ian with a gleam in his eye. "Make sure the appeal drags out until enough extra rail has been laid."

A smile spread across Parker's face. "I think I can handle that."

A waiter came by with snifters of brandy.

"To new ventures," said Parker raising his glass in a salute.

The men fell silent then, savoring the brandy and the moment.

"Parker," said Ian at length, "while you are in Harrisburg, I want you to take care of another matter."

"What is that?"

"I want you to submit the paperwork to change the name of the bank."

Parker looked at Ian in surprise. "Why?"

"The Lumbermen's Bank of Rossburg was originally set up to serve that trade," said Ian. "Since the decline of the lumber industry, the bank has expanded its services to serve the greater community. I think the name needs to reflect that change."

"What are you thinking of changing the name to?"

"The People's Bank of Rossburg."

Parker nodded in approval. "I'll take care of it."

CHAPTER SEVENTEEN

Another Reality

Mary Kate moved among the patients in the women's ward, giving them water, talking with them, and reading to them. She had been back from an exhilarating month in England for three weeks now, and she liked her new job working in the hospital. Emily thought she was crazy. She couldn't abide the hospital. But for the first time, Mary Kate felt a sense of accomplishment, and she could understand why Andrew did what he did.

A new patient had been brought in. A priest was giving her last rites, and her husband stood solemnly beside her bed along with their five children.

A nurse came up behind Mary Kate. "Sad, isn't it?"

Mary Kate turned to her. "Is the woman going to die?"

"Most likely."

"What happened to her?"

"Self-induced abortion."

Mary Kate was aghast. In her sheltered world, she had never heard of such a case. "Why?" she asked.

The nurse shrugged. "She couldn't afford to feed another mouth. We see it all the time. Just before you came, a woman was brought in who died in childbirth with her eighth child. Her doctor had told her that she would die if she had another child. She proved him right."

"I don't understand," said Mary Kate. "If she knew the risk..."

Again, the nurse shrugged. "The church teaches a woman that she cannot deny her husband, no matter what. And obviously, that woman's husband didn't care to take the warning to heart. Few do."

Mary Kate was aghast. "That's monstrous."

"That's the life these women have," responded the nurse matter-of-factly. "The children are the real tragedy when a mother dies. The father usually can't take care of them. Relatives take in as many as they can, and the rest are sent away to orphanages or to the country to work on farms."

The nurse moved on then to other tasks.

When Andrew met up with Mary Kate in the ward to see her home, he found her greatly upset. The woman who had tried to self-abort had just died. Her husband was stone-faced, and her children were crying.

Andrew put his arm around her shoulders and walked her out of the room. "I'm sorry," he said. "Maybe this wasn't a good idea to have you work here."

Mary Kate turned to him. "Drew, that woman was just a few years older than I am."

"You aren't her."

"That's not an answer."

"I know, but there is nothing you can do about it, Mary Kate. It is unlawful for doctors or anyone else to disseminate information on how to prevent pregnancies or to dispense any device for that purpose."

"But why?"

"The Comstock Act," replied Andrew.

"What's that?"

"In 1873, Congress made it unlawful to pass any material judged to be pornographic through the mail. Medical schools can't even send books to their students through the post office—"

"What does that have to do with not being able to tell women how to prevent unwanted births?" Mary Kate interrupted impatiently.

"I am getting to that. The law was expanded to disallow the dissemination of any educational materials or devices having to do with the prevention of pregnancies," explained Andrew. "States passed similar laws, and the federal and state laws together became known as the Comstock Laws."

Mary Kate was incensed. "That's archaic. If women are forced to have children they cannot afford to clothe and feed, they are condemned to lives of poverty and, in many cases, early deaths. How can women gain any kind of independence if they don't have the right to restrict the size of their families?"

"Maybe that's the idea," said Andrew, his cynical side showing.

"How is that good for society?"

"It's not."

"What can be done about it?" demanded Mary Kate.

"I would say that the first step is for women to get the right to vote," replied Andrew. "When one firmly held convention is knocked down, it is easier to knock down others."

Mary Kate shook her head. "Too many women will die before that happens."

Andrew took her gently by the shoulders. "Mary Kate, I deal with these kinds of issues all the time. You have to learn to let go of them. You do what you can and move on. If you don't, they will eat you alive."

"I don't know if I can let go of this, Drew. This is so barbaric."

"If you don't, I can't have you continue to work here."

Mary Kate looked up at him, her eyes reflecting her inner turmoil. "What can I do?"

"Why don't you keep a journal? Write down everything you are feeling. Get it out. You will feel much better."

"Is that what you do?"

"Sometimes."

She took a deep breath and gathered herself. "Well, I know one thing for certain," she said. "I shall never marry."

Decidedly, this was not what Andrew wanted to hear.

* * * * *

Over the next several months, Mary Kate encountered more distressing instances at the hospital of women dying from giving birth too many times too close together; staggering numbers of botched self-induced abortions; and cases of women infected by their husbands with venereal disease. Most, but not all, were from the lower East Side.

One incident, in particular, had a profound effect on Mary Kate. She was passing through the ward one day when a woman, who had just delivered a ninth child, mistook her for a nurse and begged her to tell her how to avoid a tenth. She couldn't get the woman's distraught face out of her mind, and it prompted her to finally take Andrew's advice to write down her frustrations. Once she started writing, Mary Kate's outrage poured out of her, and what had started out as a journal turned into four treatises.

Andrew sat in the parlor one day reading them. He set aside the last one entitled: *The Condemnation of Women and Children to Poverty by the Church and State* and regarded Mary Kate with a measure of concern. "This is powerful stuff," he said. He gave a half-hearted laugh. "I didn't know you could write."

Mary Kate beamed with satisfaction. "They are going to be printed into pamphlets and distributed."

"Are you sure that is wise?" he questioned.

"It's a call to arms to women. I haven't violated any laws, Drew. I'm not disseminating reproductive information. I'm merely expounding on the evils of disallowing it."

"I see that. They are cleverly written to that end, and you ably make your case—perhaps too well. For that, you will be targeted and harassed for committing the unforgivable sin of inciting women to question the rights of their husbands," he warned.

"The real sin is that women are being forced to bear children to the detriment of their economic status and to the endangerment of their health," retorted Mary Kate. "But you needn't worry, Drew. The president of the National American Woman's Suffrage Association had the same fear. She offered to print and distribute them under the banner of the association. No one will know that I authored them except her, Emily, and you."

Andrew still had grave misgivings. Society, men, and the Church took a very dim view of having their hypocrisy exposed. But he could see that there was no dissuading her from it. She was driven by a sense of purpose he had never seen in her before.

"What disturbs me the most," continued Mary Kate, "is that a man seems to place his own self-gratification above the health and welfare of his wife. How can he possibly profess to love her if he doesn't care that another pregnancy could kill her?"

"He probably cares, but Society and the Church absolve him of any responsibility or guilt," said Andrew. "He is taught that the woman is the weaker vessel...that he has dominance over his wife and his rule is absolute...that a woman's primary purpose is for procreation and whatever happens is the will of God. For a man living in the lower East End, his home is probably the only place where he has any feeling of power at all—what are you doing?"

"I'm writing this down."

"Whoa, I don't want the sky falling on me, Mary Kate."

"Don't worry. I won't quote you." She paused, thoughtful for a moment. "Drew, could you love your wife enough to set aside your needs for the sake of her health?"

The bold question caught him by surprise. He stood up and walked over to her. "Yes," he said looking into her eyes, "I could. But there are ways to work around the problem."

He kissed her on the cheek. "I have to go. You and Em try to stay out of trouble. Remember one thing, Mary Kate, no one wants to change the status quo when it works to his benefit. Unfortunately, the status quo usually benefits those most who are in a position to affect change. Be prepared for a long battle."

CHAPTER EIGHTEEN

A Wedding

Philadelphia—June 1905

As the carriage pulled up in front of a stone fortress that was the Tanner estate, Maven felt a measure of uncertainty. This was the prenuptial ball and the first of a round of social events that would precede the wedding of her son to Abigail Tanner.

Sensing Maven's nervousness, Parker reached over and squeezed her hand. "You will do fine," he said.

Maven gave him a tremulous smile. "I have not seen Patrick in two and a half years. I had not expected to be invited to his wedding. I hardly know what to say to him."

"He wanted you here, or he wouldn't have invited you. Let him take the lead."

A servant dressed in black coat and tie stepped forward with a gloved hand to help Maven from the carriage and escorted her and Parker to the entrance. In the twilight, Maven took note of the topiaries and the manicured lawn and was instantly reminded of the old Cyrus Morgan mansion in Rossburg that was now an apartment house. Inside, a butler pointed the way to the stairs garlanded in greenery that led to the ballroom on the second floor.

"I'll bet Ian could show these guys a thing or two about throwing a ball," remarked Parker, looking about him. He took her arm. "You look beautiful by the way, Mrs. Stanton. These society matrons will have nothing on you."

Though she was far from feeling at ease, Maven had to laugh. "You are prejudiced, I fear."

At the top of the stairs, another servant came forward. "Mr. and Mrs. Stanton, please follow me. The family would like to greet you privately."

Maven and Parker followed the servant down the hall. He opened a door and stepped aside to admit them to a private parlor. It was opulent but tastefully furnished in shades of yellow, green, and red. A huge, gold-framed mirror hung above a Victorian marble fireplace, and rose-colored drapes hung from ten-foot high windows.

A stout man with a large mustache and wire-rimmed glasses greeted them warmly. "Mrs. Stanton, I am pleased to finally meet Patrick's mother," said Joseph Tanner. "You have been something of a mystery. I see where your son gets his good looks. And Parker...how many years has it been?"

"Too many, Joseph," said Parker, returning a hearty handshake.

"I had always hoped you would return to your father's law firm so we could enjoy a few more hi-jinks."

Parker shook his head. "You know how it was with Father and me—like oil and water. I am pleased to have made my own way."

"Yes, your father was certain you would return with your tail between your legs. He was much annoyed when it wasn't the case. He was a hard man, but I can't complain. He gave me my first job."

Maven's eye found Patrick standing quietly in the corner with a young woman. He came forward, then, and kissed her on the cheek. "Hello, Mother, you are looking well." He shook Parker's hand. "I'm glad you could make it." His manner was formal, a bit stilted. "I would like you to meet my fiancée Abigail Tanner," he said, drawing forth the young woman.

Maven smiled. "'Tis pleased I am to meet ye, Miss Tanner," she said.

"Please call me Abigail," said the young woman returning a warm smile. "I am so happy that you are able to attend our wedding. Patrick wasn't sure that you could come. He said that you have been busy opening a trade school for women. I find that very commendable."

Maven looked at Patrick, who quickly averted his eyes. "Thank you, Abigail. But I wouldn't have missed such an important occasion as this. I hope we shall see more of each other," she said, glancing again at Patrick. "Time is too precious to waste. One day we shall wake up and find that we have little of it left."

"I quite agree with you, Mrs. Stanton," said Tanner. "My time with Abigail's mother was far too short. I keep telling Patrick that he shouldn't work so hard. The lad spends too many hours at the office. Well, shall we take ourselves off to the ballroom now? I believe guests are arriving."

Throughout the evening, the chasm between mother and son saw no closure, and Maven was much saddened. Abigail and her father and Maven and Patrick had led off with the first dance of the evening, a waltz. Patrick had held his mother stiffly and refused to meet her eye for more than a moment.

After Tommy's death, he had become a much more serious child. But Parker had managed to coax a lighter more playful side from him over time. After the family secret had come out, that side of him seemed to have retreated again. She had hoped that he would find someone else who could reignite that light inside of him. Abigail was friendly and warm, but she was still the product of an elite society that indulged in excesses, felt entitled, and was emotionally reserved to the point of indifference. Patrick was none of these. But, then, she hardly knew her son anymore, thought Maven sadly.

Finally, the evening came to an end.

As Maven and Parker prepared to leave with the first wave of older guests, Patrick appeared. "Will I see you at the luncheon tomorrow?" he asked. "I know this isn't your cup of tea, Mother, so if you would rather beg off—"

"She will be there," said Parker. "Now that your mother is an entrepreneur, she is going to have to learn to rub elbows with the moneyed. I'll leave you two to talk for a few minutes. I see a cousin I want to bedevil." He walked off, leaving mother and son alone to pick up the pieces of their broken relationship.

Patrick shifted uncomfortably and averted his eyes. Maven smiled. He did that when he had committed an act that he thought she would disapprove of.

"Abigail is a lovely, young woman," she said, breaking the ice.

Patrick looked at her, hearing the unspoken question in her voice. "But..."

"Are ye certain that this is *your* cup of tea?" asked Maven. She glanced around her. "This be a very different world from the one you were raised in, Patrick—one with a different code, a different set of values."

"Ian should be proud. I learned from the best how to fit in where I don't belong," he responded coldly.

Maven refused to take the bait. "Abigail is very different from Mary Kate."

"What are you trying to say, Mother?"

"Ye still be angry, Patrick. By committin' to another, ye think ye've moved on. But ye haven't, and ye won't as long as your anger continues to be the drivin' force. If ye are not honest with yourself, ye cannot be honest with Abigail, and your marriage will suffer. Perhaps ye should give yourself more time."

"Like you once said, Mother, there are different types of love—"

"Mrs. Stanton," said Abigail, suddenly appearing. She smiled brightly and took Patrick's arm. "I hope you and Mr. Stanton enjoyed the ball."

"Very much so, Abigail. Your home is quite lovely. Will ye be residin' here when you return from your weddin' trip?" asked Maven.

"Oh, no. Patrick and I will be residing on the Main Line," replied Abigail. "Father wanted to give us the house for a wedding present, but Patrick refused. He insisted upon paying for it himself."

Maven smiled. "It pleases me to hear that."

CHAPTER NINETEEN

The 14th Amendment

October

"Mary Kate, hurry up. We'll be late to the rally," shouted Emily. "Carrie Chapman Catt is speaking, and I don't want to miss any of it. Mary Kate!"

"I'm coming, Em."

Mary Kate threw aside the society section of the Philadelphia newspaper and wiped a tear from her eye. She thought that time would have healed the hurt by now. But it hadn't. Apparently, it wasn't the case with Patrick, she thought with a touch of bitterness.

She straightened her hat and pulled on a jacket, then stopped to look one more time at the picture of Patrick and his wife upon their return from their wedding trip for another jab to the heart before rushing off to join Emily.

When the girls entered the hall, they found it filled with women of every walk of life this Saturday afternoon. The air was electric, and Mary Kate's somber mood lifted as she threw herself into the moment. Banners proclaiming democracy for women and pictures of the movement's icons—Susan B. Anthony, Elizabeth Cady and Lucy Stone—stretched across the front of the room. Mary Kate smiled proudly. They had come a long way from the clandestine meetings in the homes of fellow suffragettes and in the back rooms of shops.

A member of the Women's Trade Union League of New York took the podium and the crowd quieted.

"The word 'suffrage' describes voting as a right rather than a privilege," she said in a loud, clear voice. "In 1787, founding fathers included the word 'suffrage' in the Constitution, maintaining that it is an inalienable right of citizens to vote. Men of illiteracy and ignorance have the right to vote. Women do not, regardless of their level of education. Men with backgrounds of criminality have the right to vote. Women do not, regardless of their good standing in the community. By this measure, ladies, we are not citizens but slaves to a patriarchal society."

At this, there was an outpouring of agreement and indignation. The speaker put up her hands to quiet the assemblage again.

"But take heart, ladies. The 14th Amendment has granted citizenship to slaves," she said on a facetious note. "And under Article 1, the 14th Amendment gives *all* citizens the right to vote, making no distinction between genders. Now, in 1874, the Supreme Court ruled that women's political rights are a state's rights issue. Wyoming, Colorado, Utah, and Idaho have long given women the right to vote. It is time that the women of New York march to demand their rights of citizenship, too."

Emily and Mary Kate joined the women who jumped to their feet, adding to the thunderous applause that reverberated throughout the hall. By the time Mary Kate returned to the brownstone, she was irrepressible. All thoughts of Patrick and his wife had been pushed to the farthest recesses of her mind.

Andrew sat in the parlor listening, inwardly amused, as she excitedly recounted the highlights of the meeting. Her blue eyes sparkled and her cheeks were flushed, and he was having a difficult time paying attention to what she was saying.

"Slaves, huh...that's a pretty big leap," he said.

"Well, it's true," returned Mary Kate. "This is a country of men's laws, and, as long as women are denied the right to have their say, they shall forever be enslaved and repressed. But that's our tongue in cheek argument. Our larger argument is Article 1 of the 14th Amendment."

As she outlined the ladies' intention to march to the elections office, Andrew became concerned. "Easy, Mary Kate. The police are under pressure to put a stop to suffragette activities and will not stand for civil disobedience," he warned. "There could be violence, and I'll not have you or Emily hurt. Mother and Father would never forgive me. They have adopted you, you know," he added lightly. "Where is Emily anyway?"

"She had to stop at the printers to pick up pamphlets for the next rally."

Andrew stood up to leave. "Tell her she is expected at the folks for Sunday brunch. They are expecting you as well."

"But I—"

"Sorry, no 'buts.' That's what happens when the Stodderts take you in. Take heart. It's usually only once a month."

When Mary Kate saw him to the door, Andrew took her lightly by the shoulders. "Remember my warning, and relay it to Emily," he said on a sober note. "You have never seen what the police can do when pushed too far. They don't find the movement amusing anymore. They can no longer write you off as a bunch of nuts. And it won't matter that you are women, only that you are violating the law and challenging their authority."

"We'll be careful," said Mary Kate.

Just then, Emily came in, and Andrew dropped his hands.

"What are you doing here?" she asked in surprise.

"Just delivering a message from the folks."

"Sunday brunch?"

When Andrew nodded, she groaned. "That usually means Mother has someone for us to meet."

"Mary Kate is invited as well. She can be the buffer."

"Perhaps I should stay here," suggested Mary Kate.

"No way," chorused Andrew and Emily.

Emily followed her brother to the door, a mischievous gleam in her eye. "You could have telephoned the message, you know."

Andrew grinned. "I could have. Father will send his carriage for you."

CHAPTER TWENTY

Sunday Brunch

"Mother, how could you! You are supposed to be a free thinker. Arranged marriages are a thing of the past," Emily admonished her mother in a low voice, as they approached the Stoddert parlor to welcome their guests.

"I am not arranging anything, just making suggestions and providing opportunity," Mrs. Stoddert whispered back. "Mrs. Duncan, Portia, how well you look," she greeted, entering the room. "And Mrs. Langley, where is that handsome son of yours?"

Mrs. Langley giggled. "Lawton is with the men in the drawing room."

"Will Dr. Stoddert be joining us as well?" asked Mrs. Duncan hopefully. At this, her daughter blushed and primly lowered her eyes.

Emily groaned. She reached behind her and pulled Mary Kate up alongside of her for support before following her mother into the room.

After an hour of lemonade and light conversation, the ladies were joined by the men. As they all filed into the dining room shortly thereafter, Mrs. Stoddert drew Emily aside. "Where is your brother?" she asked anxiously.

Emily shrugged. "I am not my brother's keeper, Mother." She glanced at Mary Kate. "But I'll wager he will be here this time."

When they were seated, Emily leaned over to Mary Kate seated next to her and whispered: "Drew does this every time. He calls at the last minute to say he has some emergency at the hospital. It drives Mother to distraction."

"Maybe it is true," said Mary Kate.

Emily gave her a skeptical look. "I'll take that bet."

At that moment, Andrew walked in. "Sorry I'm late," he said. "There was an emergency at the hospital." He kissed his mother on the cheek, greeted everyone, and dutifully took his chair next to Portia Duncan.

Emily chuckled. "See what I mean? He usually doesn't show up at all." She glanced at Mary Kate. "I wonder why he did this time?"

The rhetorical question went over Mary Kate's head.

Mary Kate loved Emily as a sister and was very fond of Mr. and Mrs. Stoddert. And she was fond of Andrew. They were all so easy to like—no hidden secrets, no subterfuge—just good-hearted people—so uncomplicated, so unlike her family.

As course after course was served, Mary Kate sat back enjoying the comic relief of the event, hard pressed to suppress a few giggles as Emily and Andrew subtly subverted their mother's efforts. Surreptitiously sending her children quelling looks from time to time, Mrs. Stoddert pressed on, valiantly presiding over the brunch with great aplomb, grace, and the sheer will to prevail.

Her hope for any successful match at all faded, however, as she monitored the body language of her daughter and son. Emily was barely able to conceal her boredom with Lawton Langley, often interrupting him with pointed remarks that left him flummoxed. If she could have managed it, Mrs. Stoddert would have given her daughter a well-placed kick under the table. Drew was polite and attentive enough to the shy, awkward Portia Duncan, but it was plain to see that there was no spark on his side either.

Mrs. Stoddert was about to admit defeat, when she noticed something curious. Her son seemed to direct much of his attention to Mary Kate, often stealing glances at her when she wasn't aware. It couldn't be, Mrs. Stoddert thought in amazement. Yet, to her keen eye the signs were there. She looked at Mary Kate but was unable to gauge the nature of her interest in Andrew.

When the brunch finally ended and the last guest had departed, the family gathered in the parlor.

"Really, Mother, you are supposed to be enlightened!" exclaimed Emily, flopping on the sofa. "You really are slipping back into old habits. I must insist that you attend the next NAWSA rally. You are in sore need of more indoctrination. Isn't that right, Mary Kate?"

"Mother is enlightened—when it doesn't concern her own children," interjected Andrew.

"Well, if she wishes to put herself out, why must she subject the rest of us to such punishment? Lawton Langley is an insufferable bore. Portia Duncan is frightfully dull and never has an original thought. And poor Papa...the pomposity of Mr. Duncan and Mr. Langley far exceeds their fortunes."

Andrew looked over at an amused Mary Kate and winked. "Come now, Emily. It wasn't all that bad. Lawton talked about himself for only an hour this time—when you weren't interrupting him. I believe he actually put a question to you once. Reminds me of someone else I once knew," he added with a mischievous twinkle in his eye. "His name was Horace."

Mary Kate and Emily burst into laughter.

"Oh, you two are impossible!" exclaimed Mrs. Stoddert. "I am only looking after your interests. A mother is compelled to do that when her children are not so inclined. I don't know why you persist in foiling my efforts."

Emily looked at her father with pleading eyes. "Papa..."

"Don't look to me," he said. "When your mother is meddling in your affairs, she isn't meddling in mine." He picked up the newspaper and took a seat by the window.

"What say you, Mary Kate?" asked Emily.

"Oh, no, you'll not put me in the middle of this," responded Mary Kate.

"Smart girl," said Andrew. He kissed his mother on the cheek. "It has been fun, Mother, but now I really must be getting back to the hospital. Do you girls want to ride back with me or continue to be subjected to Mother's meddling, however well-intentioned it might be?"

Emily jumped to her feet. "We'll ride with you."

Mary Kate barely had time to thank her hostess before Emily ushered her out of the room after Andrew.

"Don't forget about the Hospital Benefit Ball," Mrs. Stoddert called after them, as the young people grabbed their hats and coats from the butler and maid and hurried out the door. "Humph, some children would be grateful," she grumbled.

Mrs. Stoddert stood pensively at the window and watched as the trio stepped into the carriage and set off. "Mr. Stoddert, what would you think of a match between Mary Kate and Andrew?" she asked at length.

Ogden Stoddert set aside the newspaper he was reading. "I think, Mother, that if you don't stop your matchmaking, Emily and Mary Kate will have you ejected from the women's movement, and Andrew will be forever engaged with hospital emergencies."

Mrs. Stoddert met her husband's response with a dismissive sniff. "Sometimes affairs of the heart need a little nudging."

"Where are you going?" asked Mr. Stoddert.

"To ensure that Andrew attends the ball."

"Andrew rarely attends these things. How are you going to do that?"

Mrs. Stoddert smiled. "A mother has her ways."

Mr. Stoddert shook his head and went back to his paper.

CHAPTER TWENTY-ONE

Waiting To Be Noticed

Emily again checked the watch pinned to her blouse that Andrew had gifted her, as she impatiently awaited her brother in the reception area of the hospital. She tapped her foot and looked around her at the place that he might as well call home. It was cold and cheerless, certainly not very welcoming or comforting. She made a mental note to have her mother talk to the board about livening the place up.

After what seemed an interminable time to her, Andrew finally appeared. "Sorry, Em, I had to finish with a patient."

"Drew, this area could do with brighter paint, some plants, and a few pictures on the walls that aren't portraits of board members and administrators. It is so sterile. Honestly, I don't know how Mary Kate works here."

Andrew looked around him. "It is a hospital, Em," he replied wryly.

"Hospitals are frightening enough without the décor adding to it."

"I'll make a note of it. Now, what are you doing here? You've made it clear more than once that you would rather have a tooth extracted than step foot in a hospital. Is something wrong?" he asked on a more serious note.

"Depends on what you call wrong. I came here to give you a heads-up. You will need to make certain that your tux is available for Mother's ball next Saturday."

"I don't do social events, Em. You know that."

"Drew, it is for the benefit of the hospital. I should think you could make an exception."

"I appreciate Mother's efforts and good intentions, but I can serve a greater good working here than entertaining some debutante at a ball. I'll leave the fundraising to others."

"You really are becoming a cynic, Drew. But I think you may want to reconsider attending the ball this time." She smiled, then, and her eyes twinkled with amusement.

It immediately put him on guard. "Why?" he asked warily. "What are you being so smug about?"

"Guess what arrived this morning by messenger for Mary Kate? I'll give you a hint—it came from Mother."

Andrew groaned. "She didn't."

"She did. She sent Mary Kate her very own invitation to the ball. Mary Kate was hesitant to accept. I told her that you would be pleased to escort her."

"How…how the devil could Mother have guessed?"

Emily laughed. "I didn't have any trouble, and she is a mother 'looking after the interests of her children,'" she mimicked. "Look on the bright side. Mother must approve of Mary Kate."

* * * * *

The ballroom at the Stoddert mansion was resplendent with flowers in fall colors, small potted trees, and garlands of brilliant fall foliage entwined around Grecian columns. Mr. and Mrs. Stoddert stood at the entrance receiving guests—Mrs. Stoddert artfully reminding everyone that this was a benefit ball. When Andrew appeared with Mary Kate on his arm, she nudged her husband and smiled smugly.

"Mary Kate, how lovely you look," greeted Mrs. Stoddert.

"Thank you for inviting me," replied Mary Kate.

"I am pleased that you could come, dear. And Andrew, such a surprise…you never attend these events. Ogden, look who is here."

Mr. Stoddert raised a brow at his wife's play of surprise. "Welcome, Miss Douglas," he said, giving her a warm smile. He looked at Drew. "Glad you could get away from the hospital for the evening, son."

"I couldn't let Mary Kate enter the lion's den unprotected," Andrew replied lightly. "And I suppose it behooves me to attend since the ball does benefit the hospital."

"How strange," replied Mrs. Stoddert. "You didn't seem to think so before. But I am grateful to whatever—or whoever—is responsible for your change of heart this evening."

"Don't push it, Mother," warned Andrew. He glanced at Mary Kate and was relieved to see that she appeared to be oblivious to the underpinnings of the exchange.

"Where is your sister?" asked Mrs. Stoddert.

"She's coming with Teddy Whitehouse."

"That Bohemian?" Mrs. Stoddert made a face. "I hope he knows that this is a formal affair."

"Don't worry, no one will notice that he's not wearing socks," said Andrew.

"What! You are joking...aren't you?" asked Mrs. Stoddert in alarm.

Andrew just smiled and led Mary Kate off.

"Drew, you shouldn't let your mother twist in the wind like that," Mary Kate chastised him.

"Mother is a survivor," he assured her wryly. He nodded to some gentlemen and silently paid court to a couple of grand dames sitting across the room. When a waiter passed by, he snagged two flutes of champagne from the tray and handed one to Mary Kate. "Mother was right about one thing. You look beautiful tonight."

Mary Kate gave a light-hearted salute with her champagne glass. "Thank you, sir. You clean up pretty well yourself. I hardly recognize you without your stethoscope and lab coat."

As she looked about the room, he took advantage of the moment to study her classic profile and to admire the shapely silhouette of her figure in the fitted, black silk chiffon gown. Her blonde hair was pulled back in a lose roll and held in place by a jeweled clip. When Mary Kate turned back to him, he quickly shielded his interest.

"I see a few young ladies who would like to command your attention," she said with a teasing glint in her eye. "I wouldn't want to interfere with your mother's efforts to find you a match."

"Why do you think I brought you this evening?" he quipped. He set their glasses on a tray and led her to the dance floor. "Let's show these people how to dance."

As Andrew twirled her around the floor in time to a waltz, Mary Kate gave herself up to the moment.

"Oh look, there is Emily and Mr. Whitehouse," she said, glancing across the room. "And Mr. Whitehouse is most appropriately attired right down to his socks," she added with a giggle. "Your mother can relax."

Andrew laughed. "Em will find some way to keep Mother on edge for the rest of the evening."

When the dance ended, Andrew refused to relinquish Mary Kate and quickly led her into the next waltz and the one after that until she was breathless. "Drew, I must stop. I need to catch my breath," she said, clutching a hand to her chest.

"Perhaps you are in need of more fitness exercises," he suggested.

Emily, her escort, and a group of young people joined them then. The conversation was lively, followed by more dancing. Mary Kate hadn't enjoyed herself this much for a very long time and was disappointed when the evening came to an end. After making their farewells, Andrew escorted Mary Kate to the Stoddert carriage that awaited them and handed her in, also reluctant to have the evening end.

"It was a lovely ball, wasn't it?" she said with a sigh of contentment as the carriage set off.

"This was one of Mother's more interesting guest lists," admitted Andrew. "Emily must have had a hand in it." He laughed then. "I am reminded of the time when Em secretly changed the guest list for a dinner Mother was having. Mother practically had a stroke trying to explain to Alva Vanderbilt Belmont how she ended up seated between two of Emily's musician friends. Emily was seeking revenge on Mrs. Belmont at the time, you see."

"For what?" asked Mary Kate.

"She forced her daughter to marry an insufferable British nobleman despite the fact that Consuelo was in love with another—Winnie Rutherford—and had planned to elope with him," explained Andrew. "It wasn't pretty when Mrs. Belmont found out about the plan."

"What did she do?"

"She locked Consuelo in her room and threatened to kill poor Winnie. Then she pretended illness until Consuelo buckled. By all accounts, the poor girl is miserable. Emily had always liked Consuelo and never forgave Mrs. Belmont."

"So what happened at your mother's dinner party?" quizzed Mary Kate, captivated by the story.

"Well, as it turned out, Mrs. Belmont liked the young men and hired them to entertain at several of her less formal events," replied Andrew. "But, then, Mrs. Belmont can be a bit unconventional herself when it serves her interest."

"I am beginning to feel sympathy for your mother," said Mary Kate.

Andrew chuckled. "Don't worry about Mother. She is less straitlaced than she pretends to be and much sharper for all the shenanigans of her children. Emily and I keep her on her toes."

"I'm sure your mother appreciates that," responded Mary Kate dryly. She glanced at him, curious. "Drew, why haven't you opened a practice uptown? It would afford you more leisure time than the hospital does. Then you could attend more of your mother's charity events," she added impishly.

Andrew laughed. "I believe you just answered your own question."

"Seriously, Drew, why have you not opened a practice uptown?"

"Well...I guess I don't care to be a keeper of the secrets of the elites," he replied.

"You and Emily are members of the elite," noted Mary Kate, "but you do not like them much, do you?"

"There are some whose company I endure quite well, though one young lady in particular can be a handful at times," he quipped.

"Drew, be serious."

"You are an elite as well, Mary Kate. Do you like Horace?"

"Well, no, but that's different. He's one person. You dislike the class I think."

"I can't speak for Emily, but as a doctor dealing with death and illness every day, I have learned not to take myself too seriously. The elites live in a different reality, and I wish not be a party to those illusions. Most haven't learned yet that wealth and power don't buy everything."

"Like respect," interjected Mary Kate soberly.

"That is one of the things."

"Is that why you didn't join your father in the shipping business... become a titan of industry as the sons of such men are expected to do?" she asked.

"Actually, I did play that part for a while and did it quite well, if I do say so myself," replied Andrew. "Then I came to view life differently and decided to go into medicine."

"Your father must have been disappointed," said Mary Kate.

"He was at first. But he came to understand."

"My father is the wealthiest and, perhaps, most powerful man in Rossburg. He must be very good at playing the game, too," she remarked with a touch of scorn.

Andrew looked at her. "There is nothing wrong with having money, Mary Kate. I much prefer it to the alternative. What matters is how one makes it, whom he hurts in the process, and how he allows it to shape him. Your father strikes me as being honest and fair-minded."

"It comes to me that I don't really know who my father is or of what he may be capable." She turned away then and looked out the window.

Andrew didn't pursue the matter. He wondered what circumstances in her past could possibly warrant such anger, resentment, and bitterness for all this time...circumstances that she could not confide to even Emily, as close as they had become.

The carriage soon pulled up in front of the brownstone. Andrew stepped down, handed out Mary Kate, and followed her up the steps.

"There's a light on in the parlor. Emily must be home," she said. Andrew opened the door for her. She turned to him. "Thank you for escorting me, Drew. I know how you dislike these events. I enjoyed the evening very much."

"Then it was my pleasure." He made no move to leave but continued to look at her, searching her face for the smallest sign.

"Is there something else?" she asked quizzically.

Andrew hesitated for a moment before responding. "No, I guess not."

Mary Kate regarded him curiously. He was acting most strange. "Well, good night, then."

He hesitated again. "Good night, Mary Kate."

Mary Kate entered the townhouse and closed the door. She peeked into the parlor, but Emily wasn't there. She was about to start up the stairs, when there came a light tap followed by a more determined knock on the door.

Mary Kate hurried to open it. She blinked in surprise when Andrew strode past her into the foyer. "Drew, did you forget something?"

"Yes, Mary Kate, I did." He cupped her face and kissed her, his caress tender but passionate. When he released her, he said: "I love you,

Mary Kate. I have for a long while—probably from the first moment I met you."

Mary Kate stared at him dumbfounded.

"You couldn't guess?" he asked.

When she shook her head, he didn't know whether to feel annoyed, dismayed or hopeful.

"Drew, I-I hardly know what to say," she stammered. "I'm not sure that I am ready to—I mean I haven't given any thought to entering into a relationship with anyone."

Andrew was uncompromising. "Give it some thought now, Mary Kate. I know that you came to New York because of a broken relationship. I don't know the details, but I'm guessing it is the reason that you left Rossburg and won't talk to your parents. It has been nearly three years. That's a long time to hang on to a hurt. It is time for you to move on."

"I have moved on," she responded indignantly. "I've made a life here. I'm involved in the women's movement. I work in the hospital—"

"You are fooling yourself, Mary Kate. You're just going through the motions. You haven't moved on."

Mary Kate bristled. "How can you know that?"

"You still haven't been able to reconcile with your parents, and you keep everyone at arm's length. You're not really engaged in life. If you were, I wouldn't have had to tell you how I feel about you. I haven't been trying to keep it a secret."

"You don't understand," she retorted.

"Maybe not, but given a past experience and my profession, what I do understand is that time is fleeting," he said, softening his tone. "None of us know how much of it we have, and I will not waste any more of mine. I want to spend the rest of my life with you. I don't know if you can feel the same way about me that I feel about you, but I'll give you two weeks to think about it. I'll expect an answer then."

Mary Kate stared after him as he walked out the door, too stunned to speak.

"He may be my brother, but he's right."

Mary Kate turned to see Emily standing at the top of the stairs.

"Sorry, I couldn't help overhearing," she said, descending the staircase. "Drew fell head over heels for you at my New Year's Eve party, you know. He has been waiting for you to notice. I guess he got tired of waiting."

"I-I didn't know."

"Maybe you didn't want to know," suggested Emily.

"What do you mean?"

"C'mon, Mary Kate, my brother has been practically wearing his heart on his sleeve for a long time. Even Mother picked up on it." Emily laughed lightly. "Horace had him tied in knots until he learned that you had no interest in the guy. Didn't you wonder about all the times Drew interfered with your dates...all the times he happens by here...the invitations to dinner?"

"He invites you, too," said Mary Kate.

"He may include me in the dinner invitations, but haven't you noticed how often I have 'other plans' so Drew can be alone with you?"

Mary Kate was speechless. As Emily continued to tick off incident after incident, she realized that Emily was right. No one could be that obtuse. She simply hadn't wanted to notice that Drew had deeper feelings for her. It was more convenient for her to regard him as a brother.

Emily paused for a moment. "Did Drew ever tell you why he went into medicine?"

"No, not really."

"He was engaged once. Her name was Zenia."

"Drew has never mentioned her."

"It took him awhile, but my brother has learned not to live in the past," said Emily, giving her friend a meaningful look.

Mary Kate ignored the innuendo. "What happened between them?"

"Zenia fell ill with tuberculosis and died just before their wedding date," replied Emily. "She had contracted the illness while studying abroad. By the time anyone realized that she was sick, the disease had progressed too far."

"Oh...I am so sorry. Drew never said. It must have been terrible for him."

"He was devastated," said Emily. "He became obsessed with finding a cure and corresponded with anybody he could find who was working on the problem. After Zenia died, he travelled throughout Europe seeking out doctors and scientists in the field and investing heavily in their research."

"Is that when he decided to become a doctor himself?" asked Mary Kate.

Emily nodded. "He took his medical training in England. He felt that the doctors there were more advanced in their knowledge of respiratory illnesses. When he obtained his degree, he returned home. He had found no cure for tuberculosis, but he had gained enough knowledge on how to better treat and contain the disease. Did you know that Drew is a recognized authority in the field in America?"

"No, I had no idea," said Mary Kate, acutely aware of how little she knew about him.

"One of the technologies he invested in was the x-ray," continued Emily. "He brought back an x-ray machine with him. It can detect tuberculosis early enough to treat and has gone a long way in controlling outbreaks like the one of a few years ago. Drew also helped to fund and set up a wing in the hospital dedicated to the treatment of lung diseases. There is still no cure for the White Plague, as people call it, but thanks to him and others like him, someday there will be."

Mary Kate was astonished by everything she had learned. Now she understood the philosophical side of Andrew's nature.

"Why didn't Drew tell me any of this?"

"He has never been one to toot his own horn." Emily paused. "I know my brother better than anyone. He is a good guy, Mary Kate. He doesn't love lightly, and I don't want to see him be hurt again. Please consider your decision very carefully, and be sure of it."

CHAPTER TWENTY-TWO

Reckoning with the Past

Mary Kate was completely thrown off balance. The hospital and the suffrage movement had provided her the perfect vehicles around which to center her life now—a safe distraction from the past. She couldn't imagine any other man filling the void in her heart left by Patrick. And in her youth and naivety, still ruled by turbulent emotions, she decided that there wasn't any point in giving someone else a chance to try.

She was dedicating her life to the women's movement, resolving to remain unmarried and uninvolved and had discouraged any man's attention that ran counter to that end. It hadn't been difficult. But Drew...Drew was different.

She couldn't dismiss him, as she was able to dismiss the other young men. He occupied an important place in her life and in her affections. She enjoyed his company and was drawn to his intelligence, wit, good nature, and boyish charm. He reminded her of Patrick in this way, she thought, surprised by the realization. She also valued his level-headed advice. Again, as with Patrick, he was a counterbalance to her impetuous manner. She trusted him, respected him, and now that she was forced to consider it, she had to admit that she found him quite physically attractive.

As Andrew's deadline loomed nearer, Mary Kate filled her time working at the headquarters of the National American Woman Suffrage Association, trying to avoid notice of the passing days, trying to avoid thinking of him. She wasn't so successful at night. She didn't want to say "no" to him, but neither was she prepared to say "yes." It annoyed her that, by forcing her to view their relationship in this different light, Drew was forcing her to reconsider the course of action she had already made her mind up to—a life path that she felt comfortable in following. She wasn't ready to rethink that and consider another course.

* * * * *

Emily tapped on the door and poked her head into Mary Kate's bedroom. "Still abed? Well, you look as though you had a good sleep," she remarked facetiously, noting the dark circles under Mary Kate's eyes.

"You can thank your brother for it," replied Mary Kate irritably. She sat up in bed. "How dare he give me an ultimatum of that nature?"

Emily shrugged. "That's Drew. He's a patient guy, but he knows what he wants, and he is results-oriented. Do you want to discuss it?"

"No."

"Good." Emily looked about the room, noting the absence of a suitcase. "Aren't you going to Philadelphia with the group?"

Mary Kate shook her head. "They have enough volunteers without me."

"I think you should go."

"Why?"

"Because Patrick is there."

Mary Kate looked at her friend in surprise. "How do you know about Patrick?"

"I saw the paper in the parlor. It wasn't difficult to figure out. You need to see him and sort everything out. You won't be able to give Drew an honest answer until you do. I'll help you pack. You can use my train ticket."

"No. I can't go, Emily."

"Yes, you can. It is time to put this behind you." Emily pulled out a suitcase, ignoring Mary Kate's string of excuses, and began to pack a bag for her.

Two hours later, Mary Kate found herself on a train bound for Philadelphia, panic building inside of her with each mile that brought her closer to her destination.

When the train chugged into the train station, Mary Kate joined the other ladies on the platform to await transportation to the Bellevue-Stratford Hotel. Because of Philadelphia's historical significance in the nation's quest for independence, the NAWSA decided it would be symbolic to launch a rally for women's rights here.

After everyone had been settled into their rooms, the band of 25 met in the lobby. The leader gave each attendee a pack of fliers to hand out during the speeches before leading the procession to the park. If the ladies were nothing else, they were organized and armed with determination and every permit they could think of.

The press was on hand to greet them. Young mothers with their children and nannies with their charges began to collect. Secretaries appeared in the windows of a building, and salesmen and customers emerged from stores. Police soon followed as the crowd grew.

While the first speaker spoke about the 14th Amendment Solution, Mary Kate and several women quickly handed out their literature. Along the way, the leaders had learned some tricks, one of which was how to write effective speeches on a short piece of paper. And three of the speakers that followed were able to say their piece before the police moved in to shut down the rally.

As the crowd started to disperse, a few men called out derogatory remarks to which several ladies in the crowd took great exception, and it resulted in a spirited shouting match. But the conflict ended without serious incident and with encouraging support for the cause, and the suffragettes returned to the hotel in high spirits.

Mary Kate was tired and went to her room, while the others sought out food. It had been a good day, she thought. She had been too busy to think about Patrick or Andrew. She removed her hat and was taking off her jacket, when there came a knock on the door. Thinking it to be a member of her group, Mary Kate opened it and was surprised to find a young woman she didn't know instead.

"You are Mary Kate Douglas?" Before Mary Kate could answer, the woman continued. "I heard someone call you by name at the rally, and I discovered that you are staying here. I must confess that it took me awhile to work up the courage to approach you."

Mary Kate furrowed her brow in bewilderment. "I'm sorry. Do I know you?"

The woman shook her head. "No, but I know you. I am Abigail O'Brien...Patrick's wife."

Mary Kate was so stunned she stood rooted to the spot. The sober, young woman looked different from her picture in the newspaper.

"May I come in, Miss Douglas?"

Mary Kate collected herself. "Yes, of course. Please come in."

Abigail entered the room. She looked at Mary Kate and an uncertain smile trembled on her lips. "I'm not sure why I am here, Miss Douglas. I guess I just wanted to see you...to know what you are like. You have been a part of my marriage for so long—from the beginning I dare say," she said in a low, quiet tone.

Again, Mary Kate's brow knit in bewilderment. "I'm sorry, Mrs. O'Brien. I don't understand."

Tears glistened in Abigail's eyes, and she averted her gaze for a moment. "A part of me has always known that Patrick married me because he couldn't marry you for some reason. I don't know the circumstances. My husband is a very private man, and I haven't felt invited to ask. I think that Patrick loves me...on some level. I thought that with time the issue would resolve itself. But it has not, and the truth of the matter is that you still stand between us."

Mary Kate was completely taken aback. "Mrs. O'Brien, I promise you that Patrick and I have had no contact in three years."

"I know that Patrick has been faithful to his vows, Miss Douglas. But the heart is a different matter. You are quite beautiful. I can understand his attraction to you. But I won't be shut out any longer or share his affections with another woman even in memory. I guess I'm a little selfish that way."

"What is it you want me to do?" asked Mary Kate.

"There appears to be unfinished business between you and my husband, Miss Douglas. I want you to meet with him and finish it—one way or the other—before you leave the city. Patrick needs to make a choice. If he chooses you, I will step quietly aside." Abigail held out a business card. "His office is at this address." She paused. "He spends most of his time there."

Mary Kate hesitated, then took the card from her. She couldn't ignore the pain in the young woman's voice or the hurt in her eyes.

"You know, Miss Douglas, I support your cause," said Abigail. "I have supported women's right to vote for a long time, but a woman in my circumstance must sometimes keep private her interests for the good of her husband's career."

Mary Kate heard the unspoken question. Would she be willing to make such sacrifices for Patrick?

A couple of days passed before Mary Kate summoned the courage one late afternoon to take a cab to the address on the business card. She hesitated outside the building for several minutes before finally entering the law firm of Tanner, Williams and O'Brien.

A receptionist looked up. "May I help you?"

Mary Kate's throat was dry, and she swallowed hard. "I would like to see Mr. O'Brien please."

The receptionist looked in her book. "Do you have an appointment?"

"No, I—I'm family. I'm in town with a group until tomorrow morning."

The girl's face lit up. "Are you one of those suffragettes?" she asked in a low voice.

Mary Kate smiled. "Guilty as charged."

"How wonderful! I'm not supposed to let anyone in without an appointment, but seeing that you are family and a suffragette, I'll make an exception," she said in a conspiratorial whisper. The receptionist stood up. "I'll let Mr. O'Brien know that you are here."

"Wait. I'd like to surprise him," said Mary Kate "Can you just tell me where his office is?"

The receptionist wavered. "I don't know. Mr. O'Brien is a stickler for rules—"

"I promise you it will be all right," Mary Kate assured her. "I will take full responsibility."

"Well, in that case and since you are family, I suppose there is no harm in it. Mr. O'Brien's office is down the hall, second door on the right. His name is on the door."

"Thank you."

Mary Kate walked down the hall to the office. She stood outside for a few minutes, trying to stop the shaking in her knees before raising a hand to tap lightly on the door.

Her breath caught in her throat when she answered: "Yes, Miss Warner, what is it?" His tone was polite but brusque. It was clear he didn't appreciate the interruption.

Mary Kate opened the door and walked in. "Hello, Patrick."

Patrick looked up from the brief he was working on and stared at her in disbelief. "My God," he murmured, slowly rising from his seat. "Mary Kate—what are you doing here?"

Mary Kate smiled and closed the door, her heart pounding. "I'm in town with the suffragettes."

"I wondered if you might be among them," he said. "I saw in the newspaper that you were in the group that went to England last year for a convention."

"I have followed you in the papers as well," she admitted. "I know you married. I see you made partner."

"It helps when you marry the boss' daughter," replied Patrick lightly.

They looked at each other. The awkwardness between them began to ease. To their surprise, an easy familiarity drifted in and settled over them like a fine mist, and comfortable memories rose to the fore to afford them a safe haven from which to engage.

Patrick came from around his desk and pulled up a chair for her. "You look well," he said. "You haven't changed a bit…just as impetuous as always. You could have given me some notice, you know. Pardon me while I pick up my jaw from the floor."

Mary Kate laughed. "Still the same droll wit." She looked around her as he returned to his seat behind the desk, and she shook her head in disapproval. "I wondered how I would find you. I had hoped not to see that you are a buttoned up corporate lawyer working to preserve the status quo. But I suppose I shouldn't be surprised," she said with a dramatic sigh.

Patrick grinned. "And you're still tilting at windmills. The 14th Amendment Solution isn't going to work, you know. Susan B. Anthony tried that trick in 1872 and was arrested for it. And in 1874, after other challenges, the Supreme Court ruled that citizenship does not give women the right to vote—Minor v. Happersett."

Mary Kate snorted. "Humph, it is questionable whether women *are* citizens. We don't seem to have any rights."

"You have the right to own property now," pointed out Patrick with a glint of amusement in his eye.

"One right does not make for equality," she retorted in no mood to be humored. "Why do men feel so threatened by women?"

Patrick shrugged. "When women start demanding the same rights as men, it upsets the balance."

Mary Kate gave scornful huff. "You mean imbalance. What's wrong with men and women sharing equal status?"

"It is not the tradition."

"Why not?"

"Men have always been recognized as being the superior sex."

"Patrick O'Brien!"

He laughed and raised his hands in a defensive gesture. "Hey, I'm just telling you what centuries of convention holds. You are swimming upstream, Mary Kate, against a mighty strong current."

She sighed heavily. "Which side are you on?"

"Whichever side hires me."

"Ugh, lawyers are such prostitutes."

"Only until you need one," he countered.

"All right, then. There is a faction within the National Woman Suffrage Association that believes women should work to achieve suffrage on a national level through a constitutional amendment. Others feel that it needs to be achieved at the state level by amending state constitutions. What is your advice?"

"Clients pay a lot of money for my advice."

"I'm not a client. I'm your sister," she said on a sober note.

There...it was said aloud. A long silence followed as they struggled to acknowledge the relationship in their minds unemotionally for the first time, to become more comfortable with it rather than angrily resigned to it.

Patrick was the first to break the silence. "Then, as your brother, I would advise you to pursue both courses. Suffrage can be achieved faster and easier on state levels. Some of the states already have it. But it is easier to undo an amendment to a state constitution than it is to undo an amendment to the federal constitution. And women would have the benefit of voting in those states while continuing to fight for it on the federal front." He gave her a considering look. "Do you really believe in this cause, or do you just enjoy stirring the pot?"

"I believe in everyone moving forward, Patrick. Unfortunately, if it involves women, it requires a lot of pot stirring."

Patrick opened a drawer and took out a bottle of whiskey and two glasses. "In the interest of equality, then, how do you feel about the partaking of spirits?"

"I'm a modern woman," responded Mary Kate proudly.

Patrick was amused. "Of course, you are." He splashed a small amount in a glass and handed it to her.

"I've missed crossing swords with you," she said, taking a sip.

"You did keep my wits sharp debating the illogic with you," he acknowledged.

Mary Kate gave a huff of frustration. "Of course, a man would consider a woman's view illogical. Men can only think two dimensionally," she retorted. She gazed around her again at the bookcase lined with law books, the cherry paneled walls, and the fine leather furniture. "You have gone over to the dark side, Patrick."

He shrugged, unapologetic. "What can I say? I like to eat. And who are you to talk? As I hear it, you live pretty well—a brownstone on Fifth Avenue. Admit it. You would much rather have money than not."

She lifted her chin a notch. "It empowers me to fight for the betterment of women."

Patrick burst into laughter. "You haven't changed, Mary Kate. You have a rationalization for everything."

Mary Kate glared at him. "It's true. Who is going to listen to a poor, working class woman? At least I am not an elitist."

"Yes, you are. Elitism is a condition of the pocketbook, Mary Kate. You can't escape the mantle. You might as well wear it."

"Elitism is also a state of mind that I reject, Patrick."

"You can't have it both ways."

"Then, let us concede that it depends on how one chooses to wear the mantle," said Mary Kate, recalling Andrew's words."

Patrick lifted his glass to her. "I can agree to that."

They lapsed into silence, again, both considering the same thought. Mary Kate was the first to say it.

"You know, Patrick, I'm not sure that a marriage would have worked between us even if we hadn't been related."

"Probably not," he admitted after a long pause. "We are too different."

"And we enjoy the fight too much," she noted.

"Like siblings," he added without thinking.

They looked at each other, the full import of his words suddenly hitting them; the realization of a simple truth freeing them, at last, from the burden they had carried for so long. Neither had to say a word. The expression on their faces spoke volumes.

"How do you want to handle this?" asked Patrick at length.

Mary Kate thought for a moment. "I think that we should keep the nature of our relationship within the family for now, for the sake of our mothers. They're working together on your mother's school, you know."

Patrick shook his head in amazement. "Never would have imagined that in a million years. Have you been back to Rossburg at all?"

"No. Mama and Papa have made separate trips to New York to try to convince me to return home. I wasn't very conciliatory. I refused to see Papa. Morgan and I corresponded for a time before he became too busy being a teenager." Mary Kate chuckled. "I get the impression that he is not quite the student that my parents had hoped. How about you?"

"Parker and Mother were here for the wedding. She and my wife correspond often. Mother refuses to use the telephone. She thinks everyone in town is listening in. I see Parker when he comes to Philadelphia on business. They're careful not to pressure. I think they are waiting for me to make the first move." He paused. "I'm not ready to go home, Mary Kate, and stand shoulder to shoulder with Ian."

Mary Kate nodded. "Perhaps after we fix our own lives."

"Have you met someone?"

"Possibly. I haven't decided yet." Briefly, she told him about Andrew.

"He sounds like a good man. He must not know what a handful you can be."

Mary Kate made a face at him and took a sip of her drink. "Your wife was at the rally yesterday," she slipped in casually.

Patrick's face registered surprise. "Abigail—I never would have imagined her at a suffragette rally. I asked her once how she stood on the subject. She didn't seem to have an opinion on it."

"She has to keep a low profile to protect your career," said Mary Kate.

Patrick looked at her. "How do you know that it was Abigail?"

"She heard my name spoken at the rally and came to see me afterwards at the hotel."

Patrick furrowed his brow in bewilderment. "Why?"

"She believes that you married her on the rebound...that there are three people in this marriage," replied Mary Kate. "She wants us to resolve whatever unfinished business you and I have and for you to make a choice."

Patrick was flabbergasted. "But how would she know about you? I never told her."

"I don't know, but she does, and she is really hurt. Is she right, Patrick? Did you marry her on the rebound?"

Patrick ran a hand through his hair as he struggled with the question. His mother had asked him that before the wedding. He had always placed a high value on integrity. He was finding it difficult to accept that he might not measure up to his own yardstick.

"What did you tell her?" he asked.

"Nothing. Abigail is a casualty in all of this, too. If you love her, you need to tell her everything, or you are going to lose her. No woman wants to feel that she is a consolation prize."

"She has never said anything."

"She plays her part. On the surface, she may be demure and deferential, but underneath she knows her mind, and she has her pride. She has put up with the situation because she loves you, but she isn't going to suffer in silence any longer, Patrick. At first, I didn't think she was right for you, but I've changed my mind. Abigail is just the woman you need. She's strong, smart, and a fighter. I know the type well. Look to our mothers."

Patrick looked at her, the sudden insight a surprise to him. The day seemed to be full of them.

Mary Kate rose. "I should be off now. Thanks for the drink."

Patrick stood up to see her to the door. "Don't sell yourself short, Mary Kate. You are cut from the same cloth as our mothers—except for the demure, deferential part," he added with a grin. He paused. "You know...I think I like you more as my sister."

Mary Kate smiled. "You aren't so bad for a brother."

As she walked past the receptionist, she heard Patrick yell: "Miss Warner, call my wife and tell her I will be home early tonight. And have the florist send flowers."

CHAPTER TWENTY-THREE

Moving Ahead

It was a cool, crisp fall day, and Andrew walked the several blocks from the hospital to his townhouse in the gathering twilight to clear his head. He filled most of his waking hours with work, but, still, thoughts of Mary Kate loomed large in his mind.

After handing her the ultimatum, he had purposely avoided seeing her to give her time to think. Two days yet remained for her to give him an answer, and he had no clue as to what it would be. His sister had told him that Mary Kate had gone to Philadelphia with the suffragettes, ostensibly for a rally. But he knew that Patrick was there. What was he to make of that?

He turned the corner to the brownstone and was brought up short at the sight of Mary Kate sitting on the front steps. He didn't know if it was a good sign or not. He didn't find the sober expression on her face encouraging.

"Mary Kate, what are you doing here? You still have two days," he joked lightly. "I've never known you to be early for anything."

She looked up at him, her manner serious. "Please sit down, Drew. I need to talk with you."

Andrew sat down next to her on the step, his hopes dwindling by the second.

"I went to Philadelphia," she said.

"I know. Em told me," he replied quietly.

"I saw Patrick."

Andrew stared out at the street. "And?"

"I need to tell you something." In a tone devoid of emotion, Mary Kate told him everything about Patrick and their relationship.

Andrew looked at her at a loss for words. He had been prepared for just about anything but this.

"We always enjoyed needling, debating, and sparring with each other over issues. We have a similar kind of wit and humor, and we felt connected," she continued. "But now, after talking it over, we realize that what we mistook for a romantic connection was, in fact, the bond of siblings. We have decided to keep the story within the family for our mothers' sakes, but I wanted you to know."

Andrew reached over and took her hand. "I'm sorry, Mary Kate. It is difficult to discover that one's parents are not infallible…that they make mistakes, too, as everyone does."

"They shouldn't have kept the secret, Drew."

"I'm sure that your mother and Patrick's mother made the only choice they thought they could for the sakes of all concerned. It couldn't have been easy for them to keep the truth from your father."

"All Mama will say in their defense is that I don't know the circumstances."

"Your mother is right. They may be your parents now, but you did not know those people then," said Andrew. "You have no idea what was going on in their lives at that time, what was in their hearts and minds."

"I don't care," she retorted. "It is still wrong what they did."

"Judgment can be a tricky thing, Mary Kate. All any of us can do is live life the best way we can and hope that the choices we make—sometimes selfish choices—don't negatively impact others down the road. Unfortunately, it may be years later until we know. It is called unforeseen circumstances and unintended consequences."

Mary Kate gave a humorless laugh. "Do you know the joke of all this, Drew? After years of avoiding each other, our mothers are now working together to open a school to teach job skills to women. Can you imagine—working together after all of this?!"

"Life is messy, Mary Kate. Some people are able to move past the messes; others aren't. It sounds as though your families have found a way to do it. What about you and Patrick?"

"We have come to terms with everything. We decided that we like each other better as siblings."

"But you both still remain angry with your families."

Mary Kate nodded. "Even though Papa didn't know, Patrick feels that my father disrespected his mother. As for me, I don't know why I'm still angry."

"It came as a great shock that the man you thought you wanted to marry is, in fact, your half brother. It takes time to get over something like that."

"Drew, I can't stop thinking what if Patrick and I had crossed a line before the truth came out?"

"But you didn't. Have you ever asked yourself why you didn't?"

Mary Kate shrugged. "We told ourselves that we were observing the rules of society. I think the truth of it was we just enjoyed being in each other's company and didn't feel the need for anything else at that point. Oh, we held hands and Patrick kissed me a few times, but it was just a peck. It was never more than that. I guess we assumed that passion would magically follow the wedding." She turned to Andrew with a look of disbelief on her face. "How could we have been so naïve?"

"You and Patrick were young and too inexperienced to understand that you were attracted to each other on a different level, and the observance of the rules of society only helped to obfuscate the truth. Perhaps one could even say they afforded you cover against a closer examination of your feelings," replied Andrew. "And now, you have discovered that you and Patrick are happier just being siblings. Consequently, what you both thought you wanted you realize now is not the case. Ergo, you don't need to be angry anymore."

Mary Kate shook her head. "I've spent hours on the train considering all that, and I'm still angry."

"It could be something as fundamental as having been told you couldn't have what you wanted, even though you no longer want it," said Andrew.

Mary Kate huffed. "That's silly."

"Is it? How many times were you told 'no' in your life?"

"You sound like Emily."

"There are a lot of things that play into one's emotions, Mary Kate—some he is aware of, some he isn't."

Mary Kate threw Andrew a look of annoyance. He had a way of making the ridiculous sound plausible enough that she was forced to consider the matter, and she fell silent for a long while.

"It is time to let go and move on," said Andrew, breaking into her thoughts. "You have no reason not to now, and I think you will find that your anger subsides once you do."

He gave her a few more minutes to herself, then nudged her. "Now that you no longer need to be angry, what is next for you?" His tone was light, but hope resonated in his voice.

She looked at him, a mischievous gleam coming into her eye. "Well, this young man has been pestering me to take notice of him. I am thinking of giving him a go."

A broad smile spread across Andrew's face. "I understand that he is a brilliant doctor, much deserving of your attention and affections."

"Perhaps, but I am a modern woman," she rejoined. "I don't know how well he can handle that."

"Oh, I have it on good authority that he is well up to the task," said Andrew. "However, he will insist upon being allowed an opinion from time to time."

"Hmmm, perhaps—from time to time."

"Is everything a negotiation with you?" he asked.

Mary Kate laughed. "I guess it runs in the family."

"Then, I shall insist upon sealing the bargain." Andrew leaned over and kissed her in a soft, lingering caress.

Mary Kate was surprised at how easily she was able to respond to him. The moment didn't feel strange or awkward as she had feared it might; it felt natural, comfortable, right. It was her first real kiss, and she felt a stirring she had never felt before.

Still, she had one condition. "Drew, I want to keep the change in our relationship to ourselves for awhile. I have to be sure that this is what we want without the pressure and influence of our families."

Andrew took her hand again. "Whatever you want, but have you forgotten about Emily? My sister is like a bloodhound when it comes to ferreting out secrets."

"I can handle Emily," Mary Kate assured him.

Andrew was doubtful, but he didn't debate the matter.

CHAPTER TWENTY-FOUR

Irons in the Fire

The clerk looked up at first indifferent, then becoming wary as a throng of women filed into the headquarters of the Board of Elections on West 41st Street in the Borough of Manhattan.

"Can I help you?" he asked.

A tall, thin woman of middle years stepped forward. "We are here to register to vote by the right granted to us under Article I of the 14th Amendment."

The man looked past her at the group. The women returned his stare unflinchingly, presenting a most formidable front. He had heard about these militant women.

"Lady, I don't know anything about that. I just know that women can't vote. I can't register you," said the clerk, dismissing the group with a degree of disdain.

"Then, we shall not leave until you do," replied the woman who was obviously the leader. At this, there came a loud chorus of shouts from the other women.

The clerk turned to his runner who stood watching the exchange with open-mouth astonishment. "Fetch the police, boy."

"Yes, sir."

At the police station, Chief Michael O'Hara was in the midst of a storm of his own at the moment. Outraged church officials and members of the New York Christian Association surrounded him in his office waving copies of Mary Kate's treatises on the reproductive rights of women.

"This cannot be allowed to continue," shouted the Bishop, throwing a pamphlet on the desk entitled: *The Enslavement of Women by Society and the Church.*

"Nor this!" exclaimed a member of the Christian Association, angrily jabbing at another pamphlet—*The Needless Deaths of Women: The Injustice of the Comstock Laws.*

"What are you going to do about this, Chief?" demanded Father Donohue. "This is inciting women to—to—"

"To think," supplied another church official. "It has been reported to me that some wives have denied their husbands their marital rights because of this venomous material. It is an affront to men, God, and the scriptures."

Chief O'Hara raised his arms to quiet the group. "There is nothing I can do," he said. "I've consulted the city attorney, and he says there is nothing illegal in these pamphlets. Even if we knew the author, we could not arrest her. And in distributing these pamphlets, the suffragettes are exercising their rights to free speech."

"What about the rights of men?" blustered the Bishop.

At this point, a sergeant rushed into the chief's office. "Sir, a runner just came from the Board of Elections. He said that a group of women have taken over the office and are demanding to be registered to vote."

The religious leaders smugly folded their arms and looked at O'Hara, their complaints justified.

* * * * *

With his son in tow, George Biederman stormed into Ian's office at the finishing mill and threw down a document on his desk. "What is the meaning of this, Douglas?"

Ian casually picked it up and perused the contents. It was all for show. He knew very well what it said. "It would appear that the state legislature has overturned the Rossburg Passenger Railway Company's monopoly on the city streets. 'Tis grantin' a charter to the Valley

Citizens Passenger Railway Company to connect proposed lines by way of Market Street. Must be a new company."

"I know you are behind this, Douglas. How long did you think you could hide behind a sham corporation? I don't know what you are up to, but it won't stand. Others have tried to overturn the Curtain Charter and failed."

"Theodore Roosevelt was nae president of the United States then. Perhaps ye've heard how he hates monopolies. His antitrust policy appears to be havin' an effect."

Biederman's face was flushed with anger. "I will appeal this."

"Oh, I was under the impression that the Rossburg Passenger Railway Company was Horace's company," said Ian, feigning confusion.

Biederman pulled his son forward. "Tell him, Horace."

Horace assumed an indignant air that bordered on pomposity. "I shall file immediately and am confident of winning the appeal, Mr. Douglas. I wouldn't waste my money if I were you."

Ian smiled. "Let the chips fall where they may, gentlemen. Oh, and, Horace, congratulations on your engagement to Amos Wadkins' daughter. I am sure she will meet your needs."

Both father and son bristled. The Wadkins girl was bucktoothed and wore glasses and was, by all accounts, shy and retiring. But her father, though not as rich as Ian, was rich enough. Ian felt sorry for the girl.

The Biedermans had no sooner stormed out than Parker Stanton walked in grinning. "I take it they heard. They nearly knocked me off the stairs as they rushed past."

"They're probably headin' straight to their attorney. Is everythin' in order?"

"You'll officially have the charter tomorrow," said Parker. "It will become public knowledge then that you are the owner of the Valley Citizens Passenger Railway Company. George will know for certain then."

"It makes no matter. He knows it now. Make sure the appeal that the Biedermans file is drawn out long enough to scare Horace into layin' a sizable amount of track."

"Not a problem. It took some doing, but I was able to get the judge we needed."

Ian was thoughtful for a minute. "Parker, maybe we should give Horace a little more incentive."

"What are you thinking?"

"What if I gather a crew and start layin' tract as soon as possible?"

Parker smiled. "Horace will run to the nearest judge for an injunction, but he'll get the message."

"In about three weeks, float the rumor that his appeal is goin' to be denied. Make it look like it is comin' from the judge's chambers," instructed Ian.

"Will do." Again, Parker smiled. "It has been a long time since we've had a fight this good—not since you challenged Cyrus Morgan and Franklin Jeffries. Brings back memories of the old days."

Ian's mind scrolled selectively back through the past. "Aye. We were too young and stupid then to realize the odds we were up against. How is the school doin'?"

"It has been open for six months and has more applicants than it can accommodate," replied Parker. "Of course, many are nonpaying, but Eleanor's fundraising has provided enough scholarships for the next year that they shouldn't have to touch their reserves."

"How does Maven like havin' the school electrified?" inquired Ian. "She was pretty resistant to it."

Parker grinned. "She was slow to admit the merits of it, but I don't think I will have to twist her arm too hard to get her to accept electricity in the house now."

Ian laughed. "We'll pull her into the modern age yet."

Ian's foreman rushed in then. "Mr. Douglas, your wife just called. She wants you to come home straightaway. And she said to bring Mr. Stanton with you."

Ian and Parker looked at each other.

"Did she say why?" asked Ian, concerned.

"No, Mrs. Douglas didn't say."

"I'll meet you at the house," said Parker.

When Ian arrived home, he found Eleanor packing a suitcase. "Are ye goin' somewhere? What's wrong?"

"Where is Parker?" she asked.

"He's on his way. Eleanor, what is this about?"

"Caroline and that detective Mr. Granger telephoned. Mary Kate has been arrested," she replied. "Our daughter was among a group of women who marched on the Board of Elections demanding to be registered to vote."

"Bloody hell—is she all right?"

"The women are sitting in jail. Some sustained injuries, but Mary Kate is okay. I'm leaving on the 6:45 p.m. train."

"I'll go with you," said Ian.

Eleanor shook her head. "No, it is better if Parker and I handle this. I'll need money."

"I'll wire John Rinker at the bank in New York. Are you sure you are up to this? Ye've nae been feelin' well."

Eleanor waved off her husband's concern. "I'm fine."

CHAPTER TWENTY-FIVE

In a New Light

It was ten o'clock the next morning when Eleanor and Parker arrived in New York City. Caroline was waiting for them with a cab at the station and gave them an update on the situation on the way to police headquarters.

"Dr. Stoddert was allowed to treat the women who were injured," she said. "He was going to call Mr. Douglas, but he had his hands full, so I told him I would take care of contacting you."

"Have the women been arraigned?" asked Parker

"Yes, yesterday afternoon," said Caroline. "The judge bound them over for trial next Tuesday."

"What's the charge?"

"Illegal assembly, inciting a riot, threatening elections officials, and resisting arrest. This is a total prefabrication. I was there covering the story. These women did nothing more than present their case and voice their protests. Some didn't even know they were being arrested and were roughly handled when they tried to walk away."

Eleanor looked at Parker in alarm. "The judge can't hold these women in jail for five days, can he?"

"I'm afraid so," he replied. "Did the judge set bail, Mrs. Thompson?"

"Yes, at $5000."

"Caroline, how many of these women are from affluent families?" asked Eleanor. "Surely, that should cause an uproar."

"Those families have bargained quietly for their daughters' releases and a dismissal of the charges."

"In other words, they greased a palm," said Parker.

Caroline nodded. "Chief O'Hara calls it a contribution to the Policemen's Fund."

"How many women are left in the jail?" asked Eleanor.

"Fifteen," replied Caroline. "They either have families living elsewhere and are unable to help or who cannot afford the bail. These are the ladies the police intend to make an example of. The Stodderts are in Europe, so Dr. Stoddert tried to post bail for his sister and Mary Kate, but they refused to leave the other women. He is out arranging bail for all of them now."

When they arrived at the police station, Parker approached the officer on duty. "We are here to see about one of the women that you have jailed," he said.

The officer looked up from the desk at the well-dressed older man. "Which one?"

"Mary Kate Douglas."

The officer checked his list. "She ain't bein' released before the court date on Tuesday," he said, his manner surly. "About time these women get taught a lesson."

Eleanor stepped forward. "Officer?"

The man looked up again, and she smiled sweetly. "May I see the person in charge, sir?"

"Who are you?"

"A woman who can make your life very difficult if you do not take me to whoever is in charge."

She continued to smile and her voice was even, her tone pleasant, but there was no ignoring the command in her presence. She was obviously "one of them." He disliked the privileged. Still, he remained in awe of them and knew enough to fear them. And the chief had instructed the sergeant to pass through to him anyone of affluence who was connected with the jailed suffragettes.

"Wait here," he ordered. "What are your names?"

"Mrs. Douglas, Mrs. Thompson, and Mr. Stanton."

A few minutes later, they were shown into the office of Chief of Police Michael O'Hara. The chief, an older man with gray hair and mustache, regarded Eleanor with a measure of appreciation and immediately came forward. "Mrs. Douglas, I presume. I am Chief O'Hara," he said, his manner ingratiating. "The officer tells me that you are here about your daughter's release. You understand there are serious charges pending."

"Yes, I understand that."

The chief waited for her to continue. When she didn't, he prompted her. "I'm sure we can come to an understanding, Mrs. Douglas."

Eleanor gave him a disarming smile. "Good, then you will release my daughter and Miss Stoddert, as well as the other women who are still detained."

The chief was taken aback for a moment. "Mrs. Douglas, these women have broken the law," he said, his tone becoming patronizing. "I gather that you are from out of town. With all due respect, I don't believe you know how things are done here. Perhaps I should talk to the gentleman," he said, looking to Parker to intervene.

"That will not be necessary, Chief O'Hara. I understand very well how things are done here," replied Eleanor, her smile still in place. "These women were exercising their First Amendment right of free speech under the Constitution of the United States, and the men under your command falsely imprisoned and engaged in brutality against them."

The chief was hard pressed to hide his growing impatience. "Mrs. Douglas, I'm afraid you are misinformed. It is the opinion of the law that these women acted illegally. However, I am sure it is possible to mitigate your daughter's circumstances."

"Yes, Chief, I quite agree with you," Eleanor responded sweetly. "This is my attorney Mr. Stanton. He has connections to the law firm of Tanner, Williams and O'Brien in Philadelphia and, by extension, to

Williams and Wycliffe of this city. I am sure you are acquainted with Williams and Wycliffe, as it is one of the most prestigious law firms in New York."

"Yes, but I fail to see what they have to do with this matter."

"On behalf of the women, Mr. Stanton has instructed the firm to file a lawsuit against you, the police department, and the city for false imprisonment and police brutality. I would advise you to retain an attorney, Chief O'Hara."

O'Hara blinked in astonishment. "Now, now, Mrs. Douglas, there is no need to go to this extreme," he stammered. "I'm sure we can come to an agreement."

Eleanor's blue eyes locked unwaveringly on his, and there was an uncompromising edge in her tone. "Were you to release the women immediately into my custody and drop the charges, Mr. Stanton might be able to persuade Williams and Wycliffe to withdraw the suit."

Caroline came forward, then. "Chief O'Hara, I am a reporter for the *New York Times*. I was at the elections office yesterday, and the pictures that I took tell quite a different story from that of your officers—or perhaps you were there. If you do not take Mrs. Douglas' suggestion, I think you will find that you and the police department become the story, sir."

The chief bristled. "Extortion is against the law, madam."

"So is a public official soliciting and accepting bribes," interjected Eleanor. "What is it you call it? Oh, yes, a contribution to the Policemen's Fund. I'm sure Mrs. Thompson's editor would find that interesting as well."

Perspiration beaded on the chief's forehead, and he took out a handkerchief to mop his brow. The managing editor of the *New York Times* was not a friend to him.

Parker sat back enjoying the scene immensely. He was transported back to another time when Eleanor had "suggested" to the Rossburg chief of police that it wouldn't be advantageous to his career to arrest

Ian for murder. As then, this was Eleanor's show, and she was carrying it off beautifully.

"I would advise you to take Mrs. Douglas' proposition, Chief—and quickly," interjected Parker. "You know how lawyers hate to halt an action once it is initiated."

The chief mopped his brow again and walked briskly to the doorway. "McCrory, release the women," he shouted to an officer.

"Which ones, sir?"

"All of them!"

"I assume you will make a recommendation to the court to drop the charges," said Parker.

O'Hara glared at him and nodded.

As Parker ushered the ladies out of the chief's office, he leaned over and whispered to Eleanor: "Great bluff. Remind me to never play poker with you."

Eleanor whispered back. "Who said I was bluffing?"

Stanton looked at her in surprise. "Mrs. Thompson really has pictures?"

Eleanor just smiled, leaving him to wonder.

"I have to get back to the paper now," said Caroline. "Eleanor, I hope that I will see you before you return to Rossburg."

"Of course. Thank you, Caroline, for your help."

As Caroline walked out the door, Eleanor turned to Parker. "I want you to retain Williams and Wycliffe today."

"Why? The charges are being dropped."

"No doubt there will be other arrests after this. I want notice sent to Chief O'Hara that Williams and Wycliffe are the attorneys of record for any suffragette who cannot advocate for herself. Perhaps, next time, the police will be more mindful of how they treat these women."

"What if the firm opposes women's suffrage and declines to represent?"

"They're lawyers, Parker. The only thing they believe in is making money."

"Ouch."

"Sorry. Present company excepted."

Just then, a young man rushed into police headquarters to the officer in charge. They conversed for a few minutes and the officer pointed to Eleanor and Parker.

The young man approached them. "Mrs. Douglas, I am Andrew Stoddert."

Eleanor smiled. "It is a pleasure to meet you, Doctor. My husband has spoken highly of you."

"Thank you. I came to bail out the suffragettes, but I understand that you have secured their release."

"Yes. I had some help."

"The lady is being modest," broke in Parker with a laugh. "The chief was in fear for his well being by the time she was finished with him." He extended his hand. "I'm Parker Stanton the family attorney."

Andrew returned a hearty handshake. "I am pleased to meet you, sir. Mary Kate has spoken of you."

"Mrs. Douglas?"

Eleanor turned to see a nattily dressed, middle-aged man in a plaid suit. "Yes?"

"I am Samuel Granger of the Granger Detective Agency. I am here to see to your daughter's release."

"No need, Mr. Granger. It has been arranged."

The detective gave her a patronizing smile and his tone held a note of reprimand. "There was no need for you to make the trip, Mrs. Douglas. Mr. Douglas hired me to look after your daughter's interests."

"Indeed. It would appear that you didn't do your job very well, Mr. Granger. My daughter was in jail for nearly 24 hours," replied Eleanor, feeling an instant dislike for the man.

Granger drew himself up. "The wheels of justice turn slowly, madam," he said, pompously reciting the age-old axiom. "I warned your husband that your daughter had fallen in with an undesirable group of women that would lead her afoul of the law. I would advise Mr. Douglas to have a heart to heart with her. There is a limit to what I can do, you understand."

Eleanor had had enough of overbearing, condescending men for the day. "Thank you, Mr. Granger, but you needn't concern yourself. Your services will no longer be required."

"I beg your pardon, madam?"

"I am firing you, Mr. Granger."

The detective was taken aback for a moment. "With all due respect, Mrs. Douglas, your husband hired me. You cannot fire me," he informed her with a tight smile.

"With all due respect, Mr. Granger, I can and I just did."

The detective's smile faded. "Rest assured, madam, I will be calling your husband."

As he stormed out of the police station, Andrew and Parker exchanged glances, hard pressed to hold back snickers of amusement.

A few minutes later, the suffragettes came filing out from the lockup. They were silent. They looked tired and disheveled, but they were unbowed. Mary Kate and Emily were the last to appear.

When Mary Kate looked over to see her mother and Parker Stanton, her step faltered. She hadn't considered that someone would notify her family. She realized now it was a silly assumption.

Unsure of the reception she would receive, Mary Kate slowly walked over to them. "Mama, I wasn't expecting to see you."

"Your father wanted to come, but I thought it best that Mr. Stanton and I handle this," said Eleanor.

"I didn't intend to inconvenience you and Papa."

Eleanor looked at her. "Inconvenience—you are our daughter, Mary Kate. Nothing else matters to us but that you are unharmed."

Mary Kate had learned not to expect much emotion from her mother and was surprised by the concern she saw in her mother's eyes and heard in her voice.

"I see you have met Drew," she said, seeking to cover the awkwardness she felt at the moment. She brought Emily into the circle then and introduced her.

Emily smiled. "I am happy to meet you, Mrs. Douglas, Mr. Stanton and am very grateful to you for getting us all released. I wasn't relishing another night in jail."

"Let's hope that the police exercise more discretion in the future," replied Eleanor returning a smile.

She suddenly felt weary and put a hand to her head to quell the onslaught of a headache. "I think the girls could do with some food and rest," she said, forcing a lighter tone. "Dr. Stoddert, if you will see Mary Kate and Emily home, Mr. Stanton and I shall find our way to the Astor Hotel. I am sure that Mr. Douglas is most anxious for a report. Perhaps we can all meet for breakfast at the hotel tomorrow morning after a good night's rest."

With all in agreement, everyone dispersed.

On the ride to the brownstone, Mary Kate and Emily were uncharacteristically subdued. The arrest had been an eye-opener for them. Though they had been warned, the girls had airily dismissed concerns about police action. The complete lack of regard and the contempt the police had shown the suffragettes had come as a shock to both. Mary Kate was still feeling the effects of the arrest when her mother appeared on the scene, throwing her for another loop. She had expected recriminations and a demand that she return to Rossburg. She got neither.

Andrew watched Mary Kate struggle with her emotions as she stared out the window of the cab, and he left her to her thoughts. It was obvious that she had much to sort out. When they reached the townhouse, he helped the girls out. Emily hurried up the steps, unlocked the door, and disappeared into the house, eager to take a bath and crawl into bed. Mary Kate and Andrew followed behind.

At the door, Andrew laid a hand on Mary Kate's arm. "Perhaps you could give your mother the benefit of the doubt," he said.

"You don't know her, Drew."

"Neither do you, I suspect," he responded.

Mary Kate looked at him but was too tired to debate the matter.

He kissed her on the cheek. "I'll pick up you and Emily tomorrow morning at eight thirty. Get some rest."

At the Astor Hotel, Eleanor put in a call to Ian to reassure him that all was well, while being careful not to disclose certain details in case a party might be listening in. After they hung up, she ate a light dinner. Her headache and cough had ceased and she felt better, but her confrontation with the police chief had taken more of a toll on her than she had expected. Lines of fatigue marked her delicate features.

She changed into her nightgown and slipped on a velvet robe, then sat down at the vanity to brush out her hair. Suddenly, there came a knock on the door. Eleanor laid aside the brush and rose to answer it. She expected to see Parker when she opened the door. Instead, she found her daughter standing there looking tired and conflicted.

"Mary Kate, is everything okay?" she asked, alarmed.

"No, not really, Mama. May I come in to talk?"

"Of course. If you are worried that your father and I are going to force you to return home, you needn't be concerned."

Mary Kate entered the luxurious suite of the newest hotel on Broadway. "No, that's not it," she said. "I went to see Caroline Thompson, and we had a long talk. She told me what you had done to secure the release of the suffragettes today. I wanted to thank you."

"I admire the courage of you and these ladies. It was the least I could do to stand by my daughter. I am proud of you," said Eleanor.

For the second time today, her mother surprised Mary Kate. Andrew and Mrs. Thompson were right. She really didn't know her mother. They didn't know each other.

She led Eleanor to a chair and pulled up another to sit opposite her. "Caroline also told me a little about your friendship and your life growing up in Rossburg. I want to know more about you, Mama, and I want you to know about me."

Eleanor was taken aback for a moment. Tears welled up in her eyes. "Yes, I think it is time that we did that."

Neither knew where to start. Finally, Eleanor said in a tremulous voice: "I'm sorry, Mary Kate. I'm sorry that I wasn't the mother I should have been to you." She wiped away a tear that rolled down her cheek. "I have tried to make amends, but I fear that I have only succeeded in putting more distance between us. Please know that you are not at fault. The shortcomings are mine."

Mary Kate had never expected to hear such a confession. She had always thought that she that was the reason why she and her mother could not seem to connect…that she had been so displeasing as a child. But after talking with Caroline and getting an inkling of what it meant to be a child and a young woman in high society in those days, she was beginning to understand her mother's reserve now, why she had such difficulty showing emotion. And the floodgates opened to let out years of hurt, pain, and misunderstandings on both sides.

"It's not easy to admit that I failed at the one job that is supposed to be instinctive to women," said Eleanor, dabbing at her eyes.

Mary Kate took her mother's hands in hers. "You were set up to fail, Mama. Women and children of the power elite were instruments used to ensure the status and power of their men through bartered marriages with no thought to love. And the rigid rules of polite society were designed to keep women numb to their feelings and desires. It is still the case today. That is what you and I must fight to change." She paused. "I don't blame you, Mama."

Eleanor looked at her, her eyes glistening with unshed tears. "But I do deserve blame, Mary Kate. Regardless of the reason, I was self-centered…your father and I were in a difficult place then. And you suffered for it."

"We both did, Mama. So, let's not suffer anymore."

They talked long into the night, holding back little. They laughed. They cried, revealing themselves to each other as they slowly began to build a new relationship block-by-block.

* * * * *

At the persistent knock on his door, Andrew hurried down the stairs, still in his robe. It was seven o'clock in the morning, and he was in the process of getting dressed to leave to pick up Mary Kate and his sister for breakfast at the hotel. Thus far, he had only finished part of his grooming and was annoyed at the interruption. He hoped it wasn't an emergency at the hospital. This breakfast was an event that he didn't want to miss.

When he opened the door, Mary Kate swept past him into the foyer. Andrew looked at her in surprise. "I did say eight thirty, didn't I?"

"You were right," she said.

His brow knit in confusion. "About what?"

"There is a side to my mother I didn't know. I went to see her last night, and we talked for a long time."

"And?" asked Andrew, trying to gauge her state of mind. She appeared tired, but there was a charged energy about her.

"It was revealing and cathartic," replied Mary Kate. "Mama is going to stay on for the week. We have more mending to do."

"Did you get much sleep?"

"A few hours at the hotel. By the way, breakfast has been moved to an early dinner. I called Emily to tell her."

"I'll get dressed and take you home," said Andrew.

"No, I want to stay with you." Mary Kate took off her jacket and draped it over the banister, then started up the stairs. Halfway up, she turned and looked down at him. "Are you coming?"

Andrew's jaw dropped, and it was a few minutes before he recovered his wits and bounded up the stairs after her. When he entered his bedroom, she was removing her skirt. He watched wordlessly as she methodically took off her blouse and stripped down to the knee length union suit.

"Given the history of your parents, are you certain that you want to do this?" he asked as she sat down on the bed to remove her shoes and stockings.

She looked up at him with large blue eyes. "Yes. I have to live my life the way I want to according to my needs, Drew. Not the way someone else decides I should."

"Is this about your mother?"

Mary Kate took a moment to frame her thoughts. "I was away at school most of the time, but growing up I can't remember my mother ever crying, and I never saw her really laugh much. She was so proper...her emotions always so controlled. I didn't think she felt anything. Last night, I saw her laugh and cry, and I learned that she does feel things. She just had been trained not to show it. I don't want to be that way."

"You have to remember that your mother grew up in a different time in a much more structured society," said Andrew. "Women were taught to repress their emotions as a matter of class. It is hard to undo that kind of training."

"I know. I understand that now. Mrs. Thompson explained how it was for her and Mama growing up." She looked at him. "Not much has changed, Drew. And I refuse to allow social conventions to dictate my life. I don't want to be told what to feel. I want to experience life."

"This is an important step for a single woman, Mary Kate. It should be about something more than thumbing your nose at social conventions."

She stood up and went to him. "I love you, and I trust you, Drew. I know that you love me, and you allow me to be who I need to be. That's all that matters."

"You are sure that you don't want more time to reconsider."

"No. I've been thinking about it since leaving the hotel."

Andrew studied her closely. There was no hint of uncertainty in her voice or in her manner. All he saw was the passionate nature that he loved about her.

Mary Kate raised herself up on her toes and looped her arms around his neck. "As I've never done this before and you have knowledge of anatomy, I shall have to yield to your expertise on the matter."

Andrew smiled. "It's not that clinical."

Pressing his lips against hers, he put his hands on her hips and slowly traced the curve of her buttocks and thighs beneath the fine Cambria material of her union suit. She caught her breath as a shiver went through her, but she didn't flinch, and his hands moved higher.

"If you recall, the matter does require some planning and protection," he murmured against her ear, trailing light, feathery kisses along the column of her neck. "I would hate to end up a mention in your next pamphlet."

Mary Kate gave a light laugh. "I am sure you have something for the occasion around here."

"And how do you come to assume that? Condoms are illegal, remember?"

"You are not a priest, and as Em tells it, you are no saint either. And she said that these things can be easily obtained on the black market."

Andrew lifted his head and looked at her. "How would she know?"

"I don't know. She told me not to ask."

"Remind me to have a talk with my sister." He paused. "Mary Kate, there is another alternative, you know. You could marry me first."

"No. I will not be dictated to by a group of men who set themselves up as the conscience of society but who have no problems using women for their own gratification."

Andrew chuckled. "Always the rebel." He lowered his head and kissed her with more intimacy, slowly taking greater liberties with her as the archaic rules of polite and proper courtship gave way to a new age.

CHAPTER TWENTY-SIX

Chess vs. Checkers

When Parker Stanton got off the train from New York, Ian was standing there waiting.

"Where is Eleanor?" he asked.

"She decided to stay another week. She is going to call you tonight," replied Parker.

Ian looked at him in bewilderment. "Why?"

"She wants to attend some suffragette rallies and march in a parade on Fifth Avenue with Mary Kate."

Ian was dumbfounded. "Are ye tellin' me that I may have to bail out my daughter *and* my wife?"

"Them as well as any other suffragettes that may be arrested. You now have Williams and Wycliffe on retainer," Parker amusedly informed him. "But I wouldn't worry too much. Eleanor pretty much put the fear of God into the police chief."

"What? Bloody hell, Parker, you were supposed to handle things," said Ian with a measure of exasperation. "What happened in New York?"

As Parker recounted the details, Ian was incredulous.

"By the time Eleanor was finished, Chief O'Hara couldn't release the women fast enough," said Parker with a laugh. "By the way, she fired Detective Granger."

Ian snorted. "I know. I got an indignant call from him. It seems that he has never been fired by a woman before."

"How did things go here?" asked Parker.

"Apparently, smoother than in New York," responded Ian shortly. "I just got the permit. My foreman gathered a crew together, and they'll be ready to start layin' rail next week when the supplies come in."

"When do you start work on the other power plant?"

"Next week, along with the rail."

"Is that wise?" asked Parker. "Biederman is sure to notice. He keeps a close eye on what you're doing."

"Hopefully, he'll think the plant is bein' built to service the new trolley system. That was the purpose of all of this, remember?" Ian chuckled. "It should serve to make George more nervous about the outcome of Horace's appeal on the Curtain Charter. It will bother him that I am feelin' confident enough of my position to build the plant."

Parker shook his head. "I hope I never have you for an enemy. Has Morgan been behaving himself?"

"He was suspended from school for two weeks," replied Ian. "I put him to work in the mill. Maybe a little hard labor will convince him it is in his best interests to be a better student."

"Eleanor won't be happy that Morgan is working in the mill, you know."

"It appears that I will have some time now to come up with a convincin' argument," replied Ian dryly.

*****

Ian's crew began to lay trolley rail a week later, working at night so as not to disrupt traffic.

When Horace brought his father the news, Biederman shot out of his seat and ordered his son to bring the motorcar around. He couldn't believe that Douglas would have that much gall and had to see it for himself. When he and Horace arrived at the site, Biederman sat silent in the car chomping angrily on his cigar.

Horace glanced at his father nervously. "What should we do?"

"Rip up all the rail tonight after the crew leaves," Biederman ordered brusquely.

Horace looked at his father as though he had lost his mind. "I can't order my men to do that. Douglas obviously has a permit."

"And we have an appeal pending. Take me to my attorney."

"Why?"

"To get an injunction against Douglas' rail."

"It's a little after the fact, don't you think?" questioned Horace with a touch of sarcasm. "I could still be held liable for the damage."

"Then I suggest you tell your men to act expeditiously and not get caught."

"Douglas will know we are behind the act."

"It doesn't matter as long as he can't prove it," replied Biederman. He threw his son a look of recrimination. "You failed with Douglas' daughter. See if you can get this right."

The next morning, Parker rushed into Ian's office.

"I know," said Ian.

Parker was taken aback by Ian's casual attitude. "Well, I don't understand what you are smiling about. Your track was destroyed. You'll have to start over, and Floyd Cross just served me with this injunction. You can't lay any rail until the lawsuit is settled. You know who is behind this, but I'm told that the police haven't turned up any proof so far." He paced back and forth across the office, his agitation increasing.

Ian laughed. "Parker, settle down. The trolley company is a ruse, remember?"

Parker stopped pacing and dropped into a chair. "Sorry. I don't like the idea that Biederman thinks he has the upper hand. He's coming after you hard."

"Do nae worry," said Ian. "Horace's track at the upper end of Third Street will be meetin' with the same fate as mine."

"As your attorney, I did not hear you say that," admonished Parker. "Besides, George will instruct Horace to put guards around. He'll be expecting you to retaliate."

"That is why I will wait a couple of weeks…let the Biedermans think they have won a victory," replied Ian. "Horace can nae afford to guard all the tracts for long. When he pulls the guards from the feeder lines, that's when I will strike…and I will leave a callin' card."

Parker straightened upright in the chair and looked at him aghast. "Are you insane? You will be handing the Biedermans the rope with which to hang you."

"Calm down, Parker. They can nae afford to accuse me of sabotage when they are guilty of the same act."

"But we have no proof of that."

"Police make mistakes," said Ian. "And they do nae like to get their hands dirty." He reached into his desk drawer and pulled out a dirty, crumpled envelope. "After the police left the site this morning, I had the crew turn out and conduct their own search. One of the men found this beneath a pile of twisted rail. I think you should pay a visit to the name on this envelope and explain to the man how much trouble he is in and the merits of him working with us."

Parker looked at Ian incredulous for a moment, then gave a hearty laugh. "Tommy O'Brien was right. You do have the luck of the Irish. Oh, I almost forgot. The mayor wants to see you in an hour."

Ian took out his pocket watch and looked at the time. "Eleanor is arriving on the ten o'clock train. The mayor will have to wait."

"I can meet Eleanor for you and drive her home," offered Parker.

"Thanks, but it has to be me. Tell Archie I'll drop by his office at two o'clock."

Parker nodded. "How is Morgan these days?"

Ian chuckled. "Too exhausted to cause any trouble. He is counting the days until he can return to school."

Parker grinned. "Can't wait to hear the story you give Eleanor." He picked up the envelope from the desk. "I'll get back to you on this."

At ten o'clock, the train chugged into the station right on time. Eleanor felt a measure of disquiet—a throwback to the past. Her father used to promise to meet her at the station upon her arrival home from boarding school or from the Grand Tour. But something always came up and, in his stead, would be a surrogate to meet her. She could still feel the disappointment and hurt that she had been such a low priority on his agenda.

She gave a sigh of resignation. Ian was a busy man, too. It was silly of her to think that he might drop everything as well to meet her at the station. She looked out the train window and unenthusiastically scanned the crowd. He would probably send his mill foreman. Then her eye fell on the tall, handsome, middle-aged man standing on the platform with his arms full of flowers, and she was filled with a sense of well-being. When she stepped down from the train, Ian was there.

The look in his eyes and the warmth of his smile gave her to know that he was happy to see her. "Mrs. Douglas, how glad I am that you are home," he said, handing her the flowers and kissing her on the cheek. "I've greatly missed your presence."

Eleanor smiled up at him. "I thought you might send a foreman to meet me."

Neither the moment nor the memory was lost on Ian, and he tucked her arm in his. "Never, my love, never. It will always be me who meets your train. How is Mary Kate?" he asked, steering her toward the motorcar.

"Our daughter is an amazing woman, Ian."

"So is her mother. I heard how you threatened the police chief of New York City. I thought I might end up having to bail you out as well."

Eleanor laughed. "Not to worry. I would have had good representation. I retained Williams and Wycliffe to represent the suffragettes when needed."

"Parker told me," said Ian with the lift of his brow. "Since when did you become a subversive? Mary Kate and her group seem to have had quite an effect on you."

"They have helped me to view some things in a different light. After all, this is a new age," she announced proudly.

Ian looked at her, much amused. There was a glow about her. Her eyes shone with excitement, and her voice reflected wonder. She was like a young girl again—without the baggage.

"I met Dr. Stoddert," continued Eleanor. "He is a nice, young man. He said to tell you that Mary Kate is seeing the light. I don't know what he meant by it, but I do believe he is smitten with our daughter."

"Oh, and how do you feel about that?" questioned Ian.

Eleanor thought for a moment. "Caroline thinks very highly of Dr. Stoddert and his family. I think he would make a good match for Mary Kate. He seems to know just how to handle her."

Ian chuckled. "I wouldn't mention that to Mary Kate. It would mean the kiss of death for Dr. Stoddert."

"How is Morgan? Has he behaved while I was away?" asked Eleanor.

"I think you will find him a changed young man," Ian assured her, helping her into the car.

Eleanor glanced questioningly at him, but, as he offered no further explanation, she didn't pursue the matter and was soon onto another topic. She had lots to tell. Ian had never seen her so animated, so energized. The crown of reserve and sophistication that she had always worn as Rossburg's proud queen of society seemed to have slipped off her head.

After sharing a private midday meal with his wife, Ian left to keep his appointment with the mayor. Mayor Archibald Kramer was a pragmatic man with a passion for efficiency. He liked his i's dotted and his t's crossed and was prone to overreaction when something didn't fall into line with his dictates. Ian wondered what the fly in the ointment was this time.

When he arrived at City Hall, the secretary waved him through. "The mayor has been waiting for you, Mr. Douglas, and he is not in a good mood."

Ian nodded and opened the door. When he walked into the mayor's office, he could see that the man was clearly disturbed. "Somethin' wrong, Archie?" he asked, settling into a chair.

The mayor tapped the report in front of him. "This competition between you and Horace Biederman over the transit system is what's wrong."

"If this is about the destruction of my rails last night—"

"No, no. It's about who is going to be responsible for maintaining the roads beneath all these trolley lines. Look, I'm all for an expanded transit system, but the city can't afford to repair the trolley roads it has, let alone the feeder lines that will be added if the Court of Appeals overturns the Curtain Charter."

"Have you talked with Horace?" asked Ian.

"Yes...when he first came into possession of the company. He maintained—or rather his attorney for him—that the previous owner of the trolley company had not been charged with the responsibility and that there was nothing in the contract or in correspondence from the city to suggest that Horace should be held legally responsible either. The city immediately brought a lawsuit, but the courts came down on his side. You were mayor for a number of years, Ian. You see my problem."

Ian thought for a moment. "I think I might have a resolution to your problem, Archie. How soon can you get my company permits for five or six trolley lines?"

The mayor looked at Ian in surprise. "Biederman has an injunction against you until the appeal is settled."

"He has an injunction against layin' rail, not against collectin' permits."

"Well, the City Council meets in two days. You'll have to submit applications before then. But I don't know how the council is going to feel about getting in the middle of this dispute between you and Biederman. The papers are already calling it the 'streetcar war.' And how is this going to solve the problem of maintaining the streets? When the courts ruled against the city, precedent was set. Council members are reluctant to issue any more permits. I'm caught between a rock and a hard place."

"I have a plan, Archie."

The mayor regarded Ian warily. "Is it legal? I'm up for re-election. I can't be getting caught up in questionable shenanigans."

Ian assured him everything was aboveboard. As he laid out the specifics, the mayor smiled.

"I think the council will go for that," he said. "I'll call the city attorney right away. I dare say you will have the permits by the end of the week."

"Good. I'll have Parker submit the applications today. You can announce the permits, but keep the rest of it quiet."

"Shouldn't be a problem. Everybody on the council wants this business settled."

At dinner that night, Eleanor regarded her son with curiosity. She had been in her room dressing for the evening meal when he came home. And he had gone straight to his room. This was the first that she had seen him. Though he was happy to see her, he was oddly subdued and seemed exhausted. He had also bathed—on a midweek day. He usually had to be prodded to it on the customary Saturday nights.

"How is school, Morgan?" she asked.

The 15-year-old looked at Ian and saw the warning glint in his father's eye. "Fine," he mumbled.

"Why are you so tired?"

Again, he exchanged looks with his father. "Morgan has been working at the finishing mill, Mother, as part of a school project," said Ian.

"Oh? What kind of a project?" asked Eleanor.

"I have to work at one of Papa's companies and do a report on it," the boy replied moodily.

"Why the mill, dear, instead of your father's bank?"

"I wasn't given a choice."

"It'll be just for another week," explained Ian. "The foreman said that Morgan is doin' such a fine job he would like to hire him for the summer. As the lad seems to do much better with physical endeavors than with mental exercises, I believe the mill to make a better fit for him for the summer than the bank, Mother. What do you think?"

Morgan eyes widened, and the panicked teenager immediately appealed to his mother for support. "Mama…"

"Perhaps your father is right, dear."

Morgan looked at her in disbelief. He had always been able to count on her to take his side. With his last line of defense gone now, he let out a tortured moan and excused himself.

When their son left the room, Eleanor laughed. "We really shouldn't tease the boy that way."

Ian refrained from telling her that he wasn't joking. He set aside his napkin. "I have a few business matters that require my attention in the study. I won't be long to bed. Will I find you awake?" he asked.

Eleanor could hear the hope in his voice. A telltale blush spread across her features, but she met his eye. "Yes," she said without any ambivalence.

Ian smiled. "Then I shall make haste."

An hour later, Ian finished his work and went to his room to change into a robe. He had missed her, and he approached his wife's suite with an eager step. She was waiting for him. Dressed in a blue silk and satin peignoir, her hair hanging loose over her shoulders, she looked radiant and alluring. With a smile that held promise, she slipped the robe off her shoulders and let it drop to the floor.

Ian's pulse quickened. He walked over to her and ran his hands over the sleek, fitted nightgown, feeling the curves of her small waist and slender hips. He gathered her in his arms, then, and kissed her in a long, lingering embrace. She responded with an ardor that surprised him. He needed no further invitation. He lifted her in his arms and carried her to the bed, laying her gently on the mattress.

Quickly, he divested himself of his robe and slid in alongside of her, holding back his need out of respect for the modesty that had been ingrained in her. This night, however, to his further surprise, she met him with noticeably less inhibition, and he was able to direct her to a greater fulfillment than she was used to experiencing. He didn't know what had happened to her in New York, but he liked this new Eleanor.

CHAPTER TWENTY-SEVEN

A New Suffragette

Eleanor picked through the array of dresses in her closet, finding each one unsuitable for an afternoon at the racetrack for one reason or another. It was a beautiful autumn day, chilly but sunny with calm winds, and she finally settled on the blue wool walking suit trimmed in silver fox fur. The maid arrived and helped her to dress.

"Which hat do you prefer, madam?" asked the maid.

Eleanor thought for a moment. "I think the gray one." The drop brim would shade her face from the sun and from the dust stirred up by Ian's motorcar.

The maid picked up the hat and placed it on top of Eleanor's upswept hair. Taking a last look in the mirror, Eleanor gave a nod of satisfaction. She slipped on a duster, picked up a white chiffon scarf and a pair of gray kid leather gloves from the dresser and went to meet Ian.

She found him outside admiring his new motorcar—a sleek, shiny green runabout with red leather interior. It was the latest design from his motorcar company. Eleanor sighed. She couldn't quite fathom her husband's fascination with it. The contraption was open to the elements and ungodly noisy, but she supposed it was preferable to smelling the byproducts of horses. Ian cranked the car and helped her in, then took his seat beside her.

"Are you sure ye do nae want these?" he asked.

Eleanor looked at the goggles he held out to her and pushed them away. "No thank you," she said, looping the scarf over her hat and tying it under her chin. "It is quite enough that one of us looks silly."

"Suit yourself." Ian put on his goggles and set the car in gear. "Soon, Eleanor, these carriages will be closed to the weather and you will nae have to worry about the dust and dirt," he shouted over the noise.

Eleanor looked doubtful, but she had been wrong before about his vision.

As they bounced along the road on their way to the racetrack, Eleanor gripped the side of the motorcar and fanned away the dust. Thank heavens they had to go only a short distance. When they arrived at the park, Ian nosed the motorcar into a spot in the parking area. Among the throng of horse drawn carriages, he proudly noted that there were two dozen cars present, all purchased from his company.

Ian handed Eleanor out of the car and took her arm. He was guiding her toward their seats in the stands, when the elder Biedermans approached them.

Eleanor suppressed a moan and drew upon her training to force a credible smile. "Good day, Mr. and Mrs. Biederman. Lovely day, isn't it?"

"Indeed," replied Mrs. Biederman.

"Too bad about your trolley rail, Douglas," commented Biederman, his tone smug. "Something needs to be done about the hooligans roaming the city."

"No need to worry, George. It will be handled," responded Ian with cool confidence.

Biederman's eyes narrowed, and he regarded Ian sharply as he tried to divine the meaning behind that remark, but Ian gave away nothing. Biederman turned to Eleanor. "I understand that your daughter was arrested in New York with some suffragettes. I hope she hasn't fallen in with a group of subversives. Perhaps it is best that a match was not made between our children after all."

Eleanor inwardly bristled. Her careful smile remained in place, but her chin went up a notch. "Yes, I quite agree with you on that last score. And I would hardly count women who seek the right to vote and control their own destinies as subversives, Mr. Biederman."

"It is foolish nonsense and a danger to society, Mrs. Douglas. Women don't know about such things. They need to leave politics to men."

"That would be all well and good, sir, if men legislated for the good of women and children. As it is, they legislate only for the good of themselves. Don't you agree, Mrs. Biederman?"

The plain, stout woman became flustered. "Yes—I mean no," she stammered when her husband glared at her.

"These suffragettes are nothing more than radical rabble-rousers," Biederman continued to expound.

Eleanor cocked her head and fixed bright blue eyes on him. "I believe you do business with Mr. Kissling of New York, do you not, Mr. Biederman?"

"Yes, Mr. Kissling transports freight on my train line. He is one of my largest customers," responded Biederman, puffing up his chest with self-importance.

"How nice," replied Eleanor. "I wonder what Mr. Kissling would say if he heard that you consider his wife to be a radical rabble-rouser. Mrs. Kissling is quite influential in the movement, you know."

Biederman's chest deflated. "Well, I-I didn't mean that all the women are rabble-rousers," he sputtered.

Eleanor turned to Mrs. Biederman. "I am thinking of forming a group of my own to aid the suffragette cause," she said to the woman. "I shall send you an invitation."

She took Ian's arm then and swept past the dumbfounded couple.

"Well, you certainly handled that well," remarked Ian when they were out of earshot.

"That man is insufferable," grumbled Eleanor. She looked up at her husband suddenly concerned. "I hope I haven't made things more difficult for you."

Ian patted her hand. "I can handle the likes of Biederman."

He regarded his wife with open admiration marveling at the change in her. Her emotions were much less tightly held, her responses to his overtures less reserved. And she was speaking her heart and mind more openly these days. He decided he liked this new age of women.

CHAPTER TWENTY-EIGHT

The Streetcar War

George Biederman angrily brushed past an astonished secretary and stormed into his attorney's office. Floyd Cross calmly looked up. He was becoming accustomed to the brash temperament of his most demanding client.

"What is it this time, George?" he asked, mildly interested.

"I want Douglas arrested."

"Isn't that the job of the police?"

"The whole damn force is incompetent or else Douglas has them all in his pocket. Horace's rail on the upper Third Street line was vandalized last night. I know it was Douglas, but the police say they can't do anything about it."

"Unless there is proof, they're right." Cross leaned back in his plush leather chair. "You know, George, Douglas maintains that Horace is responsible for vandalizing his Market Street feeder rail. I would advise you to call it a draw and back away."

"Remember who you are working for, Floyd."

"I am." The attorney shoved a sheet of paper in front of Biederman.

"What's this?"

"It is an affidavit taken from one of Horace's workers recounting how he and other members of the crew were paid extra wages to tear up Douglas' trolley line."

"Where did you get that?"

"Parker Stanton sent it over this morning. If there are any further attacks on Douglas' trolley line, he is prepared to take the affidavit to the State Attorney General. George, if charges are filed, Horace could go to jail."

Biederman paled. "Who is the worker?"

"Stanton won't say, and he warned against you or Horace taking any retaliatory measures against the crew to force the man's identity."

"How do we know the man even exists?"

"Without a name, we don't."

"Douglas is lying. He's bluffing."

"I don't think you can afford to find out." Cross leaned forward in his chair. "I've known Ian Douglas for many years—since I joined my father-in-law's firm in 1878. I watched Douglas bring down the most powerful man in Rossburg when he was just a kid working in a sawmill. Now, he is seasoned and has money, position, and powerful connections. So call it even and let the matter go, George. My experience is that Douglas doesn't bluff unless he knows he can win. And right now, he appears to have proof of Horace's wrong doing; Horace has no proof of his."

Biederman ran a hand across his face in anger and frustration. He'd be damned before he would let Douglas win this battle.

"Something else you should know," said Cross, reluctant to add more fuel to the fire. "The City Council just granted Douglas's trolley company six more permits."

Biederman looked at his attorney in disbelief. "They can't do that. Horace got an injunction."

"The injunction applies only to the laying of rail."

"Why the hell didn't you get it applied to permits, too?"

"The judge didn't see the need. Whichever way the court rules, it's a moot point. But if Douglas is applying for permits, he must be hearing what I'm hearing."

"What's that?"

"The Court of Appeals is not leaning in Horace's favor. Of course, if it turns out not to be the case, Douglas' permits will be worthless, and Horace has nothing to worry about. My advice to Horace," said the attorney, "is to expand his lines as fast as he can while the Curtain Charter is still in effect."

Biederman let out an expletive and rushed out of the office. As he stood on the corner waiting to cross the street, Ian pulled up alongside in his motorcar.

"Hello, George. It looks as though the hooligans that tore up my track got Horace's as well," he said. "The police need to step it up. Can nae have criminals runnin' the streets, ay." Ian smiled then, and motored on.

"This isn't over, Douglas," Biederman shouted, shaking his fist in the air.

Biederman quickly made his way to his motorcar and sped across town. By the time he stormed into Horace's office, he had cursed Ian every which way he knew. When he told his son what had transpired at the attorney's office, Horace was horrified.

"My God, I can't go to jail!" he cried.

George Biederman snorted and rolled his eyes. "You're not going to jail, Horace. Douglas is bluffing. We have a bigger problem if he wins the appeal."

"What shall we do?" asked Horace.

"Corner the market on supplies and start laying rail now—night and day if you have to."

CHAPTER TWENTY-NINE

Up Against a Wall

Andrew sat propped up in bed watching Mary Kate as she pulled on her skirt and wrapped a wide belt around her waist. He let out a sigh and crawled out from under the covers.

"When are you going to let me make an honest woman of you?" he asked, drawing on his trousers and fastening them.

"We've been through this before, Drew. You know how I feel about marriage. It consumes a woman's identity, her independence, her sense of self."

"In your case, that's not a valid argument, Mary Kate, and you know it. I'm not that kind of man. And neither is your father. Your mother is pretty independent. From what you have told me, Patrick's mother is as well. And my mother certainly isn't under my father's thumb. Marriage isn't necessarily antithetical to a woman's independence."

Mary Kate twisted her hair on top her head and pinned it in place. "This is a new age. An emancipated woman should no longer feel the need to marry to satisfy her needs, intimate or otherwise." She turned to him. "I thought you said you could handle a modern woman."

"We've been lucky so far, Mary Kate. But we're playing with fire, and the odds are not in our favor. Condoms aren't reliable. I don't relish your father taking a shotgun to me for getting his daughter pregnant."

"There must be other ways."

"The rhythm method has proven to be highly ineffectual and so is early withdrawal."

"Aren't there other devices available on the black market?" she asked.

"There is the womb veil, but for it to be reliable, it needs to be fitted to women individually."

"You could do that for me. You're a doctor," said Mary Kate.

"The ones made in America are inferior and not worth the risk, and it is illegal to import such devices," replied Andrew. "If I were caught fitting a womb veil to a married woman, much less to a single woman, I could not only be barred from practicing medicine but jailed as well. I can't take that risk."

"It is so unfair, Drew. This is 1906."

"I know. But that's where we are until the Comstock Laws are changed. Hopefully, you women will do that one day."

Mary Kate sighed mournfully. "Well, then, I suppose the only answer is to abstain."

"You could abstain?" he asked half joking.

"It would be difficult," admitted Mary Kate. "I rather like partaking of the forbidden fruit with you."

"I have another option—marry me. Then we won't have to worry about it."

Mary Kate frowned. "If we were married, you wouldn't feel the need to be as careful, and then, I most assuredly would become pregnant."

Andrew looked at her and shook his head in wonder. "Mary Kate, your logic sometimes escapes me. What is wrong with that? I'm 33 years old. I rather like the idea of being a father."

"And you would be a good father, Drew. I just wouldn't make a very good mother."

"Why not?"

"The women in my family don't do motherhood very well."

Andrew walked over to her and took her by the shoulders. "Then, why don't you be the one to break the cycle? You be the new role model for your family."

Mary Kate pulled away from him. "I'm not sure I know how to do that."

"You'll figure it out. I have never met a woman with more heart and determination than you."

"What about the movement? I can't abandon it."

"You wouldn't have to. You can do both," said Andrew. "There are suffragettes who are married and have children. Look at it this way. You'll have five or six progenies to indoctrinate."

"Five or six!" she exclaimed.

"I suppose that can be a point for negotiation. But, I'm serious, Mary Kate. I want us to get married. I love you and want to come home to you every night instead of stealing moments when we can. And I don't want to have to worry about besmirching your reputation. This may be a new age, but we're not there yet. Being an unwed mother still carries a heavy penalty in society for both mother and child, whatever the class."

"Are you giving me another deadline?" she questioned archly.

"No. But you, of all people, know the harm of unintended consequences."

Mary Kate sobered. "I'll think about it," she said. "I'm late for a rally. Emily will wonder where I am." She gave him a quick kiss and hurried out the door.

"Try not to get arrested," he called after her.

Mary Kate walked down the street, her thoughts ponderous with Andrew's marriage proposal being uppermost in her mind. Marriage seemed a betrayal to the commitment she had made to herself to work for a more progressive and equal society for women. But Andrew was right. Women were a long way off from realizing that goal and from being sexually liberated. And she knew from experience that the consequences could be huge for such indulgence.

The modern woman in her demanded that she walk away from Andrew, embrace a life of celibacy, and sacrifice herself to the noble cause as many had done and continued to do so. But she loved him. She came to a stop in the middle of the sidewalk as the war between her heart and head raged on.

A half hour later, Andrew was about to leave for the hospital, when Mary Kate came bursting through the front door.

"Yes," she said, gasping to catch her breath from running. "Yes, I will marry you. But there will be no year-long engagement, no society wedding, and I must be financially independent."

Andrew was too astonished to speak.

"Well?" she asked, when he failed to respond. "Are the terms acceptable? Remember, I know a good attorney if you try to renege," she warned him impishly.

Andrew laughed and pulled her into his arms. "Whatever you want," he said. "But I have one condition of my own."

"What is that?"

"You can't change your mind."

"Deal," she replied.

She raised herself up and looped her arms around his neck, and Andrew gathered her to him in a passionate embrace.

CHAPTER THIRTY

A Win or a Loss?

Ian was monitoring the construction of his new electric plant, when Parker pulled up in his motorcar. "Biederman blinked," he shouted. He got out of the car and walked over to Ian. "Floyd Cross wants a meeting tomorrow afternoon."

"Tell the mayor. I want him there, too," said Ian.

Parker nodded. "Are you sure you don't want to wait for the verdict on the appeal? My source tells me it is imminent. What if it actually does turn out to be in your favor?"

"Then it will open up the field to other companies, and Biederman will nae have a monopoly for long." Noting the doleful look on Stanton's face, Ian smiled. "Contrary to what you may think, Parker, this is not a missed opportunity. There are bigger things on the horizon."

"If you say so. When is your car company going to manufacture an enclosed motorcar? It is getting damnably cold motoring around now. I'll have to get out the horse and carriage."

"We're working on it." Ian laughed. "Maven won't ride in a motorcar anyway. You'll still need the horse and carriage."

"I'm working on her," said Parker. "When is Mary Kate due to arrive?"

"Two days. Eleanor has been flitting about the house all week getting everything in order. Mary Kate is bringing Dr. Stoddert with her."

Parker raised a brow in question. "What do you think it means?"

Ian shrugged. "With Mary Kate, one can never be sure."

"Well, Dr. Stoddert is a good man—and Mary Kate is coming home. I would take it as a good sign. You know that Patrick's wife is expecting a baby next spring?"

Ian nodded, his manner more subdued. "Eleanor told me. She was at the school when Maven received the news."

Parker put a hand on his friend's shoulder. "Mary Kate is coming home, Ian. Patrick will come home, too. You'll see." He walked over to his car and climbed in. "See you at Cross' office tomorrow," he said shouting above the noise of the motor.

At two o'clock the next afternoon, Ian, the mayor, Parker, and Horace and George Biederman sat around a table in the conference room at the law office of Floyd Cross. Ian leaned over and spoke quietly to his attorney.

Parker nodded. "George, I must ask you to leave the proceedings."

The elder Biederman looked at him in astonishment "What are you talking about? I'm not going anywhere."

"I'm sorry, George, but Horace is the principal owner of the company, is he not?"

"You know that he is."

"And you are not. Therefore, my client is asking you to leave."

"I'm an investor, dammit. I have a right to be here to protect my investment."

"Mr. Stanton is correct," said Cross. "Mr. Douglas is within his rights to ask you to leave. You cannot be part of the negotiation if you are not a principal in the company."

Biederman's face turned red. Uttering an expletive in German, he stood up and stormed out of the room.

"Now, Mr. Douglas, Mr. Horace Biederman wishes to put forth an offer for your company, which is to include the six permits you were recently granted by the City Council assuming that they convey. This is the offer."

Cross shoved a folded piece of paper across the desk to Parker who picked it up, read it, and passed it to Ian. The amount was twice what

Ian actually had invested in the venture. As he considered the offer with nerve-wracking deliberation, Horace shifted restlessly in his seat.

"For this amount, the power plant be nae part of the offer," Ian finally responded.

"Agreed," said Horace. "We—I—don't need it."

"Will there be a problem transferring ownership of the permits?" asked Cross, looking at the mayor.

"No, but the permits were granted with two stipulations," said the mayor. "Work must begin within six months from the date of the permit and be completed within one year from the start of the work. And the company will be responsible for maintenance of these streets."

"What! Y-you can't do that," sputtered Horace. "Can he do that, Floyd?"

"Sorry, Horace. The city can impose any stipulation it chooses to if it has the authority to issue the permit—which it won't have if you win the appeal."

Horace licked his lips nervously as he recalculated. If he were to win the appeal, he will have just purchased a worthless company and laid out a lot of money for track he wouldn't have had to do at this time.

If he were to lose the court case, Ian's permits would give him a leg up on his competitors. But he would be under a deadline to produce, and the dates of the permits weren't staggered, which would require a larger outlay of cash. On top of that, he would be responsible for maintaining city streets permitted after the date of the lawsuit. Neither alternative looked particularly attractive to him.

The secretary entered the office then and whispered something to Cross.

The attorney nodded and looked at his client. "I would advise you to accept the conditions, Horace. The Court of Appeals just turned down your appeal," he said. "You will no longer have a protected interest in the streets."

Everyone had a different response to the news. Ian and Parker were surprised. It was always a possibility, but neither had expected Ian to actually win the appeal. The mayor was ecstatic. Horace wasn't sure how he felt as he quickly signed the papers and handed over the check. He seemed to be on the losing end whatever the verdict. Floyd Cross was just plain curious. He had expected Ian to fight for more money, given the value of the six permits now.

When Horace emerged from the office, his father was waiting for him in the reception room, and he told him about the appeals court decision.

"Did Douglas take the offer?" asked Biederman anxiously.

Horace nodded.

Biederman smiled expansively and clapped his son on the back as they walked out of the building. "And they say no one ever gets the better of Ian Douglas in a deal," he chortled.

Horace inwardly cringed. Tomorrow would be soon enough to tell his father about the stipulations attached to Douglas' permits, he decided.

Ian shook hands with Cross and smiled. "Like old times, ay, Floyd? Just a new dog with old fleas. 'Til next time."

"Indeed," murmured Cross, his brow knit in perplexity.

When Ian left, Cross approached Parker as he gathered up his papers. "Stanton, what is Douglas' end game?" he asked.

Parker looked at Cross in confusion. "What are you talking about, Floyd? Ian doubled his investment and settled an age-old dispute with the city on the maintenance of streets into the bargain."

Cross snorted. "C'mon, Stanton, you forget my father-in-law was Cyrus Morgan's attorney. I know Douglas. He has an end game. Otherwise, he would have negotiated for more money. What did he really want to accomplish with this deal?"

Parker smiled. "It will come to you, Floyd."

CHAPTER THIRTY-ONE

Going Home

November 1906

As the train pulled into the Rossburg station, Mary Kate's apprehension mounted. It had been nearly four years since she had been home. Andrew had insisted that they do her parents the courtesy of announcing their engagement in person.

Noting her uneasiness, Andrew reached over and took her hand. "You will do fine," he said.

Mary Kate gave him an uncertain smile and looked out the window. Her parents and Morgan were standing on the platform waiting. The train lurched to a stop. As she stepped off, she looked about her surroundings. Nothing seemed to have changed much; she felt oddly comforted by that.

Andrew took her arm and gave her a smile of encouragement, and she walked to the platform with more certainty. Her family looked so happy to see her she felt a tug on her heart and measurably contrite that she had stayed away for so long and was here now only because Andrew had pushed her into making the trip.

Eleanor reached for her husband's hand and smiled up at him. "Mary Kate has come home...maybe not to stay, but she has come home."

Ian nodded and squeezed her hand. He allowed himself to hope. Being estranged from the daughter he cherished had been extremely painful to him.

With a tremulous smile, Mary Kate approached her mother first and hugged her.

"We are so pleased you have come," said Eleanor. "And Dr. Stoddert, welcome."

"This can't be Morgan," said Mary Kate. He was nearly as tall as their father and in that awkward stage between boy and man.

Morgan grinned and gave her a hug. "Hi, Sis. Can't call me your little brother anymore. I'm taller than you."

Mary Kate laughed and slowly moved on. She couldn't delay it any longer. She looked up at her father. He smiled, and she saw the love and hope reflected in his eyes. A wrenching sadness at the years that had been lost to them hit her full force, and tears brimmed in her eyes. She didn't know what to say. Ian held out his arms to her, not certain what to expect. When she stepped into them, he enfolded her the way he used to when she was a little girl.

"Welcome home, Princess," he murmured.

A sob caught in her throat at the use of his pet name for her, and the rest of her anger crumbled. "I have missed you, Papa."

Eleanor blinked back tears and took hold of Morgan's arm. Her family was whole again.

When Ian released Mary Kate, he kept his arm around her shoulders, afraid to let go of her. He reached out a hand to Andrew. "Nice to see you again, Doctor."

On the carriage ride home, light-hearted bantering helped to ease the awkwardness of a long and difficult separation fraught with emotion. When they entered the house, the housekeeper took their coats. Morgan predictably went to the kitchen, while the others filed into the parlor. A welcoming fire roared in the fireplace, dispelling the chill and gloom of the gray November day.

"I do believe it may snow this evening," observed Eleanor.

A maid immediately entered with a tray of tea and cakes.

"I think that Dr. Stoddert and I will retire to the study for something a bit stronger," said Ian. "Is that agreeable to you, Doctor?"

"Yes sir," replied Andrew. "If you don't mind, I have something I wish to discuss with you, Mr. Douglas."

Ian and Eleanor glanced at each other and smiled. "Certainly, Dr. Stoddert," he responded.

Ian ushered Andrew into his inner sanctum and closed the door. "Have a seat," he said, motioning Andrew to a comfortable chair by the fire. "What is your drink?"

"Scotch, sir."

"A man after my own heart." Ian poured two tumblers of Scotch, handed one to Andrew, and settled into a chair opposite the young man. "My thanks to ye, Doctor."

"For what, sir?"

"For bringin' Mary Kate home. I suspect ye be the reason she is here."

"Mary Kate was ready to come back, sir. She just needed an extra nudge."

"For that, I am forever in your debt," said Ian with quiet emotion. He took a sip of his drink. "Now, what did you wish to speak to me about, Doctor?"

Andrew took a bracing gulp of Scotch. He had reached the point in his life and in his profession where he was confident and self-assured, but Ian Douglas was an imposing figure and Mary Kate's father. He respected that enough to feel a measure of uncertainty.

"Well, sir," he began haltingly, "I would like to have your permission to wed your daughter. I have asked Mary Kate to marry me, and she said 'yes.' It would please me to know that I have her parents' consent as well."

Ian leaned back in his chair and was silent for a moment. He was touched by the deference the young man showed him. "I appreciate your courtesy, Dr. Stoddert. I'm sure ye know that I lost the right to have a say in Mary Kate's life a long time ago. But for what it is worth, Mrs. Douglas and I would be most pleased to welcome ye into our family." He paused. "Ye know, Doctor, I only bet on what I think are sure things, and I rarely lose. I will tell ye now that my bet was on you to win Mary Kate's trust and affection."

Andrew smiled. "Thank you, sir. It was no small feat I can tell you. Please know that I love your daughter very much and will do everything I can to make her happy."

"I believe that ye will," said Ian. "Perhaps now would be a good time to discuss the dowry."

"With all due respect, sir, I have more than enough resources to support Mary Kate, and knowing her as I do, she would view a dowry as a gross violation of the modern woman's code. I would like to suggest that you deposit Mary Kate's dowry into an account that I have set up in her name. It is important to her to know that she is financially independent." Andrew gave a light laugh. "Opening an account in a woman's name quite flustered the teller. I had a time of it convincing the bank president that I knew what I was doing."

Ian chuckled. "It helps when you own the bank. I set up such an account for Mrs. Douglas some years ago." At the look of surprise on Andrew's face, Ian smiled. "This may be a new age, Doctor, but you and I be nae so different, and Mary Kate be more like her mother than she may care to think. Well, it seems that we are done here, but let's draw this out a little longer, shall we? It, at least, gives the appearance that I am in charge of my household."

The corners of Andrew's mouth turned up in a smile. "I believe you are right, Mr. Douglas. We are not so different."

In the parlor, Eleanor sat in her chair doing needlepoint and watching Mary Kate out the corner of her eye with amusement as her daughter restlessly leafed through a magazine. They had finished their tea, and the maid had cleared away the tray a half hour ago.

Finally, Mary Kate threw the magazine aside and got impatiently to her feet. "What do you think they are doing in there? It shouldn't take this long for Drew to tell Papa that—" she caught herself and stopped.

"Tell Papa what, dear?" asked Eleanor, suppressing a smile.

"Nothing, Mama."

Mary Kate paced around the room. The ticking of the clock was getting on her nerves. It seemed an eternity before she finally heard the sound of voices in the foyer as the men approached the parlor. Eleanor set aside the needlepoint and rose from her chair.

When Ian and Andrew entered the room, the women stared at them expectantly. "Well?" they asked in unison.

Ian laughed and clapped Andrew on the back. "There is to be a wedding, Mother. Dr. Stoddert asked permission to marry our daughter, and I was pleased to grant it for the both of us."

"Oh, I knew it!" exclaimed Eleanor happily. "Of course, you shall have our blessing."

Mary Kate breathed a sigh of relief, surprised to find how much her parents' acceptance of Andrew really did matter to her.

Eleanor clapped her hands together, her eyes shining with excitement. "There is so much to do. Wherever shall we start? We must pick a date, Mary Kate."

"Now, Mama, there is to be no fuss," Mary Kate quickly informed her.

"But, of course, there will be. You are our only daughter." Eleanor turned to Andrew. "How did your parents embrace the news, Doctor?"

"We haven't told them yet, but I know they will be pleased. They have a great fondness for Mary Kate. I thought it important to approach you and Mr. Douglas first."

Eleanor looked pointedly at Mary Kate. "How very traditional of you, Doctor."

"Don't get used to it, Mama," warned Mary Kate. "That's one of the things I have to change about him."

Just then, Morgan entered the room chewing on a turkey leg. "What's going on? I could hear Mama from the kitchen."

"Your sister and Dr. Stoddert are gettin' married," said Ian.

Morgan stopped eating and looked at the happy couple in surprise. "Really? Congratulations, Sis. How much did they pay you, Dr. Stoddert? As I remember it, Mary Kate can be a real pain in the—"

"Morgan Douglas!" exclaimed his mother. "Mind your manners and your tongue, young man."

Andrew laughed. "Not to worry, Morgan, I made sure it was worth my while."

Mary Kate was aghast. "Drew, you did not accept a dowry—"

"Come along, Doctor…Morgan. I think we men shall seek sanctuary elsewhere while the ladies discuss their plans," intervened Ian.

Morgan handed the turkey leg to Mary Kate and followed his father and Andrew out of the room. "I hope you don't expect me to wear a penguin suit," he yelled over his shoulder.

"You will wear what is required for a proper wedding," Eleanor yelled back.

Mary Kate groaned. "Mama, that is so traditional."

"There is nothing wrong with a little tradition, my dear. It lends a measure of stability to even a more modern world," her mother lectured firmly.

"If Papa had followed convention, you wouldn't be married to him."

"Be that as it may, my daughter will have a proper wedding."

As Eleanor and Mary Kate's debate carried into the foyer, Morgan looked at Andrew gravely. "Are you sure you really want to get married, Dr. Stoddert?"

"It does give a man pause, doesn't it?" responded Andrew with a laugh.

* * * * *

Mary Kate sat bundled up on the front porch. She knew her that mother would be looking for her, and she needed a moment of quietude. Her mother was irrepressible. She was every mother of the bride unleashed. At supper, most of the conversation swirled around guest lists, wedding dates, and conventions. Mary Kate knew this was going to happen. She had tried to tell Andrew, but he wouldn't listen. At least, he could retreat with her father into the study.

When the front door opened, Mary Kate inwardly moaned expecting it to be her mother. Instead, her father sat down next to her on the wicker settee.

"It's pretty cold out here," he remarked.

"It's the one place Mama won't find me for awhile," replied Mary Kate.

Ian patted her hand in consolation. "A daughter's wedding is every mother's dream. Your mother is very good at plannin' big events. If the details do nae matter to ye, then let her handle everything."

"You are missing the point, Papa. Society weddings with all of their strict, trivial traditions are the antithesis of everything that women have been fighting for over the past 60 years. And I have more important things to do than to attend silly fittings and pick out linens, flowers and invitations."

Ian looked down at the city. The light from the lamp posts and the few businesses and houses that had been electrified winked in the dark, starless night.

"I remember the first time I brought your mother up here," he said. "It was all farmers' fields then. I told her about the house I was plannin' to build for her on this hill and of the new society that we were goin' to create. She thought I was crazy."

He looked at his daughter. "Your mother has had to take a lot of things on faith over the years with me, and we have done well. But the one thing she never got was the wedding she had always dreamed of havin'. That was my fault. I suspect this is why yours is so important to her." Ian hesitated. "I know that I do nae have the right to ask anythin' of ye, Mary Kate, but would ye consider allowin' your mother her wedding?" He smiled, patted her hand again, and stood up. "Don't stay out here too long. Can nae have ye catch your death of cold."

After her father left, Mary Kate thought about what he had said. Once again, she was struck by how little she knew of her parents. She knew about the "mistake" her father had made, and she had learned some details about her mother's life during their talks in New York, but she really didn't know anything about her father's early life or of her parents' life together. But then it usually comes as a surprise to children that their parents had a life before them.

Andrew came out on the porch then. She looked so lost huddled up on the settee, and he sat down and pulled her into his arms. "Still trying to sort things out?"

Mary Kate nodded. She felt more confused than ever. "Andrew, how much do you know about your parents when they were young?"

"I never thought about it," he replied. "I suppose as much as I figure I need to."

"Do you think children have the right to know everything about their parents' lives?"

"No, not everything...and then it depends."

"On what?"

"On how much is to be gained or lost by the knowledge."

Mary Kate was pensive for a long moment. "I think I will go into town in the morning, Drew. If you don't mind, I would like to go alone."

"I don't mind. I can check out the Rossburg Hospital tomorrow. Are you ready to go back into the house now?"

"That depends."

"On what?"

"On whether my mother is still looking for me."

Andrew laughed. "You might as well make your bed out here then."

"I told you we should have eloped."

"You'll survive. No woman has suffered terminal effects from the planning of her wedding."

"How do you know? I may be driven to drink."

Andrew chuckled. "Come on," he said, standing up and pulling her to her feet, "we'll face the challenge together."

CHAPTER THIRTY-TWO

The Tour

Maven sat at her desk in the school office looking over the inventory list and making notes of supplies that needed to be purchased.

"Mrs. Stanton, someone to see you," announced one of the students.

Maven looked up and smiled. "Thank you, Annie. Mary Katherine, what a wonderful surprise. Please come in. Your mother said ye were comin' home for a visit. She and your father were so happy when ye called."

Mary Kate returned a warm smile. She had always liked Patrick's mother. There was an air of serenity about her that, along with the pleasant lilt of her Irish accent, Mary Kate had always found soothing.

"I hope I am not intruding, Mrs. Stanton. My mother has talked so much about the school, and I wanted to see it for myself," she said. "I think it is admirable what you are doing."

Maven stood up and walked over to her. "Ye not be intrudin', Mary Katherine. 'Tis a pleasure to have ye visit. And I cannot take all the credit for the school. If it were not for your mother's fundraisin', this school would be just a dream. She is a big part of its success."

"Lately, my mother never ceases to amaze me," replied Mary Kate.

"Would ye be likin' a tour?" asked Maven.

"Yes I would, if it is not an inconvenience."

"Not at all. As I understand it, ye be doin' your part as well to help the cause of women. I should like to have the courage of you suffragettes."

Maven led Mary Kate down a long hall with cream-colored walls and shiny hardwood floors. The bright, clean feel of the place was a surprise to Mary Kate. Instead of the usual musty smell of an old building, there was the pleasant odor of varnish, Murphy's oil, and soap.

At the first door, Maven knocked softly, and a voice invited them to come in. Upon entering, they were met with the clicking sound of typewriters. Twenty young women sat at desks studiously pecking away on the machines. Maven introduced Mary Kate to the elderly instructor.

"The girls are doing very well, Mrs. Stanton," said the woman, smiling proudly. "A few have already secured positions. It is wonderful what you and Mrs. Douglas are doing for these young ladies, and I am pleased to do my part."

"Thank you, Mrs. Perkins. 'Tis kind of ye to volunteer your services," replied Maven.

They left the room and continued on.

"Are all your instructors volunteers?" asked Mary Kate.

"No. Just a few who believe in the cause and are not in need of income," said Maven. "The others are paid a modest fee. They are either retired from their jobs or are working a few hours here to supplement their regular wages. Come, ye must see our design class."

Maven pushed open the door to a frenetic scene of whirring sewing machines and young women cutting, snipping, pinning, and drawing. A number of dress forms stood along the wall with dresses draped over them in various stages of completion.

"This be me pride and joy," she said. "We design and make all the dresses here, then sell them in my shop. It is an excellent way to develop and promote bright, new talent and, at the same time, provide a large line of the latest styles for customers to choose from at a more modest price."

Mary Kate was quite impressed, and Maven's enthusiasm was contagious. "What other instruction does the school offer?" she asked, eager to see more.

"Well, we are in the process of installin' a kitchen in the back," explained Maven. "There be a number of girls interested in learnin' the art of fine cuisine. Perhaps the school can advertise a catering service. All of our courses teach the business side as well to encourage students to become entrepreneurs. Come, I want to show ye the latest course offering."

They climbed a flight of steps to the second floor. "I was really surprised at the number of students who have enrolled for this," she said, opening a door.

Here, as in all the other rooms, sunlight poured through large windows, giving the classroom a light, airy feeling. A group of 30 women sat in rapt attention listening to the instructor, a tall, slim woman in a snow-white uniform.

"This be a class in nursin'," said Maven. "The hospital has been workin' with us to develop the program and is supplyin' instructors as well as course material. There be a greater need for maternity nurses now that more women are choosin' to have their babies in hospitals."

"Really? Why is that?" asked Mary Kate.

"Women have access to pain medication in the hospital that makes childbirth less difficult. Your mother and I are also considerin' a care center so women have a safe place to leave their children while they work."

"Yes, I can see how there would be a need for such a service," replied Mary Kate.

"And last but not least," said Maven. She led Mary Kate to a room full of contractors busily running lines to a large board. "Your father be settin' up a telephone exchange for us. Here, girls will learn to be telephone operators. It seems that callers prefer female operators to male operators. They find women's voices more pleasin' and courteous," she said with a smile of amusement. "And that concludes the tour."

"I had no idea what you and my mother had accomplished," said Mary Kate, feeling new respect for her mother. "It is truly amazing what you have done. It is so important for women to be self-sufficient to have some control over their lives."

"Aye, there be a great need but limited resources. It does present a challenge," admitted Maven.

When they returned to the first floor, Mary Kate showed no inclination to leave.

"Is there somethin' else I can do for ye?" asked Maven.

Mary Kate hesitated. "I—I was hoping that I might talk with you in private if you have the time."

"Of course." Maven led Mary Kate into her office. "Please sit down."

The office was small and plainly furnished with two file cabinets, an old desk, and two straight chairs. A large window brought light into the room and provided a view of the street.

Maven took her seat behind the desk and waited for Mary Kate to begin.

"I'm engaged to be married," said Mary Kate.

Maven smiled brightly. "How wonderful. Your parents must be very pleased indeed."

"Yes, Mama is quite preoccupied with wedding plans." Mary Kate paused to frame her thoughts. "I want you to know that Patrick and I have come to terms," she said. "I have met his wife Abigail, and I like her. I think she is the right woman for him. He realizes it now, too. They should be quite happy together."

A look of relief crossed Maven's features. "I am much heartened to hear ye say that. I was concerned that…well, that he hadn't married Abigail for the right reasons. They be expectin' a wee one in the spring."

"Yes, I know. I am very happy for them and for you." Again, Mary Kate hesitated. "Patrick doesn't blame you, and neither do I. He still isn't ready to reconcile with Papa, but I believe that he soon will be."

Maven's eyes misted over. "I thank ye for that. It lightens a heavy burden."

Mary Kate was silent for a moment. "I...I'm sorry that my father hurt you," she said.

"Your father was no more to blame than I, Mary Katherine. Sometimes two people are at different places in their lives and are not lookin' for the same thing. When they are young, they do not always recognize that. Or, sometimes they choose to ignore the truth until it is too late," Maven added softly. "I am deeply sorry that you and Patrick were so affected by our mistake in judgment."

Mary Kate looked away for a moment. "Yes, unintentional consequences."

Maven folded her hands on top of the desk and leveled a more discerning eye on Mary Kate. It was clear that her young visitor was conflicted about something. "Mary Katherine, what is troublin ye?" she asked.

Mary Kate met Maven's gaze. "I love my father, Mrs. Stanton, but I don't feel that I really know him."

"'Tis understandable. Ye've been apart for a long time. Ye just need time to reconnect."

"It is more than that. I need to know who Ian Douglas is...where he came from...what manner of man he is and why."

Maven was taken aback. "Is it not enough to know the man that is your father now?"

"No," responded Mary Kate definitively.

"Perhaps ye should be talkin' with him or your mother about this," suggested Maven.

Mary Kate shook her head. "I have asked them questions in the past. Mama didn't seem to know much about my father before they married. All Papa would say was that one doesn't get anywhere going backwards and then change the subject. As I grew older, I guess I became too involved with my own life to care about Papa's anymore."

"Why is it so important to ye now?" questioned Maven.

"I love him, Mrs. Stanton, but I need to be able to respect him again."

The words were softly spoken, but Maven was struck by the force of them. "I see. Why come to me?"

"You grew up with my father. I have the sense that no one knows him better than you—not even my mother."

Maven hesitated, reluctant to become involved in another's affairs. But she found it difficult to ignore the plea in the young woman's eyes. Taking a deep breath, she took a moment to compose her thoughts.

"Your father is a complex man," she began haltingly, "perhaps due to his heritage and to the losses in his life. He was 12 years old when his family came over from Scotland. My family and the O'Briens—my first husband's family—had come to Rossburg from Ireland just six months before. Tommy O'Brien was nearly 13, and your father's sister and I were 10 years of age. As immigrants and outsiders, we were naturally drawn together and created a kind of family within a family. We vowed to always look out for one another." She smiled wistfully. "We called ourselves the Pine Street Warriors. We even had a ditty. 'We're the Pine Street Warriors. Thick as thieves the four of us be; where there's one, you'll find the other three,'" she recited.

Maven's eyes shone with the fond memory. "Your father was our leader and led us from adventure to adventure. I guess you could say that we were no strangers to mischief," she admitted with a laugh. "It was a hard life for immigrants livin' in the Basin. We all worked very hard—even the children—to keep body and soul together. Happiness was doled out in morsels, but your father made the days magical for us."

Her face clouded over as her mind continued to pull up memories of another life. "Then, as they usually do, things changed, and we were forced to grow up," she continued. "Your grandfather was crippled workin' in a sawmill, and your father had to quit school to go to work there at the age of 14 to help support the family. Your grandmother and Katherine took in laundry. After that, there were no more adventures. Tommy went to work in the sawmill as well a few years later, but we still looked after one another.

"In 1877, when your father was 17, there was a terrible influenza outbreak," she went on. "A lot of people died—your grandmother and Katherine among them. Your father blamed their deaths on poverty. Your grandfather blamed them on himself for bein' crippled and not able to properly provide for them. Several months later, he took his life."

Mary Kate gasped, horrified.

"It was a terrible day," Maven recalled sadly. "Your grandfather left a note sayin' that he was a burden, and that, by this act, he was givin' your father a chance at a better life. I suspect your father still lives with the guilt of that."

"Why?" asked Mary Kate. "It wasn't his fault."

"With a tragedy of this nature, one tends to blame himself for not seein' the signs in time to stop it. And there is always the wonder if something was said to cause it. 'Tis difficult to escape self-judgment."

"Papa never said anything."

Maven looked at her. "Nor will he. Ye must never ask, and ye must never tell anyone else. This belongs private to him to do with what he will. I only tell ye because if ye really want to understand who your father is this be an important piece of it."

Mary Kate nodded. "What were my grandparents like?" she questioned.

"They were good people—loving, hardworking," replied Maven. "You and your brother are named for the family, ye know. Morgan's middle name of James was for your grandfather. Mary was your grandmother's name and Katherine was your father's sister." Maven smiled. "You are very much like Katherine."

"Papa never told me," said Mary Kate.

"When your father left the Basin, I thought it was because he was ashamed of his roots. I realized later it was because the memories were too painful for him to stay."

As Maven continued on recounting Ian's rise to power, his fight to break the stranglehold of the powerful lumber barons and improve labor practices while fending off labor unions with a different agenda, the amorphous image of her father began to take shape in Mary Kate's mind.

"This was a very difficult time," said Maven. "There was a lot of strife, a lot of violence. Your father, Tommy, and Parker stood alone through much of it. When Tommy died, your father took it very hard."

She paused, reflective for a long moment. "I believe that all of the grief, the losses, the adversities one experiences in life become woven into the fabric of his or her being. They become part of the character of that person." Maven stopped. "This is all I can tell ye. The rest is personal."

Mary Kate nodded. "I understand." Andrew had told her much the same thing...that some things about one's parents needed to remain private to them. But she had to ask the question. "Do you still love my father?"

Maven gave a smile of forbearance. "I will tell ye what I told Patrick when he asked me that. There are different kinds of love at different times in our lives. And just as people change, love changes. It does not necessarily have to go away."

Mary Kate could believe that. She still loved Patrick but not in the same way that she had.

"Perhaps there is one other thing I can tell ye that will show ye the true measure of your father," said Maven. "When ye returned home from your Grand Tour, George Biederman approached your father about a marriage between you and his son...a 'joinin' of empires' as he put it. Your father said that it was your decision to make, that he wouldn't force ye into a marriage against your will. When your mother told him that Horace was continuing to pursue ye in New York against your wishes, your father immediately put an end to it."

Mary Kate was surprised. "I thought my parents had encouraged Horace."

"Mary Katherine, what is important is who Ian Douglas is now, not who he was 25 years ago. He loves you and your mother and brother very much. He has helped a lot of people in Rossburg. You can believe that he is an honorable man worthy of your respect."

Mary Kate nodded and stood up to leave. "Thank you, Mrs. Stanton. I am seeing things clearer now, and I believe that you are right."

"I trust that our conversation will remain between us," said Maven. "Your father is a private man, and I make it a policy not to interfere in other people's affairs. I have made an exception in your case. If I can help to bring you and your father closer together, I feel that I owe ye that."

Mary Kate returned from her trip to the school and entered the house in a thoughtful mood. She found her parents in the parlor. When she walked into the room, her mother looked up from the book she was reading, and her father set aside his newspaper.

"I hope you had a nice time in town, dear," said her mother. "If you are looking for Dr. Stoddert, he is still visiting the hospital."

"No, I want to speak with you," replied Mary Kate. "Mama, I have decided to turn over all matters of the wedding to your planning."

At this, her mother stared at her speechless, and her father smiled.

"But I have two conditions," continued Mary Kate. "I want Mrs. Stanton and her students to design and sew the wedding gown. I toured the school this morning and looked at their work. I like what they have done—I like what you and Mrs. Stanton have done—and I think it would be a good advertisement for the school."

Mary Kate braced herself for an argument when her mother rose from her chair.

"Why, I think that is a wonderful idea!" Eleanor exclaimed to the surprise of her daughter. "It would bring legitimacy to the school and perhaps business from other debutantes in town. What is your other condition, dear?"

"The wedding will take place in June."

"June! Mary Kate, that is just seven months away. I don't know if I can pull a wedding together in so short a time."

"Nonsense, Mother. I've seen you pull large affairs together in less time than that," said Ian.

"But anything short of a year, people will think it is a marriage of convenience," protested Eleanor. "There are certain proprieties that need to be observed."

"I don't care what people may think," said Mary Kate. "Time will prove them wrong. Seven months, Mama, or Drew and I will elope." Mary Kate started to leave, then turned back with another thought. "Oh, Papa...Mama, you may call me Mary Katherine if you like."

As she strode out of the room, Eleanor and Ian looked at each other quizzically.

Ian smiled then and picked up his newspaper. "Ye had best start plannin' a wedding, Mrs. Douglas."

* * * * *

Andrew and Mary Kate broke the news of their engagement to his family at dinner two weeks later. At the announcement, Mrs. Stoddert dropped her fork and burst into tears.

Emily laughed at the look of dismay on her future sister-in-law's face. "Don't worry, Mary Kate. Mother is actually thrilled to pieces, aren't you, Mother?"

Mrs. Stoddert bobbed her head as she dabbed at her eyes with her napkin and sobbed brokenly: "I feared that Andrew...that he...that he would never find—"

"What Mother is trying to say is that she had just about given up hope on Drew ever marrying," intervened Emily. "Now, she can tell Mrs. Duncan to stick her innuendoes up her—"

"Emily!" gasped Mrs. Stoddert, quickly bringing herself under control.

"What innuendoes?" quizzed Andrew.

"Nothing, dear," Mrs. Stoddert quickly responded.

"Mrs. Duncan hinted that you might be a Nancy," Emily laughingly informed her brother. "Why do you think Mother stepped up her matchmaking efforts?"

"A Nancy!" exclaimed Andrew. "Because I was not interested in Mrs. Duncan's daughter?"

"Well, you are a middle-aged bachelor," Emily pointed out.

Mrs. Stoddert glared at her daughter. "I most certainly never thought that of you, dear," she assured her son. "You know how Emily likes to create a fuss."

At this, Mr. Stoddert cleared his thought and stepped in to take control. "Congratulations, son. You are a lucky man to have won the hand of this lovely, young lady. Mary Kate, it is my very great pleasure to welcome you into our family, though you may want to reconsider that," he added wryly, looking at his wife and daughter.

"Mary Kate can take care of herself," interjected Emily.

"Let's see, a year from now would make this a Christmas wedding," said Mrs. Stoddert, already beginning to plan for the event. "The winter is never a good time to—"

"Mother, Mary Kate and I are having a June wedding," broke in Andrew.

"June—you can't mean this coming June," said Mrs. Stoddert with a nervous laugh. "Gracious, you know what people will conjecture about a wedding so quickly arranged." She shot a questioning look at Mary Kate and her son.

"No, Mother, it is not a shotgun wedding," replied Andrew to her great relief. "Long engagements are for people who need time to get to know each other. Mary Kate and I have known each other for nearly four years. We are not strangers in an arranged marriage, and we see no reason to delay beginning a life together. For those people who choose to think something more, as Mary Kate told her parents, time will tell the story."

Mrs. Stoddert was slightly mollified. "Well, I suppose that could serve to quiet a few tongues. And as long as Mary Kate's parents are agreeable—"

"Perhaps we should adjourn to the parlor for coffee and dessert where we can talk more comfortably," suggested Mr. Stoddert.

"Oh, yes, we have much to talk about, so many plans to make," said Mrs. Stoddert, already rising from her chair. "There is no time to waste. We must coordinate with Mary Kate's parents on the balls to announce the engagement. You know, Ogden, we should invite Mr. and Mrs. Douglas for a visit during the Christmas season."

"Yes, Mother," replied Mr. Stoddert, following his wife from the dining room.

Mary Kate groaned in dismay. "First my mother and now yours. This is precisely what I feared, Drew. I thought if we gave them less time, they wouldn't be able to plan so grand an affair."

"Sorry, honey," said Emily. "Didn't you know? Weddings are not for the bride and groom. If you gave Mother a month, she would still manage to arrange an extravaganza."

She took Mary Kate's arm as they walked to the parlor. "It's about time that my brother did right by you. I had thought to prod him with a shotgun myself." Emily lowered her voice. "Mother tries, but she is still old fashioned about some things. You and Drew must have a care now that she is not proven wrong to her friends about the timing of your wedding."

Mary Kate came to an abrupt stop and looked at Emily in surprise, then sent Andrew a reproachful glare.

"I didn't tell her," he said defensively. "I told you we weren't fooling her."

CHAPTER THIRTY-THREE

Challenging the Status Quo

"Congratulations," said Parker as Ian entered his office. "I hear Mary Kate is getting married to the good doctor."

Ian smiled broadly. "Eleanor is turnin' the house upside down preparin' for an engagement ball and the weddin'."

"The school as well," added Parker. "Maven and Eleanor have turned it into a training project. Not only are they using students to design and sew the gown, but they are also bringing in instructors from a culinary school and a floral designer from Philadelphia."

"That will go over well with the local businesses," remarked Ian.

"Not to worry. Eleanor has promised them all a part in the events if they agree to take on the students as apprentices when they graduate."

Ian laughed. "Never underestimate the agenda of a woman."

"I wouldn't laugh if I were you," warned Parker. "This wedding is going to cost you a fortune. Lucky for you that you have only one daughter."

"Indeed. Why did you call me to your office?" asked Ian.

"Two reasons. For one, Maven and Eleanor asked to meet with us."

"Why?"

Parker shrugged. "My guess is as good as yours, but it makes me nervous when they have their heads together about something."

"Most likely 'tis somethin' to do with the weddin'. What is your other reason?"

"The accountant came to see me. We both think that you need to cut your loses on the motorcar company," replied Parker. "You can't afford to hold onto a losing proposition, particularly now. The few sawmills still in operation are closed for the winter, which means your finishing mill will soon be running out of lumber. And you can't put up more poles until the ground thaws, so you can't string anymore electric or phone lines to increase your subscriptions. Now, I know that the cars have had good showings across the country, but the fact remains that you are not selling enough of them, Ian."

"I'm studyin' a way to produce more motorcars in less time, and we are about to introduce the closed car."

Parker shook his head. "It doesn't do you any good to produce more for less if the Association of Licensed Automobile Manufacturers has set the average cost of a licensed car at $1500. It's too high for the general population. ALAM controls the Selden patent on the motorcar and controls the industry. And don't even think about suing them," warned Parker, reading his longtime friend's mind. "The association is too powerful."

"Since Teddy Roosevelt became president, more antitrust suits are bein' successfully brought to the courts," argued Ian.

"Even if you win, in the end you lose, Ian. ALAM has more resources. They can drag out the lawsuit for years and bleed you dry."

Ian knew that Parker was right, but he could not give up on the project. It was the future, and it went against his grain to admit defeat. "There is more than one way to fight a battle," he said. "I just have to find it."

Parker sighed. "I hope you find it soon."

Just then, Eleanor and Maven were ushered into the office. Ian and Parker greeted them guardedly. Their wives had a purpose, and there was a determined air about them. As the ladies settled themselves in chairs, Parker and Ian took their own seats, their curiosity increasing as they waited for the ladies to disclose their business.

Maven was the first to speak. "As we are all busy, I shall get to the point, gentlemen. Eleanor and I wish for our names to be put forth for membership on the Board of Trade."

Ian and Parker looked at each other in surprise.

"You need support against Biederman and his faction," continued Eleanor, "and Maven and I can help give you that advantage with our votes."

"I see," replied Ian. "While Parker and I appreciate the desire of you ladies to help, there be some impediments."

"What impediments?" questioned Maven.

Ian and Parker shifted uncomfortably in their seats as they tried to figure out how to bring up a delicate point.

"The biggest hurdle is that you are women," Parker blurted out. "The association will not allow the membership of women."

"Is there anything in the bylaws that prohibits it?" asked Eleanor.

Parker thought for a minute. "Come to think of it, no," he admitted. "But that was just an oversight. Those bylaws were written at a time when women were seen and not heard."

"Then, it is time for women to be seen and heard," declared Maven. "We have talked with five other female business owners who would like to become members as well. Decisions made by the Board of Trade impact our businesses, too, and we deserve to have a say in them."

"Even if the association can't prevent you from applyin' for membership, the members have the right to vote you down, which they will do," warned Ian. "It will be an exercise in futility."

Maven was firm in her resolve. "We have to make a point."

"We'll go to the press," said Eleanor. "We can ask Mary Kate's suffragette group for support. If it's a fight the members want, we'll give them one."

Parker looked at Ian. "It might work. The time is right. Women are becoming more vocal about their rights. We could organize a public relations campaign. If there is one thing businessmen hate, it is negative publicity. Something else to consider...if the members take on these women in a public fight, their wives may see it as a denigration of them as well. I know some wives who won't stand for it."

"Perhaps, but ye be forgettin' one other problem," said Ian. "Eleanor and Maven are representatives of the same business. Only one owner can represent a business under the bylaws."

"Actually, that will not be a problem," said Eleanor. "More students are coming in from out of town, and we are beginning to experience a shortage of proper accommodations. I intend to form a separate company that will build and manage a dormitory for women."

Ian looked at his wife in surprise. "When did you decide this?"

"Maven and I have been talking about it for some time. I made the decision just now."

Parker was highly amused. "Now you get a taste of my life, Ian. What do you think?"

Ian shrugged. "It will certainly create a stir. You are sure that you ladies want to do this? It will test your mettle. It is always an uphill battle when challenging the establishment."

Eleanor regarded her husband intently. "You and Parker did it once. It is up to Maven and me to do it now."

Maven nodded in agreement, firm in her conviction as well.

"Then, until Eleanor's eligibility is established under a separate business, we need to keep this among ourselves," said Ian. "If the members get wind of what we're plannin', they will move to change the bylaws."

Maven and Eleanor stood up.

"Well, gentlemen, with that settled, Maven and I have much to do," said Eleanor. "I will leave the details of setting up the company to you, Parker. Ian, please make certain that the funds are made available from my trust fund."

As the ladies strode out of the office, their husbands braced themselves for the can of worms they were about to open.

CHAPTER THIRTY-FOUR

Shared Goals

Mary Kate stood in the corner of the room, uneasily watching the amicable interaction between her mother and future mother-in-law as they busily made plans. She had never seen her mother so animated and light of spirit. It was two weeks before Christmas, and this evening was the official meeting of the parents at the Stoddert mansion on Madison Avenue.

Among other events, it had thus far been decided that the Douglas engagement ball in Rossburg would be held a week after Christmas, and the Stoddert engagement ball in New York City would be held a week after the New Year. It was all so dizzying, it made Mary Kate's head spin.

Andrew came up behind her and put his arms around her. "Why so glum? I might think you are regretting accepting my proposal."

"I am regretting that we did not elope. Look at them, Drew. See how well our mothers are getting on? They look as though they are old friends."

"Correct me if I'm wrong, but I think that is supposed to be a good thing."

"Not if they are conspiring to plan our whole life. Don't you see? They can provide reinforcement for each other."

"I think you are being a little paranoid."

"No, she's not," said Emily, joining them. "Don't be surprised if you end up having two weddings—one in Rossburg and one in New York. Mother already has her guest list up to 300."

Mary Kate was horrified. "Can't you do something?"

Emily laughed. "Not on your life. As long as Mother is busy with your wedding, she is not trying to plan mine."

"What are you going to do when my wedding is over?" asked Mary Kate with a sly smile.

"Well then, I will turn Mother's mind to thoughts of grandchildren," Emily promptly responded.

Mary Kate was not to be outdone. "If you do that, I will call her attention to the fact that you have stepped well into the age of spinsterhood. I'll wager that will prove to be of greater concern to her than grandchildren at this point, and I will see to it that your mother steps up her matchmaking until you have suitors sleeping on your doorstep."

Emily gasped. "You wouldn't."

"I would."

As the girls squared off against each other, Drew quickly and quietly withdrew to join Morgan in the kitchen. He wasn't about to get drawn into the middle of this debate.

In the Stoddert library, Ian and Ogden Stoddert sat drinking cognac, talking business, taking each other's measure, and recalling battles they had fought over the years. Ian found Odgen Stoddert's easy-going manner a perfect foil for his well-honed business acumen. The older man liked Ian's forthright manner and keen insight. He sensed that Ian Douglas could be a formidable opponent, but he also saw a man of principle.

"My son tells me that you have a motorcar company," said Stoddert. "How is that going?"

"The company builds three models now—a two-seat runabout, a roadster, and a four-seat touring car. My engineer just finished plans for an enclosed car that we expect to begin production on soon. We've shown the runabout and roadster models around the country, and the cars have received high reviews for speed, appearance, and a quieter motor. But the company is strugglin'," admitted Ian. "We can lower the cost to manufacture, but the price still will be too high for the general population."

"Let me guess—ALAM."

Ian nodded. "The association is cripplin' the industry. But how do you know about ALAM?"

"I have become acquainted with a man in Detroit, Michigan, who started a manufacturing plant a few years ago," replied Stoddert. "He is having the same struggles with ALAM. The board denied his application for a Selden license."

"For what cause?" asked Ian.

"The reasons cited were past business failures and undercapitalization, which may or may not be valid. But I suspect there was another reason. The man priced his car at $900," said Stoddert.

Ian looked at him in astonishment. "I've cut my manufacturin' costs to the bone and still cannot come close to that price."

Stoddert nodded. "It is the case with the other motorcar manufacturers as well. The ALAM board member who stood most in opposition to this man's application owns Olds Motorcars and controls most of the Detroit market."

Ian was intrigued. "Who is it that can price his car so low?"

"His name is Ford…Henry Ford. He is about your age," replied Stoddert.

"I've heard the name," recollected Ian. "I believe ALAM filed a lawsuit against him for selling cars without the Selden license."

Stoddert chuckled. "Henry can be a stubborn man. He filed a countersuit questioning the legitimacy of the Selden patent and is continuing to manufacture and sell his cars in the meantime. ALAM has threatened to sue anyone who buys one, so Henry is offering to indemnify all dealers or owners who do."

"'Tis a smart move."

"Indeed. As I hear it, not too many have felt the need to take up Henry on his offer. The whole affair is turning into a big public relations mess for ALAM and a boon for Ford."

"How long have the lawsuits been in the courts?" asked Ian.

"Since 1903," replied Stoddert.

"'Tis a long time."

"It could be several years more before the matter is settled." Stoddert chuckled again. "I think ALAM was expecting to shake off Henry long before this, but once Henry sinks his teeth into something, he doesn't let go."

"How does Mr. Ford have the resources for such a protracted fight?" queried Ian.

"He has contributors donating to his cause, but he needs more." Stoddert paused. "You might want to join forces with him since you have a shared goal."

Ian nodded. "The idea bears consideration."

"There is something else that you might have in common with Henry," continued Stoddert. "He believes every man should have a car. He is always experimenting with faster, more efficient ways of building them so he can further reduce the price to a workingman's wage. Imagine how that would revolutionize the country? But he will have to beat ALAM first."

Ian was greatly interested. "I should like to meet Mr. Ford."

"Henry uses my shipping line to import materials and machinery, and I contribute to his lawsuit from time to time. I might be able to arrange a meeting with him for you," offered Stoddert. "He doesn't hold to office hours though, and he doesn't make appointments. It may be difficult to pin Henry down to anything."

"I will make myself available for whatever opportunity you can arrange," said Ian.

Stoddert nodded. "I'll see what I can do. I must warn you that Henry is a bit eccentric. Like all geniuses, he can be contrary, and he doesn't suffer fools. He's brusque. If you don't capture his interest with the first sentence out of your mouth, he'll dismiss you before you can put two words together for a second one."

CHAPTER THIRTY-FIVE

A New Path Forward

March 1907

"Ian, must you leave now? Michigan is so far away," said Eleanor, uncharacteristically ruffled. "Mary Katherine's wedding is just around the corner, the contractor is soon to break ground on the women's dormitory for the school, and you must speak to Morgan."

"I'm sorry, Eleanor. Ogden Stoddert was good enough to arrange this meetin' with Mr. Ford. I have to go," said Ian, closing his suitcase. He turned to his wife and put his hands on her shoulders to calm her. "The wedding plans are well in hand, and Parker can help you with any questions the contractor may have. Now, what be the problem with Morgan? Is he skippin' school again?"

"No. He's been towing the line in that respect, but he's becoming wild and reckless." She turned away from Ian, clearly agitated. "Perhaps you are right. The boy needs a firmer hand. He is certainly beyond my control."

Ian groaned inwardly. For Eleanor to make such an admission, Morgan must have really crossed the line this time. "What has he done now?"

"It has just come to me that he was racing one of your cars out Johnson Farm Road on Saturday with two other boys. A farmer has complained that the noise disturbed his cows so much the milk dried up."

Ian chuckled. "I'll talk to Morgan when I get back."

"I'm serious, Ian, I don't want him driving that machine, much less racing it. It's too dangerous. And he spends far too much time at that car garage of yours."

Ian drew her into his arms. "Ye worry too much, Mother. At least he nae be gettin' into trouble at school, and he has finally found an area of interest that keeps him out of mischief."

"Well, I wouldn't call scaring cows half too death staying out of mischief."

"Did Morgan win the race?" asked Ian.

Eleanor gave a huff of exasperation and pushed him away. "You're impossible."

Suddenly, there came a great disturbance of man and machine outside, and Eleanor and Ian hurried over to the window in time to see Morgan come riding into the yard on a noisy motorized bike.

"Papa, Mama, come see," he shouted, turning off the motor and removing his goggles.

Eleanor gasped and marched out of the room and down the stairs. Recognizing that look on her face, Ian followed close behind, more so to provide his son some protection.

"Morgan Douglas!" exclaimed Eleanor rushing out to the porch. "Where did you get that thing?"

"It's a motorcycle, Mama. I made it at the garage. I've been working on it for six months. I tweaked the motor like you said and got the speed up to 58 miles now, Papa."

Eleanor angrily rounded on Ian. "You knew about this?"

"Now, Mother, the boy be 17. 'Tis good he shows an interest in somethin'."

"I've entered the race at the Muncy fairgrounds next month," said Morgan, missing his father's gestures that warned him to keep quiet.

"Well, you can just unenter it, young man. You are not going to race on that…that thing or any other machine," declared Eleanor definitively. She glared at Ian, daring him to countermand her, and marched back into the house.

Morgan looked so crestfallen Ian walked down the steps and put a hand on his shoulder. "I'll talk to her when I get back. It'll give her time to calm down. In the meantime, put the motorbike in the stable, and don't do anything to upset your mother while I'm gone."

Morgan nodded. As he wheeled the bike toward the stable, Ian called out to him. "Well done, son."

* * * * *

Ian stepped out of the cab on the corner of Piquette and Beaubien in Detroit and stared in amazement at the three-story brick plant that housed the Ford Motor Company. The long, narrow building, fashioned after an old New England mill, was roughly twice the size of his plant in Rossburg.

Ian entered the building. The business offices were on the first floor, and he walked up to an office worker at one of the desks. "I have an appointment to see Mr. Ford," he said.

"Mr. Ford's office is on the second floor, southwest corner, but he's never there."

"Well, he'd better go in there pretty soon," said a passing co-worker. "His desk is piled high with paperwork and mail."

The secretary laughed. "That's not unusual. Tucker, this gentleman is here to see Mr. Ford. Can you escort him?"

"Yeah, sure. I think he is somewhere in the production area. This way, Mr.—"

"Douglas," said Ian.

The office worker led him up to the second floor. Like the first floor, it was divided into four sections. Tucker explained that the sections were separated by firewalls for fire prevention.

He opened a steel door, and they stepped into the first section. There was a great hubbub of activity as groups of men worked on assembling different parts of a car. Ian calculated a workforce of between three and four hundred. Sunlight streamed through the row of double hung windows that lined both sides of the brick walls. The oak plank floors were soaked with grease and oil. Tucker looked around for a few minutes before he found the foreman. Ian couldn't hear what they were saying, but the foreman pointed to another steel door.

"This way, Mr. Douglas," said Tucker. "Mr. Ford is in the next section."

They walked through the door into another section exactly like the first. Again, the escort looked around, then motioned Ian to follow him over to a man of medium height and slight build who was inspecting some machinery.

"Mr. Ford," he said, shouting over the noise, "Mr. Douglas is here to see you."

Ford straightened and fixed his visitor with piercing blue eyes. He neither smiled nor extended his hand as he waited for Ian to state his business.

Ian didn't flinch. Recalling the advice that Stoddert had given him to take his best shot first, he said: "I wish to contribute to your law suit against ALAM."

Ford's eyes narrowed. "Why?"

"We share a common vision—a car for every man. ALAM is an impediment to that goal." Ian could see that he had captured Ford's interest. "Ogden Stoddert arranged for this meetin'," he added.

"You are that car manufacturer from Pennsylvania."

"Aye—Ian Douglas."

"Ogden said I should talk with you. What's your car?"

"The Imperial. We have three models."

"I've seen the runabout. Good car. I like the motor. Price is too high."

"'Tis why I am here to see you."

Ford looked at Ian for a long moment, sizing him up. "I have a board of directors who is suing me because I want to build a car priced for the masses. They think I should build expensive cars for the few. What do you say?"

"I think ye proved your point with the Model N car, Mr. Ford. It has been a great commercial success."

"Yes, but still they sue me. They can't see the big picture. They only care about greater profits in the short run."

"A man should keep controllin' shares of his company," said Ian.

"Exactly. I just bought mine back."

"I never gave mine up."

Again, Ford fixed Ian with a long appraising look. "Come with me," he said.

He led Ian back through the production areas and upstairs to the third floor. They walked over to a door in the northeast corner. Ford took out keys and unlocked it, and Ian followed him into a small room twelve-by-fifteen-feet in size. There were several blackboards with designs and specifications scrawled on them and a drafting table where ideas were being converted into blueprints.

"This is the experimental room," said Ford. "Only my team is allowed in here. We keep our work a secret from the board." Ford pointed to the chalkboard. "These designs are for the Model T—the car of the future, Mr. Douglas."

"I thought that was supposed to be the Model N," said Ian.

Ford smiled. "The Model T is the Model N without the design flaws."

"What improvements are ye makin'?"

"New transmission, a flywheel magneto, removable head so valves and cylinders can be accessed easier…and the steering wheel and controls will be moved to the left side."

Ian was astonished at the revolutionary changes. "How many cylinders?"

"Four with a horsepower of 20."

"'Tis not much power," said Ian, surprised that a man of such vision would overlook such an important feature as speed.

Again Ford smiled, reveling in his visitor's reaction. He picked up a crankshaft and handed it to Ian.

Ian tested it in his hands. "What metal is this?" he asked, puzzled. "It is much lighter than the steel currently used by manufacturers."

"It's vanadium alloy," said Ford. "I discovered it when I examined a French racecar that had crashed during a race in Florida. The metal has 170,000 pounds of tensile strength. America's finest steel has only 60,000. I first used the alloy in the Model N. In addition to the chassis of the Model T, the metal will be used in all the parts that are subject to stress. The car will be lighter in weight, making it more fuel efficient and just as perky as the more expensive cars—and the metal will not break."

"This metal must be expensive. How can ye afford to lower the price of your cars?" asked Ian.

"Two ways," said Ford. "No one here knew how to make the alloy, so I brought in a metallurgist from France and built a steel mill to produce it."

"And the other way?"

"A more efficient way of building cars, of course." He led Ian back to the second floor to a production room. "What do you see?"

Ian looked around the room at the group of workers. "It looks to be a division of labor."

"Exactly."

"I've experimented with the idea myself. I found it didn't make much of a difference," said Ian.

Ford's blue eyes twinkled. "You did not incorporate a key element."

"What might that be?"

"Interchangeable parts. There will be no more handcrafted parts in my factory, Mr. Douglas."

It was a novel but simple concept, and Ian marveled that neither he nor his engineers had thought of it.

"I've also hired the fellow who created scientific management to do time and motion studies to determine how fast a worker should work and the best way to accomplish his task in a shorter period of time. And soon my team will install a conveyor belt system that will bring the parts to the workers to reduce more wasted time."

Ian was astounded. By the time Ford had finished with the tour, Ian had determined a new course of action.

* * * * *

When Ian got off the train in Rossburg, Parker was waiting on the platform as instructed.

"What's up?" he asked when Ian strode up to him. "Why did you telephone me to meet you?"

"I want ye to drop me off at the mill," instructed Ian. "Then go to the garage and tell the Bailey brothers I'm callin' for a meetin' in my office in one hour. Where is Morgan? Is he out of school yet? I want him there, too."

"Aren't you going home first to see Eleanor?" asked Parker in surprise.

"I'll telephone her from the mill," replied Ian. "I need to lay some groundwork before I see her, or I may not get another chance."

Parker glanced at his friend quizzically. He was wound up about something. It was not like Ian to put business ahead of Eleanor, especially after being out of town for nearly a week. And he wondered if he should be worried.

"What's going on, Ian?" he asked more forcefully.

On the way to the car, Ian quickly recounted his meeting with Ford and everything he had seen. "By the time he is done, Ford expects to be able to cut the time for manufacturin' a car from twelve hours to two and to charge the price of a workingman's wage," he said.

Parker was as astounded as Ian had been. "Do you think he can really do it?"

"His team has been studyin' this for a long time," said Ian. "The man has hired an efficiency expert. Ford has everything figured out right down to the number of parts it takes to build his car. When everything is in place, he'll have a workforce of 1500 men turnin' out a car every two hours, maybe less. And he makes his own metal, which is far superior to what is available to the rest of us."

Parker furrowed his brow, concerned. "How can you hope to compete with that? It would take hundreds of thousands of dollars to copy what he's doing, and he's years ahead of you. He'll own the market by then."

"We're not goin' to compete with him, Parker. We're goin' to close down the Sun Motorcar Company and become part of his revolution. I've taken shares in Ford's company with future stock options."

"Well, I'm all for cutting our losses on the car company, especially after everything you've told me," said Parker. "Do you really think this guy's Model T is the golden goose?"

Ian nodded. "Look at the success of his Model N. The Model T is the same car but better crafted and half the price of competitors. 'Tis no doubt why ALAM refuses to give Ford a Selden license."

Parker came to an abrupt halt. "Wait a minute. Ford's cars aren't licensed—and he's been selling them anyway? ALAM is going to shut him down. I can't believe they haven't already brought suit against him."

"The association has brought suit against him, and Ford has countersued questioning the legitimacy of the Selden license. He and ALAM have had lawsuits against each other pending in the courts since 1903," said Ian.

"Since 1903—how the hell can Ford sell his cars?" questioned Parker in astonishment.

"Until the matter is settled, he is indemnifying dealers and owners of his cars. And it is working, Parker. Buyers are not being scared off. According to Ogden Stoddert, it has turned into a media nightmare for ALAM."

Parker shook his head, highly skeptical. "I hope you haven't bought many shares in Ford's company, Ian. ALAM is bleeding him dry. That's what big corporations do in lawsuits. They drag out court proceedings with appeals, and, in the end, they always will. I warned you about that before. ALAM will win and Ford and his company will be destroyed. I don't know how the man has been able to fight it out this long."

"He has contributors, and I've agreed to be one of them," said Ian.

Parker stared at him. "You are kidding—have you lost your mind? Didn't you hear what I just said? You'll be throwing good money after bad."

"I don't think so," replied Ian. "This is the era of antitrusts, and given the fact that the lawsuits have gone on this long, I think Ford has a good chance of winnin'."

Parker gave an exasperated sigh. He knew Ian had already made up his mind.

"What about the Bailey brothers?" he asked. "They aren't going to be too happy about you closing the company. What about the employees?"

"The only reason the Baileys went into manufacturin' cars was because they did nae have enough cars to sell to keep up with the demand. I've signed a dealership agreement with Ford. The Bailey's can go back to sellin' cars," said Ian. "With the Model T, they'll have more inventory and demand than they can imagine."

"Not if Ford loses the lawsuit against ALAM," interjected Parker doggedly. "There won't be any Model Ts to sell. Did you think of that?"

"I'm bettin' he'll win," replied Ian confidently.

Parker snorted. "Pardon me if I talk with the lawyer handling Ford's case rather than trust your gut instinct." He paused with another thought. "Setting aside the lawsuits, it could be a year or more until the Model T is manufactured. You said it is still in the design stage. What are the Baileys to do in the meantime?"

"I have a plan."

Parker eyed Ian guardedly. "What is it?"

"You'll see."

An hour later, the Baileys walked into Ian's office somewhat bewildered. They had always held planning meetings at the garage. Morgan walked in a few minutes later, a little hesitant, wondering what trouble he was in now. His father had never summoned him before in this manner.

Parker sat off to the side and Ian sat behind his desk, their faces expressionless.

"Have a seat, gentlemen," said Ian.

Morgan and the Baileys pulled up chairs and sat down.

"Why are we meeting here?" asked one of the brothers.

"'Tis more private," said Ian. "What is said here does not go beyond these walls. Is that clear?"

The Bailey brothers nodded, more curious now than bewildered.

Ian looked pointedly at his son. "That goes for you, too, Morgan. That means ye do nae discuss our business with Horace Biederman or anyone else."

The boy looked surprised and his features became flushed. "Yes, sir."

With no more detail than was necessary to divulge, Ian laid out his plan to close the company. The Baileys were visibly upset until Ian told them about the dealership he had brokered for them. Morgan was crestfallen. The garage and plant were the only places where he felt connected to something.

One of the brothers asked the same question that Parker did. "What are we to do in the meantime? What about the workers?"

"We are goin' to retool and build somethin' else."

"What?" the brothers asked in unison.

Ian leaned back in his chair and smiled. "Motorcycles. My son tells me that motorcycle racin' is becomin' a popular sport."

Morgan's jaw dropped. "Sir, is this a joke?" he asked.

"Nae, Morgan. When ye not be in school, ye'll work closely with the Baileys on both the engineerin' and design aspects since you know the sport—as long as your grades do nae suffer," Ian stressed.

Morgan's smile stretched from ear to ear. "Yes, sir." He suddenly became worried. "What about Mama?"

"I'll take care of your mother." Ian looked at the Baileys. "Your shares in the company will remain the same. How does this sit with ye?"

They looked at each other and nodded. "Sounds good to us," said one of the brothers. It's a lot quicker and cheaper to manufacture a motorcycle than a car. The profit margin is higher, particularly since we don't have to pay ALAM royalties."

"Then it is settled. I say again, gentlemen, no word of this is to be made public until I make the announcement."

Morgan and the Baileys solemnly nodded and stood up to leave.

"Morgan, I want ye to remain," said Ian as the Baileys filed out of the office.

Morgan sat back down and looked at his father expectantly.

"There are conditions that come with your part in this venture," continued Ian.

"Yes, sir. I'll stay out of trouble at school," Morgan was quick to assure him.

"There is that, and ye must also agree to attend college."

The smile on Morgan's face faded. "Papa, books don't interest me."

"I have in mind the Agriculture College of Pennsylvania."

"A farming college? You want me to learn how to farm?"

Ian smiled. "Nae, son. This college has one of the largest engineerin' schools in the country."

Morgan's features brightened again. "Really…engineering?"

"Aye. College will mature ye and hone your technical skills. When ye show me that ye are responsible and can make good business decisions, I will turn the Sun Motorcycle Company over to ye. You will become the president. It will be your company to run. Have we an agreement?"

Morgan was so speechless he could manage only a nod. He couldn't believe what his father was telling him. And he stood up and departed the office in a daze. Minutes later, Ian and Parker heard an exuberant "Yahoo!" erupt from outside that split the air.

"Well, that's a relief," laughed Parker. "The way that boy looked when he left, I thought he was comatose. I see why you didn't go home first. Eleanor is going to hit the ceiling when she hears about this. How are you going to tell her?"

Ian locked his hands behind his head and gave Parker a lopsided smile. "I do nae know yet."

"Can I drop you at home?"

"I'll take a cab," said Ian "I have an errand to do on the way, and I want to stop at the florist."

"To bribe Eleanor?"

"Nae, to let her know that she is important."

"She may not see it that way."

"She is not as cynical as you."

Parker looked doubtful. "I can't wait to see how this turns out."

When Ian walked through the front door an hour later, Eleanor was coming down the stairs. Her face lit up, and she hurried to greet him.

"Ian, I am so happy you are home."

Ian smiled. "As am I, Mother. As am I." He took off his hat and set it on the table and handed her a bouquet of yellow roses.

"They're lovely." She sniffed their fragrant scent. "You always remember that yellow roses are my favorite."

"I missed ye much," he said, cupping her face and kissing her with affection.

"Ian, whatever will the staff think?" she whispered self-consciously.

"That I love my wife," Ian murmured, kissing her again. When she stepped back to collect herself, he was amused to see that he could still bring a blush to her cheeks.

"How was your trip?" she asked.

"Quite educational. I'm sorry about the meetin' at the mill. I find it necessary to make some changes to the company, and they need to be instituted quickly. I have much to discuss with ye," said Ian.

The maid appeared then to take his hat and coat.

"Polly, bring a bottle of champagne to my study," he instructed.

"Yes, sir."

Ian took Eleanor's arm and led her into his inner sanctum. Eleanor glanced quizzically at her husband He had never discussed business with her before, and he disliked champagne. When he took a box from his pocket and handed it to her, she looked at him warily. "What mischief have you been up to, Mr. Douglas?"

"Can nae a man show appreciation for his wife?"

Still somewhat guarded, Eleanor laid the roses aside and opened the jeweler's box. Delight overrode her suspicion when she lifted out an exquisite cameo necklace. "Oh, Ian, it's beautiful," she said, her blue eyes sparkling.

"I believe 'tis the one ye noticed in the window a few weeks ago. I had the jeweler set it aside before I left on my trip."

"Yes…yes, it is. I didn't think you had noticed."

He took the necklace from her and fastened it around her neck. "Anything having to do with you, my love, I notice."

Eleanor smiled and lifted her hand to his cheek. "Thank you," she said, moved by the sentiment.

The maid appeared then, carrying a tray with a bottle of champagne and glasses and set it on the table. "Shall I put the roses in water, madam?"

"Yes, Polly. Use the good crystal vase."

The maid picked up the flowers and quietly withdrew, drawing the doors closed.

Ian filled a flute with the bubbly wine and handed it to Eleanor.

"What is it that you wish to talk about?" she asked, settling herself on the leather sofa.

Ian told her about his meeting with Ford, deliberately drawing it out to allow time for her to drink enough of her champagne.

"So ye can see why I have to make changes," he said when he had finished.

"Yes, dear, I can see that." She was flattered that he wanted to consult with her, but she was bored by all the business talk and listened with only half an ear.

He refilled her glass and waited for her to take a few more sips before proceeding to explain that he intended to retool the automobile plant to manufacture something else. She didn't make the connection until he mentioned 'motorcycle' and 'Morgan' in the same sentence.

The fuzziness in her head suddenly cleared, and she jumped to her feet. "Ian, how could you! You know how I feel about this obsession he has with motorcycles. No, I will not allow you to encourage it. It is too dangerous. And you know that if he is building them, he will be racing them."

"Morgan be nae a young lad, Eleanor. He is approachin' manhood. Life is not without risk. Ye can nae continue to protect him. He has a great interest in mechanical engineerin' and has shown that he has a mind for it. Ye have to give him his head and see where it leads him."

"I know where it will lead him—straight into the hospital or worse," she retorted.

"If ye do nae allow him this chance, Eleanor, he will become another rich kid with no good purpose, and he'll engage in even riskier behavior."

In the foyer, a day maid dusted the table while keeping an ear close to the door.

Morgan walked in then and could hear the angry rise of his mother's voice. "How long have they been in there?" he asked the maid.

"Nearly an hour, sir."

"Arguing about me?"

The maid nodded.

Morgan sighed heavily and sat down to wait. He might as well face his mother now and get it over with.

Suddenly, the arguing stopped, and everything became quiet. The maid and Morgan looked at each other, wondering what was transpiring. Finally, the maid departed the foyer, no longer able to justify her presence. Fifteen minutes later, the door opened, and Eleanor emerged from the study flushed and patting her hair in place. Ian followed behind her looking amused and a bit smug.

Morgan jumped to his feet. "Mama?"

Eleanor turned, startled to see him. "Oh, Morgan, I didn't know you were here," she said, giving him a lopsided smile. "Your father and I have been engaged in—in discussing your future. And, we have come to an understanding. You may make your motorcycles, but you must go to college and take no unnecessary risks." She gave a little laugh. "Goodness, my head seems to be spinning. I think I shall need to take a rest before dinner."

Morgan stared after her in stupefaction as she regally ascended the staircase, a slight wobble in her gait.

"Your mother is right," said Ian. "There is a difference between takin' calculated risks and bein' reckless. The latter never ends well."

"Yes, sir. But how did you get Mama to agree?"

Ian put an arm around his son's shoulders. "I think it is time for us to have a man to man talk now. There be some things about women ye should understand," he said, guiding Morgan into the study.

At dinner that night, Morgan was irrepressible.

"Papa, I think I know how to tweak the motor to get the speed of the motorcycle up to 68 miles per hour."

Ian frowned. "I thought that most accidents occur at speeds of over 65. The riders lose control of the machine at that point."

"I'm working on a stabilizer that should take care of the problem. I noticed at the race in Muncy that—"

"Morgan, you promised you wouldn't race!"

"I only watched, Mama. You didn't say anything about not watching. You just said I couldn't race."

"That's right, Mother. I was there," interjected Ian with a grin.

Eleanor glared at her husband. "Well, I guess I shall have to be more precise with my instructions in the future."

"Mama, I cannot design the best motorcycles if I don't go to races and observe the competition," said Morgan, pragmatically.

Eleanor raised a brow. He was sounding more like his father every day.

"Papa, I was thinking," continued Morgan. "We should enter our motorcycles in races around the country. If we win, we'll know we're doing something right, and it will be the best advertising. If we lose, we'll know the reason why. Maybe we could even sponsor a race here…become part of a circuit. That should make merchants happy about all the people it will bring into the city."

Ian nodded. "'Tis sound thinkin', son."

Morgan beamed with pride. "May I be excused now?"

Eleanor looked at her son in surprise. "You don't want dessert?"

"No thanks. I want to work on some calculations before I start my schoolwork."

Eleanor was speechless. Morgan declining dessert and doing schoolwork without being coerced…she could never have imagined that. As her son left the dining room, she glanced over at Ian.

He leaned back in his chair and smiled at her, his manner smug.

"All right, so you may be right in your handling of Morgan," she conceded. "Hopefully, college will turn the boy's mind to a different interest."

Ian doubted it, but he kept his opinion to himself. "All that a young man wants is a chance to prove himself, Mother. Morgan has been given that chance. It will be up to him what he does with it."

Eleanor was quiet for a moment. "There wasn't anyone there to give you that chance…to guide you," she said.

"I was given that chance," replied Ian. "It took me awhile to accept that it was my father who had given it to me. And I had Maven and Tommy for support. Later on, there was Parker—and you."

Eleanor winced. "I am so sorry for the way I behaved in those early years, Ian. I am so ashamed I can scarce bring myself to think about it."

"I was as much to blame," he assured her. "We each needed something from the other that neither of us had the capacity to give at that time. What is important is where we are today." Ian smiled. "And I rather like where we are today."

Eleanor blushed, knowing that he was referring to her more ardent nature. "As do I," she confessed with a shy smile. A shadow crossed her face. "Mary Katherine lost so much in the process though. I failed her terribly."

"She has grown into a strong, independent woman, caring and passionate. The two of you have mended your relationship, and she is soon to marry a good man whom she loves," Ian pointed out. "Our daughter is happy, Mother. I don't call that failure."

He rose from the table and moved to pull back her chair. "Come," he said, putting out a hand to her. "I have just returned from a long trip. I should like to become reacquainted with my wife."

CHAPTER THIRTY-SIX

The End Game

George Biederman picked up the Sunday morning newspaper and nearly choked on his coffee when he turned to a full-page ad. The Douglas Telephone and Electric Company was announcing its expansion of phone and electric service to city residents and to residents five miles beyond the city limits for affordable rates. At the bottom of the page were testimonials from several people singing the praises of the safety and cleanliness of electricity and pledges for record subscriptions.

At this point, Horace had the misfortune of walking in, a bit worse for wear from a late night at the Crystal Palace.

"Did you know about this?" questioned his father, jabbing at the page.

Horace sat down at the table and looked at the ad. He shook his head. "Must be why Douglas wanted to keep his new power plant."

Biederman looked at Horace sharply, his son's comment provoking an unsettling thought. Had the trolley car war been a smokescreen for another agenda? No, not even Ian Douglas could be that clever to run a scheme as big as that, he decided, and dismissed the idea.

"So Douglas is running lines," remarked Horace reaching for the coffee. "Who cares?"

"Who cares?!" exploded his father. "The Rossburg Gas Company cares. Practically all the businesses in the city are turning to electric. If people start to electrify their homes now, the demand for gas will decrease. Gas stocks have been steadily declining for the past couple of years as it is. Investors will begin to pull out of the consortium. How did we not hear of this? Didn't the Douglas boy say anything?"

Horace ran a hand over his face, feeling miserable. "I don't see the kid anymore. He spends all of his time at that motorcar garage. What's the problem anyway? Just trot out your anti-electric campaign. It scares the crap out of people every time."

Biederman glared at his son, amazed by his progeny's obtuseness. "It is too late to mount an effective campaign, Horace. Douglas has momentum now. That's the problem."

At that very moment, Floyd Cross was enjoying his Sunday brunch and opened the newspaper. He was about to reach for his coffee, when he came to the same full-page ad. He didn't share George Biederman's lack of imagination, and he burst into laughter at the realization of what Ian Douglas' end game had been.

A week later came the announcement from the Sun Motorcar Company that it was ceasing the manufacture of automobiles and was switching production to motorcycles. Again, Biederman had the uneasy feeling that Douglas had some larger plan, but he couldn't grasp what it might be.

Douglas is up to something, Horace, I know it," he said, pacing the room in agitation. "First the running of new lines for electricity and now the announcement about this motorcar company…there is something going on."

"Nothing is going on," replied Horace, growing bored with his father's obsession with Ian Douglas. "The Douglas kid is into motorbikes. Douglas is just creating a company to give to the kid instead of making him earn his own way."

Biederman looked at his son. "You mean like I did for you?"

Horace bristled. "You forget, Father, it was I who negotiated the streetcar settlement with Douglas to our benefit," he said with an air of self-importance.

George Biederman dismissed his son's proud achievement with a snort. He was questioning more and more just who the streetcar battle and settlement had benefitted most. In the end, Horace's company had lost its monopoly of the city streets and was now responsible for maintaining the streets for the Douglas permits and any future permits, and Douglas had undoubtedly walked away with more money than he had invested in the venture.

Biederman poured himself a stiff drink. "Get something on Ian Douglas, Horace, and get it quick."

Horace sighed. "We hired a detective once before and didn't get anything usable, Father. Why waste the money?"

Biederman glared at his son. "Everyone has a skeleton in his closet, including Ian Douglas. Find it, and I don't care how you do it."

Across town, Parker Stanton walked into the Rossburg Men's Club and handed Ian a fine cigar. "You have a healthy grandson," he announced in a lowered tone.

Ian smiled. "When?"

"This morning. Maven is getting ready to leave on the afternoon train."

"Patrick's wife is well?"

"Yes. They named the boy Thomas after Tommy O'Brien."

Ian nodded. "'Tis fittin'." He became quiet for a moment, and his eyes reflected sadness. "I wonder if I'll ever see the child."

"They say time is a great healer," said Parker.

"Five years is a long time to heal."

"It was a deep wound, Ian. But it is healing."

"How can ye know that?"

Parker smiled. "The baby's middle name is Douglas. Maven wanted you to know."

CHAPTER THIRTY-SEVEN

A Matter of Diplomacy

Mary Kate's wedding arrived on the wings of much public discussion, conjecture, and curiosity. For Maven and Eleanor, it was a great sigh of relief that the moment had finally come.

Though she had promised her mother wide latitude in the planning of the wedding, Mary Kate was determined to weigh in on a few subjects—the pomp and circumstance that accompanied a society wedding being one of them and a church wedding being another. Mary Kate refused to entertain the thought of either.

It was too much for Eleanor, especially after they had already broken the less-than-a-year engagement rule. It would create rumors and taint the event, she had argued. But Mary Kate had remained adamant. She could not care less what people thought, and her disagreement with the Church's stand on women's reproductive rights was too insurmountable to allow her to step foot in a church with any degree of conscience.

Three months from the wedding date, mother and daughter had become stubbornly entrenched, and Eleanor was beside herself. Finally, Ian had to appeal to Maven to intervene. She agreed to do so only because there were still decisions to be made regarding the wedding, and her students were unable to move forward with their assigned tasks until these matters were settled.

When Maven stepped forward with the proposal of a garden wedding, Mary Kate was intrigued; Eleanor was further dismayed. It had never been done before—certainly not by any member of society. She had always prided herself on being at the forefront of fashion, but one didn't trifle with tradition that had been established by Queen Victoria's wedding in 1840.

If done right, the wedding would be the talk of town—in a positive way—Maven assured a very skeptical Eleanor. By the time Maven had finished laying out her vision, both Mary Kate and Eleanor were forced to consider the merits of the idea. The compromise inherent in the plan was just as clever. In exchange for Eleanor agreeing to a garden ceremony, Mary Kate would have to agree to allow her mother's Episcopalian minister to officiate and to permit her mother a sufficient amount of pomp to pull off the novel concept.

When the coveted invitations went out announcing a garden wedding, the town was abuzz. All had attended garden parties, but a garden wedding—no one had ever heard of such a thing within the circle of the elite. Thus, when guests arrived on the afternoon of the eighth of June at the Douglas mansion, they were unsure of what to expect.

Very proper servants in formal dress ushered the guests outside to an area at the back of the mansion, where a charming outdoor chapel was set up. Around a large, open-air gazebo, rows of pews were positioned in a half circle with a wide center aisle. Inside the gazebo was a beautifully crafted altar flanked by brass candelabras five feet high and elaborate floral arrangements. Potted ferns and palm trees were strategically placed to add a striking contrast.

Not to be outdone, gardeners had worked for weeks to unveil a stunning display of flower gardens, manicured shrubs, hedges, and topiaries sculpted in the forms of animals and birds. Mother Nature also did her part by supplying a perfect spring day with sunshine, low humidity, and a gentle breeze.

Against this backdrop, before over 200 awestruck guests, Mary Katherine Douglas and Dr. Andrew Stoddert exchanged their vows. There were whispers of how handsome the groom was in his impeccable formal attire and of how beautiful the bride was in her gown of white silk and French lace embroidered with flowers and seed pearls. Several of the women decided that surely it must be the creation of a New York or French designer. Eleanor smiled proudly. Henri couldn't have done so well, she thought.

From her vantage point, Maven also smiled as she overheard the glowing comments. She doubted that any New York or French designer would have survived the trial by fire that she and her students had. Caught between mother and daughter, they had had to navigate opposing styles and temperaments to find just the right balance. Many designs and much debate later, they had finally managed to meet the challenge of making everyone happy.

To satisfy Mary Kate's more modern taste, Maven and her team, in a departure from the traditional ball gown and princess silhouette, continued the skirt in a straight line from the hips and ended it in a flare at the bottom that swirled gracefully around Mary Kate's feet. They further substituted a lower scoop neck for the traditional higher round neck and added lace waterfall sleeves. A pleated satin sash fastened around the waist with satin covered buttons completed the dress. To satisfy Eleanor's need for formality, the back of the gown was gathered to create a train modest enough to suit Mary Kate and still be acceptable to Eleanor.

But the war hadn't been won yet. Mary Kate had balked at the traditional headdress and the all-around floor length veil. She found the yards of lace too smothering and complained that the veil covered too much of the gown. Her mother persistently pointed out that a veil that touched the floor symbolized a woman of good breeding and character. Finally, Maven intervened with another compromise: a simple headdress of a crown of orange blossoms—such as Queen Victoria had used—and a veil fashioned to taper back from the sides with the veil brushing the ground in the back. In the end, mother and daughter agreed that the gown was a striking blend of simplicity and elegance and tradition and modernity—perfect for the occasion.

The wedding party was small—also unconventional. Morgan stood as best man for Andrew, and Emily was Mary Kate's only bridesmaid. At the end of the nuptials, the wedding party filed into the house for pictures, and guests were directed along an enchanting pathway to where they were served champagne and a light repast on linen covered tables set with china, silver and crystal. At sunset, guests were invited inside the house to the ballroom for dancing and were formally received by the bride and groom and their parents. For those who yet remained, a dinner would be served at midnight.

The wedding incorporated sufficient formality and tradition to bedazzle the guests so that they overlooked the "peculiarities" they found. The event was on such a grand scale that the departures from the standard couldn't be attributed to a reversal of fortune for Ian Douglas, and the bride was obviously not in a delicate condition. She wore white—a concession Mary Kate felt she had to give her mother. Thus, the guests had to conclude that it was just the Douglases being the Douglases. Ian Douglas was not known for strict conformity.

When neither Eleanor nor Maven picked up any notable criticisms throughout the evening, they glanced over at each other and exchanged smiles of victory.

"Looks like Eleanor managed to pull it off," said Parker approaching Ian. "It's a hell of a wedding."

Ian grinned when Parker handed him a tumbler of his much-preferred Scotch. "Two months ago, I would nae have given ye odds," he confessed. "Maven deserves a lot of the credit. If she had nae been there to referee between Mary Katherine and her mother, I doubt we would be standin' here this night."

"They did keep Maven and her students on their toes," admitted Parker. He held up his glass in a toast. "To your good fortune of having only one daughter."

Ian laughed. "Boys are easier on the pocketbook, but they can present another set of problems."

"Ah yes, Maven said Morgan wasn't too happy about having to wear formal attire. He equated it to having to walk the plank, I believe. What carrot did you dangle in front of him to keep him on his best behavior?"

"None. His mother threatened to have him barred from the motorcycle garage and plant for a month if his behavior was nae above par," said Ian.

Parker chuckled. "That would do it."

"Aye, but Morgan admires Andrew. I think he felt honored when Andrew asked him to be best man."

Parker looked about the room. "I don't see Morgan haunting the food tables. Where is he?"

Ian laughed. "Over in the corner runnin' a finger around his collar and watchin' the clock. He is released from duty when the bride and groom leave."

At the prearranged time of ten o'clock, Mary Kate and Andrew said private good byes to their parents and slipped out to change and catch the train to New York. Ian had arranged a private car for them. In two days, the Douglases and a select group of guests would board private cars to New York as well for the post marital reception to be hosted by the Stodderts, at which time the newly married couple would be presented to New York society in equally grand style.

Mary Kate and Andrew were barely out the door when Morgan ripped off his tie and discarded his coat. Having acquitted his duties to his mother's complete satisfaction, his focus was now squarely on mechanical data and future projects.

He tore down the back stairs and into the kitchen to make his escape to his workshop in the stable and nearly collided with a girl carrying a tray full of silverware. Both came to an abrupt halt, and the silver flatware rattled precariously on the tray.

"Pardon me, miss, I—" The rest of Morgan's apology trailed off when she looked up at him with startled blue eyes, the color all the more striking against her fair skin, dark lashes, and raven black hair.

She was about his age, tall and slender; the women in his family were blonde and petite. She presented quite a contrast. He wondered why he had never seen her before.

An older woman came bustling into the kitchen then. "Annie, why are you lollygagging about when there are tables to be set up for the midnight dinner? You girls have been given this opportunity to show the talents of the school. Our reputation is on the line. We must make Mrs. Stanton and Mrs. Douglas proud," she chided lightly.

"I'm sorry, Mrs. Ulrich."

"It was my fault that she was detained," intervened Morgan. "I came into the kitchen in such a hurry I put a fright into her. She was just taking a moment to collect herself."

Annie threw him a look of gratitude and hurried off to her duties.

The older woman turned to the young man. He wore no coat or tie, and she had initially dismissed him as just another worker trifling with one of her charges. Her eyes widened when she realized her mistake.

"Oh, Mr. Morgan, please excuse me. I didn't see that it was you. May I get something for you?"

"No, thank you." Morgan hesitated. "Uh, Mrs. Ulrich, that girl Annie…is she a student at my mother's school?"

"Yes. You might say that she was our first student. Why do you ask? Has she done something wrong?" asked the woman, suddenly becoming concerned.

"No, no," he hastily assured her. "I—I was just wondering. I haven't seen her at the high school."

"Is there anything else, Mr. Morgan?"

"No…no, thank you." Morgan turned to leave and banged into a table. He flashed Mrs. Ulrich a sheepish smile and quickly disappeared out the back door.

Mrs. Ulrich's brow furrowed. "Most peculiar," she murmured and hurried off to her tasks.

* * * * *

The train climbed into the Adirondacks toward the Sagamore Resort at Lake George where the newlyweds would spend their honeymoon.

"Well, that wasn't so bad," said Andrew.

Mary Kate looked at him in disbelief. "We had two receptions, Drew."

"Yes, but we had to endure only one ceremony," Andrew reminded her.

"That's hardly comforting. I felt as though we were put on display."

"Look at it this way. The Rossburg elites now know what Mrs. Stanton and her students are capable of doing and may give the school more consideration—and our mothers are happy. Now that my mother has more time on her hands, I would venture to say that she is turning her sights on Emily about now and making my sister's life quite miserable."

Mary Kate giggled. "That is comforting." Andrew put his arm around her, and she nestled against him. "At least we won the honeymoon argument. I would much rather spend a month in the mountains than six months in Europe. Luckily, you could plead the excuse of the hospital."

"Brace yourself upon your return," Andrew warned her. "Mother will be waiting to draw you into her charity events."

"Well, if I have to attend charity balls so do you," said Mary Kate. "And there had better be no hospital emergencies. I'm on to that trick, Dr. Stoddert."

Andrew laughed. "I can't promise that there will be none at all, but I doubt there will be quite as many."

He fell silent, then, as his mind went back to his conversation with Mary Kate's mother at the wedding reception in New York. She had refused to admit anything and had waved aside his concern. But his instincts as a doctor told him that there was something wrong. Her cough seemed more persistent since he had first noticed it at the engagement ball. Her headaches appeared to be more frequent as well, and though she hid it well, he could see that she tired easier. He had given her the name of his colleague at the hospital and had strongly urged her to see him before she returned to Rossburg. He hoped that she had followed his advice.

Mary Kate nudged him. "Why so solemn? Are you having second thoughts?" she teased.

He smiled and tightened his arm around her. "Not on your life, Mrs. Stoddert."

CHAPTER THIRTY-EIGHT

Wall of Silence

"Welcome back from your honeymoon, Doctor," said a nurse as Andrew passed through the ward. "You were missed."

"Thank you, Nurse Drummond. Don't tell my wife, but I missed the hospital."

"I know your wife, Stoddert. You have to be kidding," joked another doctor. "I'm glad you're here, Andrew," he said on a more serious note. "Can we talk in the office?"

"Sure." Andrew followed Dr. Bollard into the office that they shared. "What's up? Do you need a second opinion?"

The doctor closed the door and took a file from his desk. "Mrs. Douglas came to see me upon your recommendation. I think you should see this."

Andrew took the file, his expression becoming more troubled as he read through the pages. When he was done, he looked up at his colleague. "Are you certain, Walter?"

"There is no question, Andrew. Your mother-in-law has lymphoma. The x-rays confirmed it. She requires radiation therapy as soon as possible. I'm sorry, Andrew. She's a lovely lady."

"Thanks, Walter. I'll take it from here. If Mary Kate comes into the hospital, don't say anything to her about this."

Dr. Bollard nodded. "I'll be on rounds if you need me."

After his colleague left the office, Andrew went over the file again. It was just as disturbing as the first time he had read it. "Damn," he murmured. Mary Kate was just beginning to form a closer relationship with her mother.

He ran a hand across his face and sat in deep thought for several minutes, then reached for the phone and put in a call to the chief of staff at Rossburg Hospital, whom he had come to know. When Dr. Howard came on the line, Andrew discreetly alerted him that he was sending a report that the doctor should read.

* * * * *

The maid showed Dr. Howard into the parlor at the Douglas mansion. His visit alone alerted Eleanor that something was wrong; the solemn expression on his face confirmed it.

"What is it, Charles?" she asked apprehensively.

He pulled the double doors closed and walked over to sit down on the sofa beside her. "I've known you a long time, Eleanor, and I know that you would want me to be straight with you." He paused and took her hand. "The health problems that you have been experiencing are due to an illness called lymphoma."

Eleanor looked at him, the color draining from her face. "Cancer? Are you certain?"

Dr. Howard nodded. "I'm sorry, Eleanor. Your son-in-law sent me the report and the x-ray films."

"Oh, dear God," she whispered. "Am I going to die, Charles?"

"The mass has not yet affected your lungs. There's a good chance that radiation therapy can prevent that from happening. But you must start treatment right away."

Eleanor stood up and walked over to the window. It was nearing the end of July, a beautiful summer day. The flowers were in full bloom. This couldn't be happening to her—not now when everything was so right with her life.

"The hospital doesn't have an x-ray box, so Dr. Stoddert has offered to buy one and train a technician," continued Dr. Howard. "In the meantime, you will have to travel to New York for your first treatments. A hospital technician and I will accompany you. Did you hear me, Eleanor?" he asked when she didn't respond.

She slowly turned to him. "Yes, Charles, I heard you. I have two conditions. I want to buy the x-ray box. It will be my gift to the hospital, and no one is to be told of my illness—not even my husband. All anyone will know is that we are traveling to New York to appraise and purchase the machine. Has Dr. Stoddert told Mary Katherine anything?"

"No, he is awaiting your instruction."

"Please relay my wishes to him."

"Eleanor, I don't think it is wise for you to keep your illness a secret from Mr. Douglas. He should know of it."

"My husband has enough to deal with right now. Until we know the outcome of the treatments, I don't wish to burden him with this. When do we leave?"

"Next week. I've made arrangements with Dr. Stoddert."

Eleanor looked at him in alarm. "Over the telephone?"

"Don't worry. When Dr. Stoddert sent your file, he included a code for us to use when it was necessary to correspond by phone. Your secret will be kept."

*****

When Andrew walked into his house, he found Mary Kate and his sister measuring and moving furniture.

"What's this?" he asked.

"I'm helping Mary Kate spend your money," said Emily. "We must completely refurbish this place."

Andrew looked around him. "Why? What's wrong with it?"

"Antlers hanging on the wall...really, Drew. You don't even hunt."

"It was a gift from a patient. Mary Kate never complained before," he said, looking to his wife for support.

"Of course, she didn't. She only spent time in the bedroom," responded Emily.

"Emily, behave yourself," Mary Kate chided her sister-in-law. She turned to her husband and gave him a smile designed to melt the heart of any man facing the disposal of his possessions. "She's right, darling. This place does need a little updating."

"A *little* updating!" exclaimed Emily. "I would say that you need to start from the beginning. The sofa is beyond shabby and—"

Andrew glared at his sister. "Don't you have some place to be, Em?"

"Actually, no."

"I believe you have a home of your own," he pointed out.

"Now that Mary Kate has moved out, it is lonely there. And since it is all your fault, Drew, you will just have to get used to the idea of me spending more time here," Emily airily informed him. She paused with a thought. "Perhaps I will get a job…a job working at the hospital with Mary Kate."

Andrew snorted. "I don't think so. People go there to get well." He regarded her more closely. "You are hiding from Mother, aren't you? Weren't you supposed to attend some luncheon this afternoon with her…meet some would-be suitor's mother and aunt?"

"I begged off. I told her that Mary Kate needed my help. Now, she is arranging a dinner party." Emily groaned. "The woman goes out of her way to torture me."

"She is just looking after your interests," said Andrew with a snicker.

Emily flopped into a chair. "Why is it that unmarried men at any age are considered eligible bachelors, but unmarried women older than 23 are labeled as spinsters?"

"Because a woman's worth is determined by her ability to produce children, and the best years for that are before the age of 24," said Andrew with the clinical deduction of a doctor. He realized his mistake when he saw the hostile glare the women turned on him. "I'm just explaining society's position and a medical fact," he said to his defense.

"Andrew Stoddert, if you weren't my brother—"

Mary Kate raised her hands. "Stop you two. You are giving me a headache. Drew, you are home early."

"Good thing or I might have come home to an empty house," he said, clearly out of sorts.

Mary Kate went over to him and put her arms around him. "I promise you that nothing will get thrown away without your approval. How is that?"

"Well, that's a start," he said, recovering some of his good nature. "It's Friday, and I came home early to take you to dinner and to treat you to an evening at the theater. Also, I have news that your mother is coming to New York on Monday and will stay for a week."

Mary Kate looked at him in surprise. "That's wonderful. Why didn't she call me?"

"I'm sure that she will. Dr. Howard made the arrangement. He and a technician are coming to look at the x-ray machine," Andrew smoothly replied. "They want to purchase one for Rossburg Hospital. Your mother is a benefactor and has decided to come along to see what her money is buying and to visit with you. Don't worry," he added when he saw her look around the room in a panic, "your mother is staying with Mrs. Thompson."

Mary Kate brightened. "Well, I guess I should get ready for an evening with my husband then." She looked meaningfully at Andrew and nodded toward Emily.

"Oh, all right. Emily, you are welcome to come as well," he said.

Emily rose from the chair. "Thank you, but I have plans of my own with Teddy. Maybe we'll catch you later."

As Mary Kate disappeared upstairs, Andrew walked his sister to the door. "Em, I need you to keep Mary Kate busy next week so that she stays away from the hospital," he said in a lowered voice.

Emily looked at her brother in bewilderment. "Why?"

"I can't say. Please just do it."

"It may mean that your furniture will be gone," she teased.

"Whatever it takes, keep her away."

"You really are serious about this." She studied her brother closer. "Mrs. Douglas isn't coming for just a visit, is she?" When Andrew looked away and ran a hand across the back of his neck as he did when he was disturbed about something, Emily knew. "The x-ray machine—oh, God, Mrs. Douglas is sick. She's coming for radiation treatments, isn't she?"

"I can't discuss anything," he said firmly. "Just keep Mary Kate away and don't voice your concerns to her or to anyone else."

Emily nodded. "I'm so sorry, Drew. I like Mrs. Douglas. I'll help any way that I can."

CHAPTER THIRTY-NINE

The Visit

When the train pulled into the station, Mary Kate and Andrew met the party from Rossburg.

"Mary Katherine, how nice to see you again," said Dr. Howard. He introduced the technician and turned to Andrew. "Dr. Stoddert, thank you for making the time for us."

Mary Kate hugged her mother. "Mama, I am happy you came," she said.

Eleanor smiled, buoyed by the warm greeting. "So am I. Your brother wants to know if Dr. Stoddert is having second thoughts about marriage yet."

"Tell Morgan to beware. The minute a woman enters his life, his possessions will be at risk," remarked Andrew only half joking.

Mary Kate took her mother's arm. "Don't pay any attention to him. You should have seen it, Mama. His place was such a bachelor's domicile. There were actually antlers hanging on the wall. Emily has been helping me to put a woman's touch on the house. I'm sorry it isn't yet comfortable enough for you to stay with us."

Eleanor patted her daughter's arm. "Caroline and I have many years to catch up on, and newlyweds should have their privacy. I'm feeling a bit tired after the journey. Perhaps we can all meet for dinner tonight."

"Of course," said Mary Kate. "I have some shopping to do anyway this afternoon."

"Good, then seven o'clock it is. And please invite Emily as well."

At the appointed time, the small dinner party was shown to a table in the Palm Garden Restaurant, located at the rear of the first floor lobby of the Astor Hotel. Decorated to resemble an Italian eatery, the restaurant displayed vine-covered pergolas, scenic pictures of the outdoors, baskets of ferns, and a ceiling painted to resemble a Mediterranean sky.

The mood was light. Mary Kate was surprised by how spirited her mother was as she and Caroline talked about their happier days growing up in the 19th century. Both she and Emily were horrified by how strict and stratified society was then. And Mary Kate realized that she was still learning about her mother. Andrew sat back enjoying the continuing bonding of Mary Kate and her mother as he kept a watchful eye on his patient. After a few hours, he saw that Eleanor was growing weary. He signaled to Caroline, and they moved to end the evening.

The next morning, Andrew showed Dr. Howard, the technician, and Eleanor the x-ray radiotherapy machine and explained the process. She would receive small doses of radiation every day for a week. At the end of the week, an x-ray film would be taken to assess their progress. It might take several weeklong sessions to arrest the cancer.

"How successful is this treatment, Andrew?" asked Eleanor in a low, quiet tone.

She put on a brave front, but Andrew could see that she was frightened.

"It is a fairly new technology in the treatment of cancer," he admitted. "We don't have many records beyond three or four years, but there have been reports of the shrinkage of tumors and masses." He laid a comforting hand on her arm. "Do you need more time to consider it?"

Eleanor shook her head. "No. I am ready to proceed."

Dressed in a lightweight robe, she and the others followed Andrew to a separate room where he instructed her to sit in a high-back wooden chair. The Bellevue radiologist had been waiting for them and stepped forward. Andrew and Dr. Howard moved to the back of the room.

With the Rossburg technician standing next to him to observe, the radiologist trained the x-ray field on Eleanor's neck and upper chest and turned on the machine. He put his arm in front of the x-ray to test the strength of the radiation, increasing the level until the skin on his arm turned pink. Eleanor sat ramrod straight, her chin held high. It was a display of courage and strength that Andrew would not forget.

That night, he held Mary Kate a little tighter and made love to her a little longer. He couldn't imagine his life without her. When the moment came, he made a request of her. "Mary Kate, I don't want to use the condom tonight."

Mary Kate went still for a moment. She knew what he was asking. When she looked into his eyes, she saw the depth of his love for her, and she knew that he would always be there to support her whatever the circumstances. She nodded. She was ready to take that leap.

CHAPTER FORTY

Sucker-Punched

True to her word, Emily kept Mary Kate busy throughout the week arranging appointments with decorating consultants and trips to dry goods stores, furniture stores, and importers. Before long, Mary Kate found herself knee deep in contractors who were removing wallpaper, painting, and refinishing floors.

Her mother joined them on some of the shopping trips. Mary Kate found Eleanor's input to be practical, and her decorating taste lent a more sophisticated air to Mary Kate's unconventional bent. In the evenings, they all had dinner together, usually at the home of Caroline Thompson. These were light-hearted affairs, and Mary Kate didn't know when she had laughed so much. To her surprise, she found that her mother could be very witty.

By the end of the week, the first round of radiotherapy was finished, and Eleanor was feeling the effects of the treatments. She was tired, the skin on her neck and chest was red and sensitive and her throat was swollen. Mary Kate was told that her mother had come down with a cold and was confined to bed for a few days—no visitors. Andrew then called Ian to give him the same report and that Eleanor would have to extend her stay until she was feeling better.

On the fourth day of her convalescence, Andrew was much heartened when he visited her. "You are looking better today," he said. "The x-ray film is showing that the radiation is having an effect. But I recommend one or two more treatments after you return to Rossburg. You should feel well enough to travel in a few more days. You will be given another week to recover at home before starting the next round. By that time, the machine should be in place at the hospital there. I'll send a radiologist to make certain the technician is properly trained."

Eleanor nodded. "Thank you," she said, her voice hoarse.

"Mrs. Douglas—"

"You are saving my life, Dr. Stoddert. Please call me Eleanor."

Andrew smiled. "Only if you call me Andrew or Drew," he replied. He furrowed his brow. "I don't see how you will be able to keep this from Mr. Douglas. You are too ill after a round of treatments. He will see that something is wrong. He has a right to know, Eleanor, and you need your husband's support right now to give you the strength to fight this illness."

"Dr. Stoddert is right," said Caroline, entering the bedroom. "You have to tell him, Eleanor. Otherwise, the energy you need to recover will be spent trying to keep your secret."

"Dr. Howard and his technician departed last week, and you shouldn't be traveling alone in your condition. I can return with you and help you to break the news to Mr. Douglas," offered Andrew. "I'll tell Mary Kate that I am going back with you to oversee the installation of the machine in the hospital."

"I'll come, too," said Caroline.

Tears welled up in Eleanor's eyes. They were right. She had to tell Ian, and she would need their help to give her the strength to do it. She was truly frightened. She didn't want go through this alone. After a few minutes, she nodded in agreement.

* * * * *

When Ian met Eleanor's train, he was surprised to see Caroline and Andrew and happy to see his wife. Though Eleanor brushed aside his concern, he could clearly see that she was in a weakened state.

Ian accepted that Andrew had come to oversee the installation of the x-ray machine and that Caroline had wanted to see Rossburg again. But by the time they arrived at the house, he had the unassailable feeling that something wasn't right.

Eleanor asked the maid to show Caroline to the guest room, and Andrew suggested that the three of them go into the parlor for a chat.

"What's wrong?" asked Ian anxiously as his son-in-law drew the double doors closed for privacy.

"Let's sit down," said Andrew.

When they were all seated, he methodically laid out the facts. Ian looked as though he had been sucker-punched.

"My God," he murmured.

Eleanor began to cry softly. "I'm so sorry, Ian. I didn't want you to have to know. You have so many things on your mind."

Ian immediately enveloped her in his arms as though to shield her from the darkness that had suddenly descended on them. "You are my priority, Eleanor. Without you, nothing else matters. We'll get through this," he said, struggling to keep his voice calm and steady. "Andrew said the treatments are having an effect. Whatever it takes, I will not lose you." He held her close to him as she continued to weep.

Andrew quietly left the room, his stomach tight with emotion. He went to the phone and put in a call to Mary Kate. He needed to hear her voice. When she came on the line, he smiled as she excitedly told him about all the changes she had made to the townhouse and of her ups and downs with the contractors. He even laughed when she told him that Emily had more or less moved in, having decided that Mary Kate needed her expertise.

CHAPTER FORTY-ONE

A New Chapter

Eleanor was nearly recovered from the last of the radiation therapy. Dr. Howard was pleased with the results. The treatments appeared to have been effective.

The circle of the informed had been widened to include Parker and Maven and Eleanor's personal maid who was fiercely loyal. All anyone else knew was that Eleanor was sick with a stubborn cold and, thus far, no other facts had escaped into the rumor mill. Morgan wasn't home much and didn't question anything. School had started again, and he spent most of his spare time at the plant designing and developing various motorcycle models. And Mary Kate remained blissfully unaware in New York as she finished her renovations of the townhouse.

Maven was overseeing the construction of the women's dorm while Eleanor convalesced. And Caroline had stayed on through her friend's treatments, helping to keep up her spirits. Ian heard laughter as he passed by the parlor one morning and looked in to see Caroline, Maven, and Eleanor in high spirits enjoying tea and cakes.

"Has the cook spiked the tea again?" he quipped from the doorway. He walked over to his wife and kissed her on the cheek. She looked the best he had seen her look in weeks, and it heartened him considerably.

Eleanor laughed, her eyes twinkling with amusement. "We were discussing Morgan. Maven thinks he is smitten with her assistant Annie."

Ian chuckled. "I wondered why he was hangin' around your school so much."

Caroline turned to Maven. "Annie...isn't that the girl who inspired you to open the school?"

"Aye, that she did," replied Maven. "And she has shown herself to have quite the organizational skills. I don't know what I would do without her."

"She must be a special young lady to draw Morgan's attention away from his motorcycles for more than a minute," commented Ian.

Maven gave a light laugh. "Perhaps Morgan should be forewarned that Annie is Irish. It has been told to me that Irish lasses tend to be willful."

"Parker and I can attest to that," responded Ian.

Eleanor sighed. "Well I, for one, would be much happier if Morgan's interests leaned more to a girl than to those infernal machines."

"You shall have to tell me how it turns out," said Caroline. "Now that you are recovering so well, Eleanor, I think it is time for me to return to New York tomorrow. John is probably wondering if I'm coming back, and I don't want to lose my position at the newspaper."

Eleanor took Caroline's hand. "But of course. I shall miss you, dear friend. Thank you for staying and for all of your help and support."

Caroline smiled. "You are my oldest and dearest friend, Eleanor. I could so no less."

"I will see to your travel arrangements, Mrs. Thompson," said Ian. He bent down and kissed his wife on the cheek again. "I'll be at the electric plant if you need me."

Caroline stood up. "Please excuse me while I pack, ladies. I'll join you later, Eleanor."

She and Ian left the room together.

Outside in the hall, Caroline turned to him. "Mr. Douglas, I didn't have a chance to properly thank you for paying Ben's debts when he died. I hope to repay you one day."

"Mrs. Thompson, you have made my wife laugh, and I enjoy hearin' her laugh. With you, she can connect with that part of her past in which she finds warm memories. Whatever debt you feel you owe me has been paid in full. Be ye sure ye can nae stay a little longer?"

"Thank you, but no, Mr. Douglas. Eleanor's illness has made me reconsider a few things. I am going to tell John that I am ready for us to marry."

Ian smiled. "I have it on good authority that you'll nae get an argument from him. And please call me Ian. Ye be more than friend, Ye be family now."

Caroline wiped a tear from her eye. "That means more to me than you know...Ian."

As Caroline climbed the stairs to the guestroom to prepare for her trip home, Ian walked out the front door. He was about to cross the yard to his car, when Parker came motoring up the driveway.

"What are ye doin' here?" he asked when the car came to a stop.

"I'm here to pick up Maven," replied Parker.

Ian raised a brow in surprise. "You convinced Maven to ride in the car?"

Parker grinned. "Baby steps, my friend, baby steps. I hear Morgan has his eye on a certain young lady."

"So I am told," said Ian.

Parker eyed his friend pointedly. "Annie is a good kid. She grew up in an orphanage and has no family. Maven is very protective of her."

Ian nodded, getting the message. "I'll have a talk with Morgan."

Suddenly, Morgan came roaring up the drive on a motorcycle yelling and pointing up at the sky. Maven and Eleanor came out of the house followed by Caroline.

"Goodness, what is all the commotion about?" cried Eleanor.

Morgan dropped his motorcycle and ran over to them. "Look everyone. Look up."

Everybody looked up at the sky, astounded, as a man in a biplane glided overhead. None of them had ever seen such a thing before.

As it disappeared into the distance, Morgan ran back to his motorcycle.

"Where are you going?" his mother called after him.

"It's heading toward Johnson's field. I think it's going to land there," he shouted driving off.

* * * * *

It was announced that the biplane would be on display over the weekend at the field next to Beaumont ballpark for the whole town to see. Morgan was so excited come Saturday he rushed his parents through breakfast and practically pushed them out the door. Indeed, Ian hadn't brought the touring car to a full stop on the edge of Beaumont Field before Morgan jumped out and ran ahead.

Ian helped Eleanor out of the car. "Are you sure you are up to this?" he asked, his brow knit in concern.

Eleanor looped her arm through his. "Yes, I need to resume life again and, according to Morgan, I can't miss this historic moment."

A large number of the townspeople had flocked to the field to see the crazy man and his aeroplane. Shops had closed for a few hours, and those who had to work took detours to pass by the park on their way to their jobs. People were still trying to become accustomed to a motorized vehicle. The idea that man could fly through the sky like a bird on a power-driven machine heavier than air was spellbinding and mind-boggling all at the same time.

Few people had heard of the Wright Brothers. They claimed to have achieved motorized flight in December of 1903, but their press release had been largely ignored. Morgan had come to know of the event when he read a later report of it in *Popular Science Monthly* and had been intrigued. Since then, other articles had begun to appear about enthusiasts who had taken up the challenge, further fanning his interest. Now, to actually see an aeroplane in flight and to be able to touch the wood and canvas machine that had borne a man into the air for approximately 20 minutes was a dream come true for Morgan. Still in awe, he questioned the pilot extensively and examined every inch of the plane, mentally doing the calculations that could explain such a feat.

While Eleanor went off to join a group of women, Ian remained to watch and enjoy his son's excitement.

"What do you think?" asked Parker, walking up to him.

"I think that Eleanor will be very unhappy when she finds that Morgan's new obsession is aeroplanes."

Just then, Annie passed by catching Morgan's eye. He glanced back and forth between her and the aeroplane a few times before chasing after her.

Parker laughed. "Now there was a torn man if ever I saw one."

Ian joined in the laughter. "I can see why. Annie is a pretty girl." He looked at Parker. "I had a talk with the boy," he said on a more serious note. "Maven does nae need to worry." Ian fell silent for a moment. "Given our history, would Maven have a problem with Morgan approachin' Annie?" he asked at length.

"No, I don't think so. Would you?" asked Parker.

"What do you mean?"

"Maven has seen to Annie's education, but Annie was a foundling. There is no record of her parents. All that anyone could glean from a note pinned to her blanket was that her mother was Irish and most likely a domestic. Morgan is the wealthy son of Rossburg's most prominent citizen. There was a time when that might have mattered to you."

Ian looked off into the distance. "That was another life, Parker. I have learned that the pot can nae call the kettle black."

"What about Eleanor? Would it be a concern for her?"

"I do nae believe so, as long as Morgan follows through and goes to college."

"I am glad to hear that," said Parker. He paused. "Maven and I have decided to adopt Annie. I've already begun the paperwork. If anything does develop between these two young people, it will put her on a more equal footing."

Ian nodded. "Funny how life is a circle," he remarked reflectively.

CHAPTER FORTY-TWO

The Campaign

The president of the Board of Trade called the meeting to order. It was not the usual meeting day and members looked around in bewilderment.

"Why are we having this meeting now?" questioned one of them. "We always meet the last Thursday of the month."

"We have important new business to attend here that will likely provoke much discussion and leave no time for other business," responded the president.

"Well, what is it?" questioned a second member impatiently.

"We have before us seven requests for membership into the association."

"If they meet the criteria, what's the problem?" asked another member. "It's a simple vote."

"The new membership requests are from women," said the president.

There was a moment of dead silence, followed by an outburst of laughter.

Biederman was indignant. "You called us here for that?! My time is too valuable to waste on this nonsense. Of course, women are not eligible."

The president looked decidedly uncomfortable. "Actually, George, they are."

"What are you talking about?"

"There is no wording in the bylaws that expressly prohibits the membership of women, and these women meet the criteria. They own viable businesses and have not just one sponsor as required but two."

"Who are these women?" asked another member.

The president went down the list. When he read off the names of Eleanor Douglas and Maven Stanton, Biederman jumped to his feet.

"What are you and Stanton trying to pull, Douglas?"

Ian calmly stood and addressed the members. "These ladies came to Parker and me and asked us to sponsor them for membership in the association. We agreed to do so when it was established that they were eligible."

"Well, then, we'll change the bylaws," said Edward Crandle.

Parker stood then. "If you try to do that before giving these women fair consideration, I will be forced to tell the court that the association violated the bylaws when the ladies bring suit—which they assuredly will do."

Crandle turned to Floyd Cross, the attorney for the Board of Trade. "What about that, Floyd?"

"There is a legal process. You cannot dismiss the requests of these women without due consideration," said Cross.

Having said their piece, Ian and Parker sat down.

"Whose side are you on, Stanton?" yelled out another man.

"This is not a private men's club, gentlemen," said Ian. "We are in a new age now where women have a right to be members. They own businesses that help to strengthen Rossburg's economy and will add to the stability of the association."

"If we let in women, next thing we know they'll be trying to run the organization," said Crandle. "They're already agitating for the right to vote."

Biederman suddenly smiled. "Settle down, gentlemen. The answer is simple. Memberships are accepted by a two-thirds majority rule. All we have to do is vote down the ladies—after fair consideration," he added facetiously. "Then, we change the wording in the bylaws to exclude women."

For a moment, it brought calm to the hall.

Then Parker pointed out: "A judge may see the changing of the bylaws as prima facia evidence that you never intended to give them fair consideration."

"That right, Floyd?" asked the president.

"Yes," replied the attorney.

"We'll take our chances," declared Biederman.

Ian leaned over to Parker. "What do ye think?"

"The judges tend to rule against any extension of women's rights…and some of the members may have a connection with one or two of the judges," replied Parker. "I think it is time for Plan B."

Ian nodded. "Ye might want to reconsider votin' the ladies down," he said, standing to address the membership again. "There be some among you whose businesses may suffer from the adverse publicity."

"What are you talking about?" demanded Crandle.

Just then a group of men entered the hall.

"Who are you?" questioned the president. "This is a private meeting."

"They are members of the press from Rossburg, Philadelphia, Harrisburg and New York," interjected Ian. "It would appear that, in light of the suffrage movement, they find this to be a noteworthy event."

There was silence as every man tried to gauge how this type of publicity might impact his business.

The answer became clearer when the reporters began shouting out their questions: "If the ladies meet all the criteria and there is no other provision in the bylaws, why are you voting down their membership? How many male memberships have you voted down in the last year? If the women's businesses are sound, don't their memberships benefit the community?"

It was the last reporter's question, however, that made them fully aware of the seriousness of the matter. "Are you aware that the National American Woman Suffrage Association is following this case?" he shouted out. "There is talk that the Philadelphia and New York branches of the association will march on Rossburg and call for a boycott of merchants if these women are voted down for no better reason than that they are women."

The members floundered helplessly. Finally, the president banged his gavel and declared that the vote on the new memberships would be tabled until the applications could be better reviewed.

"But you said that the applicants met all the rules for membership," the reporter reminded the president again. "What's to review?"

At a loss for words, the president again banged the gavel. "This meeting is adjourned," he said and quickly exited through a side door.

The other members promptly followed his lead. George and Horace Biederman glared at Ian as they hastily departed.

"Will the ladies grant us an interview?" a reporter from Philadelphia asked Ian.

"I think that can be arranged," said Ian.

He had had the clout to get reporters into town to cover the story. It was up to the women now to make their case.

A press conference was promptly arranged for the next day in the parlor of the Douglas mansion. The ladies came dressed in their Sunday best—prepared and determined.

The reporter from New York asked the first question. "The NAWSA is watching this event closely. Isn't this just another political statement in women's bid for suffrage?"

Eleanor and Maven exchanged glances. Their husbands had warned them about getting trapped with such a question and had advised them to keep the focus narrow and nonpolitical.

"No, it is not," replied Eleanor with the right amount of conviction. "The Board of Trade was formed in 1868 by business owners—my father among them—for the purpose of providing direction to the city on measures that best keep businesses stable. Strong businesses serve the interests of the people in a number of ways that, in turn, serve the city. Businesswomen simply want to have that input as well. The needs of businesses owned by women are not always the same as those owned by men."

"Can you give us an example?" asked the Philadelphia reporter. "Members of the Board of Trade might argue that they must make decisions based on the greater good. Many of their businesses benefit the general populace, while female-owned businesses benefit mostly women and tend to be small and inconsequential in the broader picture."

One woman drew herself up, clearly ruffled at the insinuation that her business was inconsequential. "Sir, my name is Mrs. Curtis. I own the Curtis Machine Company, which manufactures sewing machines, bicycles and typewriters. I would say that benefits the general populace, wouldn't you?"

"And I am the owner of the Lycoming Moving Company," chimed in another woman. "My husband and I started it together in 1903. Since he died two years ago, I have been the sole operator." She motioned toward the lady sitting next to her. "Mrs. Jaffres' company makes wire—"

"Your points are well taken, ladies," acknowledged the reporter.

"Regarding the charge that our businesses are small," said Eleanor, "I dare say that the revenues generated by our companies are as substantial—if not more so—as the profits of businesses owned by members of the trade association. Why don't you gentlemen explore that?"

"Another point well taken, Mrs. Douglas," replied the local reporter.

"Gentlemen, perhaps you might be interested in having a tour of our companies," suggested Maven. "I'm sure the ladies would be happy to accommodate you."

"Most certainly we would," declared Mrs. Curtis stoutly.

The other ladies nodded, and the reporters knew they had no choice but to accept their offers.

For four days, the press toured the ladies' companies and the school. The reporters came away charmed and impressed by the women. They found them intelligent, capable, feminine and, particularly in the case of Eleanor and Maven, comely. They were not the fire-breathing radicals their suffragette sisters were portrayed to be. They were smart, level-headed women who successfully ran their own businesses and wanted nothing more than the benefits a trade association offered their male counterparts. How unreasonable was that?

At the end of the week, members of the Board of Trade Association picked up the *Rossburg Gazette* to see a front-page picture of the ladies standing in front of the Board of Trade Hall. Above the image was a banner headline: LOCAL BUSINESSWOMEN SEEK MEMBERSHIP IN CITY TRADE ASSOCIATION.

Over the next few weeks, newspapers from other cities began filtering in that carried more pictures and articles about the women. Particularly galling and concerning to members were the reporters' observations that women were showing themselves to be just as capable a steward of companies as men.

George Biederman angrily wadded up a New York newspaper. "This is getting out of hand. These women are becoming celebrities. They're being called the 'Rossburg Seven' now. Soon we'll have those damned suffragettes in town."

Horace studied his manicured nails. "So what if these women get membership in the Board of Trade? They are only seven votes."

"They are Douglas' seven votes," snapped Biederman. "And that will open the door to more women and more votes for his side."

At the men's club, Ian and Parker sat reading through the same newspapers, their smiles widening at the imagined reactions of their fellow members.

"They can't put off the vote forever," said Parker.

Ian puffed on his cigar. "They'll try. We'll have to keep up the pressure. Let's see how much fire these ladies can draw."

"Why? What do you have in mind?" asked Parker curiously.

"As you said, sometimes women will see an attack on one of them as an attack on all of them," replied Ian. "I wonder what members' wives will come to think about all of this."

CHAPTER FORTY-THREE

A New Generation

Andrew chuckled as he set aside the newspaper. "Your mother and her friends seem to be making headlines enough without the benefit of your organization."

"They haven't been voted membership yet," Mary Katherine pointed out. "The sisters stand ready in Philadelphia and New York."

"I've no doubt that they do. I never underestimate the power of the sisterhood." He got up from the breakfast table and put on his coat. "I have to get to the hospital. What are your plans today?"

"Emily and I are going shopping for a few more pieces of furniture."

"Furniture—where are you possibly going to put more furniture? I hardly recognize the place as it is."

Mary Kate gave him a bright smile. "I'll take that as a compliment, sir. But in answer to your question, there is one more room to finish upstairs."

"I've lived here for 10 years. I didn't know there were so many rooms," replied Andrew dryly. He bent down and gave her a quick kiss. "I'll be home for dinner."

Andrew was halfway through his rounds at the hospital when he was called to the telephone.

"Dr. Stoddert, this is Mr. Beasley at the bank," said a stilted voice on the other end. "I am an account manager, and there is a young woman here seeking to withdraw funds from your account. She says she is your wife."

Andrew smiled. "Is she blonde, blue-eyed, and pretty?"

"Yes, sir."

"Is she angry?"

The bank manager looked at Mary Kate nervously. "Yes, quite."

"Is she accompanied by an attractive brunette who looks as though she would like to tear out your hair?"

"Uh, yes, sir." The manager's voice dropped to a whisper. "Should I call the police? Are they dangerous?"

Andrew could hardly contain his mirth. "Not unless you provoke them further. But to answer your question, yes, the blonde one is my wife. From which account is she drawing?"

"The account bears her name, but I am sure there is a mistake," said the manager.

"There is no mistake. It is her money. I suggest that you give her what she wants."

"Sir, it is the policy of this bank not to dispense money to a woman without the consent of her father or, if married, of her husband, and we certainly do not open an account in a woman's name. We only make exceptions in the cases of widows, single women over the age of 30, and abandoned women with children."

"Mr. Beasley, is your president there?"

"No, sir. He is on holiday for the week."

"Well, then, Mr. Beasley, you have my permission to give my wife the money she wants. I will come in later to change the account."

Mr. Beasley hung up the phone and smiled triumphantly at the women, considering that he had won the battle.

Mary Kate and Emily were not in a good mood when they left the bank. Their experience with Mr. Beasley served to highlight how much further women had to go to gain autonomy over their lives. A few hours of shopping, however, tempered their anger.

By the end of the day, they were in a much better frame of mind. The furniture had been delivered. The room was made ready to their satisfaction, and Emily departed. The day maid had gone for the day, and the cook had left a meal with instructions for warming. Mary Kate wanted an evening alone with her husband.

Given her experience at the bank, Andrew wasn't sure what kind of mood his wife would be in when he arrived home and was relieved that a much more relaxed Mary Kate greeted him at the door.

"Well, your day seems to have ended happier than it began," he said, taking off his hat and coat. "Perhaps this will make it better." He took out a check and handed it to her.

"What's this?" she asked.

"It's your money. I closed your account at the bank. I would suggest that you find a more female friendly place to deposit it. You might consider John Rinker's bank."

"Oh how I would like to have seen Mr. Beasley's face when you closed the account," chortled Mary Kate. "He was so smug when Emily and I left."

"Well, he didn't look so well when I left," said Andrew. "I thought I would wait a few days before transferring my funds. I don't want the poor fellow to have a stroke."

Mary Kate giggled. "I shall take this to the New York Mercantile Bank tomorrow and open an account."

"Where is Emily?"

"At her house. She does have one, you know."

"I was beginning to wonder about that," said Andrew.

Mary Kate took him by the arm. "Come, I want to show you the room Emily and I finished. Then we are going to sit down to a nice dinner by ourselves."

As they climbed the stairs, Andrew was beginning to sense an ambush. Emily wasn't present. Mary Kate was acting strange. And there was the matter of this room that she and Emily had been working on. He balked outside the door.

"Mary Kate, if this is your way of breaking the news to me that Emily is moving in with us, it is not going to work," he said in a resolute tone. "I know that she is lonely since you moved out, but she will just have to get another roommate—" His voice trailed off when Mary Kate opened the door to the guestroom to reveal a newly decorated nursery.

He turned and looked at her, speechless for a moment. "Are you...are you saying that you are having a baby?"

"No. I am saying that *we* are having a baby. You promised to help, remember? You couldn't guess?"

"Well, I...no," he admitted.

"Not very observant for a doctor, are you?"

Andrew laughed and hugged her. "Okay, so I have been a little distracted lately. Have you seen a doctor yet?" he asked, holding her at arm's length and running a critical eye over her.

"No. Can't you oversee my care?"

"I primarily oversee respiratory diseases. I haven't had much experience delivering babies. I would rather set you up with Dr. Jacoby at the hospital. He's an excellent doctor in the event of a problem, and he has a good nurse to handle routine deliveries."

"On this, I shall defer to your judgment, Dr. Stoddert," said Mary Kate.

"So, Emily knows?"

Mary Kate smiled. "Don't look so disappointed. She was actually the first one to suspect. She dragged me to the library to consult a medical journal. When the symptoms matched, Emily was so excited the librarian nearly threw us out for disturbing the silence. But don't worry. Emily has promised to let us make the announcement. You know that she is hoping for a girl."

"Of course she is," said Andrew. "It is not enough for her to brainwash my wife."

For two more weeks, Mary Kate and Andrew kept the news to themselves until they had confirmation. Emily stuck to her word, difficult as it was for her. Finally, Andrew made the announcement at the Sunday brunch. Mrs. Stoddert's reaction to the news of a grandchild was much like her reaction had been to the news of her son's engagement. She cried, and Emily had to translate her joy to everyone. Mr. Stoddert beamed with pleasure. Within minutes of recovering from the unexpected surprise, Mrs. Stoddert was busy planning a party to announce the happy event.

The following week, Mary Kate and Andrew traveled to Rossburg. Gathered around the Douglas dinner table, they again shared their news. Her parents' reaction was much the same as the Stodderts' reaction had been. Eleanor cried tears of joy; Ian smiled happily.

Morgan, however, shook his head in pity. "You're getting in deeper, Doc."

"I'm afraid so," responded Andrew, earning a glare from Mary Kate.

"We must have a party to make the announcement," said Eleanor, dabbing at her eyes with a handkerchief.

Mary Kate groaned.

"Oh, don't worry, dear. It will just be a small affair with a few of our closest friends."

"That should hold the guest list to a hundred," joked Ian.

"Well, I'm certainly not going to invite the Biedermans or the Crandles or anyone else who refuses to accept the march of progress," Eleanor declared indignantly.

"How goes the women's bid for membership on the Board of Trade?" asked Andrew.

"The association refuses to put it on the agenda," said Ian. "They fear an organized boycott if they vote against membership for the ladies—particularly if Mary Katherine's group comes to town. Some members have already seen a decline in their businesses." Ian chuckled. "I think they are beginnin' to realize that women do most of the shoppin'. But still, it goes against their grain to allow women into the association."

"How nasty has it been?"

"The association has backed off on its attacks, once it discovered that they served to make many of the members' wives sympathetic to the ladies' cause," replied Ian. "So the men sit in hope that the issue and the women will disappear."

"Well, that is not going to happen," interjected Eleanor. "The ladies are completely committed. These men have underestimated the power of the petticoat."

"The ladies of NAWSA stand ready to help if you need them," said Mary Kate.

"Mama, may I be excused?" asked Morgan, bored with the conversation. "I have some schoolwork to do."

"Of course, dear."

Mary Kate stared after her brother in wonder as he left the dining room. "Since when did Morgan become the perfect student? He always took to schoolwork like a cat takes to water."

"Your mother and I came to an understandin'," explained Ian. "As long as Morgan keeps his grades up, stays out of trouble, and goes to college, he can keep workin' at the motorcycle company."

Andrew sighed with mock sympathy. "It does not bode well when a boy's parents discover that he has a best love. It gives them ammunition."

Ian chuckled. "Unfortunately for Morgan, his parents have discovered that he has two best loves—his motorcycles and a girl."

Mary Kate looked at her father in surprise. "Morgan has a girlfriend?" In her mind, Morgan would always be her annoying little brother. She couldn't image him with a girl.

"Well, I don't know that 'girlfriend' is quite the word yet, but he certainly has his eye on the young lady," said Ian. "He does nae think anyone has noticed."

"Why that little weasel," said Mary Kate. "He teases Drew about being hooked on my line when he has been hooked himself. Who is the girl?"

"Maven's assistant," replied Eleanor.

"Annie? I met her when I visited the school. She's a lovely girl. Perhaps I should warn her."

"You will do nothing of the sort," her mother admonished her. "And I forbid you to tease your brother about it. I would much rather have Morgan preoccupied with a girl than with those motorcycles or that flying machine that came into town."

"It's called an aeroplane, Mother," said Ian.

"You've seen an aeroplane?" asked Andrew.

"Aye. Last month, a man flew a biplane overhead here and landed in Johnson's field. It was on display at Beaumont Field for two days."

"It's foolishness," said Eleanor. "If man was supposed to fly, he would have been born with wings." She rang the dinner bell, and a servant girl immediately appeared. "Louisa, we'll take our tea and dessert in the parlor." Eleanor looked at Mary Kate then and smiled. "We can plan the dinner party and perhaps a brunch, dear."

"Uh, Louisa, just make that tea for the ladies. The doctor and I will retire to the study for somethin' a bit stronger," said Ian.

Mary Kate flashed her father a look of appeal, but he pretended not to notice. She didn't garner any more support from her husband. Andrew just gave her a smile and shrugged. Smothering a moan, Mary Kate stood up and followed her mother to the parlor.

In the study, Ian poured two glasses of Scotch and handed one to Andrew. He motioned the doctor to the leather chair and took a seat on the settee.

"I have nae the heart to tell Eleanor that Morgan's interest has been leanin' more to aeroplanes than to motorcycles lately," he said with a chuckle. "I had always contended that cars were the future. Morgan contends that aeroplanes are."

Andrew shook his head in wonder. "It is difficult to keep ahead of the pace of technology these days. The once unimaginable is now within reach."

"Aye, that it is," agreed Ian. "Morgan has vision and a keen mind in the field of engineerin'. With a little maturity, I have no doubt that he can be a leader in the industry. I promised to give him ownership of the motorcycle company when he graduates college and can demonstrate a head for business. I would like ye to be a trustee, Andrew. Your father told me ye showed excellent business acumen when ye were involved with the shippin' industry. Morgan looks up to ye. He'll listen to ye."

"Thank you for your vote of confidence, sir, but I would think you to be better suited to be his mentor."

"Morgan needs to know that he is doing this on his own."

"In that case, I would be honored, sir." Andrew took a sip of his drink. "Mrs. Douglas appears well. She seems to have energy and is in high spirits. Her color looks good. No night sweats, fevers or headaches?"

"None."

"Begging your pardon, sir, but she hid her illness from you before."

"I watch her carefully, and we keep company in the same bed now. I will know if there is a change in her health," Ian assured him. He looked at Andrew. "Will she stay well?"

Andrew was silent for a moment. He believed in giving patients and their families hope when possible. But he knew Ian to be a man who dealt in facts.

"The truth is I don't know," he said. "The technology is too new for record-keeping beyond three or four years. In that time, some have relapsed and died. Until we can find a way to increase the level of radiation without damaging the skin, the therapy may not work on more aggressive tumors. But Mrs. Douglas is strong. Her latest x-ray shows that the treatments were successful. There is just as much reason to be optimistic."

Ian nodded and stared into the fire. He had been largely successful in life because he had been adept at reading his enemies and predicting their moves. For the first time in his life, he had met an adversary that gave him no such advantage.

* * * * *

Horace Biederman rose from the bed and walked over to the table to pour himself some whiskey.

"Horace, come back to bed," pleaded a pouty voice.

"In a minute," he said. He took a couple sips of drink before throwing back the contents of the glass.

When he returned to the bed, the woman nestled against him, running her fingers up and down his chest. He kissed her with little passion and threw her hard against the mattress. He liked to play rough, and it pleased him that she didn't complain. His wife was a milquetoast that he could barely force himself to lie with. The woman cried and prayed throughout the entire act. He found her so displeasing it was difficult for him to perform.

When they were sated, the woman laid her head against his chest. "You do love me, don't you Horace?"

"Of course, Jennie."

The smile that spread across his face held more the look of cunning than of love. Silly girl, he thought. His only interest in her was for the pleasure she gave him and the information she could bring to him as a day maid in the Douglas household. So far, she hadn't supplied any information of value, and he was beginning to tire of her companionship.

"One day maybe you'll leave your wife and marry me," said Jennie, her tone hopeful. She lifted her head and looked up at him when he didn't answer.

Horace gazed down at her, his eyes devoid of emotion. "Maybe." He rose to get dressed. "I have to meet my wife for dinner now," he said, drawing on his trousers and fastening them. "You need to pay closer attention, Jennie dear. I need information about Douglas I can use, not the typical gossip."

"I told you. Mr. and Mrs. Douglas don't talk much around the help, Horace."

"Then put an ear to the door. Talk to the staff. The sooner I can bring down Ian Douglas, the sooner I'll have enough wealth and power to leave my wife," he said, slyly offering her the carrot she sought.

"Why must you destroy Mr. Douglas?" asked Jennie. "He and Mrs. Douglas have always been nice to me."

Horace slipped on his shirt and began to button it. "There is room at the top for only one of us."

"The daughter is visiting with her husband," she offered up hopefully. "She is expecting a baby in April."

This had the opposite effect she had intended. His mood turned darker. Her comment only served to remind him of the great catch he had been deprived of—not only from a financial standpoint but also from the standpoint of a much more desirable bedmate and now an heir. It still rankled that the doctor had bested him.

Horace tucked in his shirt and pulled up his suspenders. As he slipped on his coat, he looked at her. "Get me what I need, Jennie, and make it soon."

CHAPTER FORTY-FOUR

Financial Panic

Parker walked into Ian's new office suite in the business district. Ian still kept the office at the mill, but this suite was the heartbeat of his business empire and, at last, reflected the success of its owner.

"Congratulations," said Parker, dropping into a seat. "Eleanor told Maven the news. How long will Mary Kate and Andrew be visiting?"

"They expect to leave next week. But if Eleanor keeps plannin' parties, Mary Katherine may leave tomorrow," Ian replied dryly.

"Well, take it from me it is much easier to be a grandparent than a parent—" Parker stopped. "I'm sorry, Ian. I shouldn't have said that."

"'Tis all right, Parker. To Patrick's child, you will always be his grandfather. Eleanor showed me the pictures that Maven gave her. He is a handsome lad at just seven months."

"Yes he is and just as smart. Speaking of smart and handsome lads, how is Morgan doing these days?" asked Parker, turning the conversation to a lighter topic.

"Anxious to prove himself," replied Ian, also eager to change the subject. "The boy has more ideas for the company than I can keep up with. I have to admit that most of them are sound. The company is returnin' a good profit."

"Looks like the apple doesn't fall far from the tree," noted Parker. "By the way, Maven said to tell you that she has it on good authority that Annie won't eat Morgan for lunch if he calls on her."

Ian chuckled. "That should be a big relief to him."

Parker suddenly sobered. "I'm actually here on a more serious matter. Have you been following what is happening with the banks in New York?"

Ian nodded. "John Rinker assures me that the crisis is confined to the trusts."

"I don't share his optimism."

"You always were a pessimist, Parker."

"No, I'm cautious. Look, Ian, ten trust banks have failed, including the three largest in the country, but only one—the Knickerbocker—was actually insolvent.

"What are ye sayin?" questioned Ian.

"I don't think that this is over. Once a run starts on the banks, panic sets in everywhere." Parker sighed heavily. "This couldn't have come at a worse time. The New York money market is always in short supply in the fall with crops being transported from the interior of the country to New York and Europe."

"Everything will calm down," said Ian. "America's higher interest rates will soon bring in gold from Europe to supply the market and spell the liquidity shortage as it always does."

Parker shook his head. "Not this time, Ian. Tight markets in Europe have sparked higher interest rates there as well, particularly in England. The gold appears to be staying home."

"How do you know this?"

"I have my sources in New York, too. The point is the economy has been constricting throughout the year. This business with the New York trusts could exacerbate the problem all the more. We could be sitting on a ticking time bomb," warned Parker. "Even your bank president is worried."

"Trusts are required to keep 15 percent in reserves, of which only 5 percent needs to be liquid in most states. Some states require none. National and state banks are generally required to keep 25 percent in reserves, all of it liquid. The People's Bank carries nearly 45 percent, and most of that money is mine," said Ian. "Asherton does nae need to worry."

Just then the phone rang, and Ian answered it. When he hung up, his brow was furrowed.

"What is it?" asked Parker apprehensively.

"That was John Rinker. The healthier trusts are refusin' to lend call money to the brokers to trade stocks, and the stock market nearly collapsed today," replied Ian. "New York city and state banks are bein' forced to put up money to keep the exchange open. John has to recall the balance of my loan."

"How much?"

"Four hundred and twenty-five thousand dollars. He can give me only to the end of the week."

"That's four days. Christ, Ian, do you have that much liquidity?"

Ian ran a hand across his face. "As my stock appears to be worthless right now, I'll have to use the bank reserves."

"That will put the liquid reserves down to nearly 25 percent," pointed out Parker. "You may be legal, but it isn't going to cover all the depositors in the event of a run."

"There are still my material assets. I'll put up the electric company as collateral until I can sell some property to bolster the reserves," said Ian.

"Why don't you put up the motorcycle company as collateral instead?" suggested Parker. "It's less of a loss to Douglas Enterprises."

Ian shook his head. "I promised the company to Morgan when he proves he can handle it."

Parker sighed heavily. "I hope you know what you're doing. This panic has the potential of being worse than the Panic of 1893."

"We weathered that one, Parker. We'll weather this one if it develops," responded Ian, sounding more confident than he felt.

Horace walked into his father's office with a smug smile. "Douglas had a loan recalled by a New York bank this morning."

George Biederman looked up with interest. "Which bank?"

"The New York Mercantile Bank."

"How much?"

"Four hundred and twenty-five thousand—by the end of the week."

"How do you know? Have you hired a private detective?"

Horace smiled. "Something better than that and without monetary cost."

"What are you talking about?"

"The information came from an operator at Douglas' telephone company. She's been listening in on his calls for me. I also have the day maid at the house passing me information."

"Mein Gott, Horace!" exclaimed his father, lapsing into German, "You are sleeping with these women? Amos is a church-going man. What if he finds out that you are cheating on his daughter?"

Horace brushed aside his father's alarm. "Amos can't say a thing. He's a frequent visitor at the Crystal Palace for more than just gambling. By the way, Mary Kate is in town, and she's pregnant."

George Biederman let out a snort of disgust. "Douglas is ahead of me in even the getting of an heir?" He looked at his son. "Maybe you should stay home and spend a little more time with your wife," he remarked snidely.

Horace bristled. "The woman either breaks into hysterics and prayer the minute I touch her, or she lies stiff as board. No man can perform adequately under those conditions."

"I suggest you find a way. Her fortune isn't secured without an heir."

"Indulge yourself with Douglas' affairs all you want, Father. Leave mine to me. Now, what about Douglas' loan recall? How can we use that?"

Biederman thought for a moment. "Our resources are tight. We have experienced substantial losses in the stock market." He pulled out three checks and filled out each one for a different amount for a total of $450,000. It was worth the gamble. "I want you to go to New York. Find three agents to open accounts in three national banks, then deposit a check in each one of these accounts."

Horace looked at his father as though he were insane. "Haven't you been reading the newspapers? The banks are in trouble there."

"Only the trust banks."

"So far."

"Don't worry about it. The money won't be in there that long."

"Why? What are you doing?"

"Forging the first nail in Douglas' coffin. Leave today."

CHAPTER FORTY-FIVE

Blindsided

The next day, the *Rossburg Gazette* screamed out the headlines: TWO MORE NEW YORK TRUST BANKS CLOSE//PANIC SPREADING//STOCK MARKET LIMPS TO CLOSE AT NEW LOW AS CALL LOAN MONEY DRIES UP.

Two weeks later, Ian received a call from his bank president. "Money has come in from two New York banks," said William Asherton.

"Depositors are probably lookin' for a safe haven," surmised Ian. "How much?"

"Three hundred thousand, so far."

When Ian hung up the phone, he leaned back in his chair, his brow knit in thought. Something didn't feel right to him. Why his bank? Why not a bank in Philadelphia or Harrisburg? He picked up the phone to call Asherton back, then thought better of it. Instead, he called Parker. "Meet me at the bank," he said.

He and Parker arrived simultaneously, and Ian told him about the deposits.

When they walked into the president's office, Asherton looked up in surprise. "Mr. Douglas...Mr. Stanton."

"I want to see the record of the deposits from New York, William," said Ian.

"Of course." He pulled out the register and opened it. "These two," he said, pointing to the entries.

"How were the deposits made?"

"By checks cleared at the New York Clearinghouse."

Ian looked at the entries. "Two different accounts, two different banks, two different amounts, all deposited within 24 hours."

Parker jotted down the names. "I'll see what I can find out."

"William, do nae accept any more deposits from new accounts until I say so."

The bank president nodded, bewildered by Ian's concern. Deposits were supposed to be a good thing.

When Ian arrived home that evening, he was met with a crisis of a domestic nature. Eleanor's personal maid angrily had Jennie the day maid by the collar, and the young woman was sobbing hysterically.

He walked over to Eleanor. "What be the problem here?"

Eleanor looked at him just as confused. "I'm not sure yet."

"Tell them," shouted the older woman, giving Jennie another shake. "Tell them what you've been about...how ye been spying on the family and carryin' tales back to that worm Horace Biederman."

Ian and Eleanor were taken aback.

"Is this true, Jennie?" asked Ian sternly.

Jennie nodded and sobbed brokenly. "I-I'm sorry, Mr. Douglas, honest I am. Horace promised to leave his wife and marry me if I helped him. But I ain't the only one," she added angrily. "I found out that he has taken up with Beatrice at the phone company, too. She's been listenin' in on your calls for him."

Ian turned to his wife. "With the exception of the cook and your personal maid, I want this house cleared of all servants now. Each one will be reevaluated tomorrow." The tone of his voice and the look in his steel-blue eyes were sure indications that he was furious.

He rounded on his heel then and went to his study whereupon he picked up the phone and called the supervisor at the telephone company. It was telling that, when the supervisor went to Beatrice's station to escort her from the building, she was nowhere to be found. A half hour later, Parker called and asked Ian to meet him at the men's club in one hour.

When Ian arrived at the club, Parker was already there. Ian told him about the maid's spying and the telephone operator's eavesdropping on his calls.

"Geez, it's a good thing I didn't report this over the phone then," said Parker. "You pay well. Why would they betray you?"

"Horace was sleepin' with them to get information he could use against me," replied Ian.

"Do you think they reported anything useful to him?" asked Parker, concerned.

Ian glared at him. "No, Parker, because there was nothin' to report."

"That's what you said when you were accused of killing Jeffries. Look where that led," noted Parker. "It doesn't have to be true...just the appearance of being true. Watch your step."

Ian nodded. "Why did ye call me here?" he questioned irritably.

"My contacts in New York checked out those accounts. It turns out that they were new accounts opened on the same day with checks written on the Rossburg National Bank. Guess who signed them—George Biederman. As soon as the deposits cleared in New York, checks were written on those New York accounts and deposited in your bank—the People's Bank of Rossburg."

"I suspected as much," said Ian. "I can nae figure the reason. What's he up to?"

The servant approached with drinks and the *Rossburg Gazette*.

Parker casually picked up the newspaper and read the headline: NEW YORK FINANCIERS CALM WALL STREET//SHORTAGE OF MONEY BRINGS INTO QUESTION SOLVENCY OF LOCAL BANK.

He paled as he quickly scanned the story. "Jesus," he murmured. He handed Ian the newspaper. "Read this."

As Ian read it, the expression on his face was one of incredulity. "What the bloody hell—why is the solvency of only my bank questioned? What about Rossburg National?"

"Rossburg National is a national bank backed by treasury bonds. The People's Bank of Rossburg is a state bank with no such assurances," explained Parker. "Look at the byline. Cecil Keaton is a hack. Ian, the story is a plant."

"That bastard! Biederman is engineerin' a run on the People's Bank. The telephone operator must have been listening in when John Rinker phoned to recall my loan. He knew I couldn't liquidate enough assets in time and figured I would have to take from the reserves."

"Why would he arrange for the deposits to be made, then? It doesn't make any sense," said Parker.

"To give the bank a false sense of security," replied Ian. "He's bettin' Asherton will use the deposits to augment the reserves to calm depositors' fears. Even so, there will be those who will be fearful enough to withdraw their funds. Then George will pull out his deposits."

"And 'someone' will leak the story to Cecil Keaton that the bank has little or no cash reserves and create a greater panic to crash the bank," finished Parker.

Ian nodded.

"I don't think Biederman can time it that well," said Parker. "As soon as the cash reserves fall below 25 percent, the state will close the bank. He can't know when that will be. If he doesn't get his money out in time, he stands to lose a good portion of it. Why not just engineer a run on the bank and let the state close it? He knows that you probably can't sell off your assets in time to forestall it. Why risk his own money?"

Ian thought for a moment. "George isn't a banker. Maybe he doesn't know about the 25 percent threshold. Either that or he is playin' a longer game."

"Maybe it is both," suggested Parker. "Whatever the case, a lot of people will be showing up at the bank first thing in the morning to demand their money. You could declare a bank holiday and buy some time."

Ian shook his head. "That would just add to depositors' fears and fuel the run."

"What are you going to do, then?"

Ian tapped his fingertips together as he considered his options. "Instruct Asherton to freeze Biederman's deposits until I can liquidate enough of my assets," he said. "Can you get legal paper for it by tomorrow mornin'? Base it on suspicion of fraud."

"Sure." Parker smiled as Ian's strategy became clear to him. "As long as George's money is in the bank, you'll have cash reserves over 25 percent. The state can't close the bank, then."

"And this will force George's hand so we can see what he's up to," added Ian. "He does nae dodge and weave very well."

Parker laughed appreciatively. "You have him in a box. He can't protest your actions without exposing his part in the fraud. He's going to be mad as hell."

"It will make him even more dangerous," warned Ian. "We'll have to watch our steps carefully. We can nae underestimate his need to win."

"Why don't you enlist Andrew's help?" proposed Parker. "He used to be a player in the business world."

"Nae. I underestimated Franklin Jeffries' need to win, and Tommy paid the price. I'll not put my family in the crosshairs of the Biedermans."

"Do you think George and Horace would go that far?"

"They've already crossed the line," said Ian. "George tried to force a marriage between Mary Katherine and his son. When that didn't work he threatened to dredge up old rumors of an affair between Maven and me. And Horace used Morgan to keep tabs on Mary Katherine and my business. The day is done that the Biedermans try to use my family and my employees for their gain." Ian looked at his old friend and confidant. "Make bloody damn sure nothing comes to the surface about Patrick," he said in a lowered voice.

Parker nodded, more worried than he let on. They had faced some tough fights in the past, but this had a different feel. The Biedermans had involved family. This made the fight much more personal.

Across town, George Biederman sat in his office, his smile widening as he read Cecil Keaton's story questioning the solvency of Ian Douglas' bank. He had the bastard now. It was too bad that the People's Bank had stopped accepting deposits well short of the $450,000 he had intended, but Douglas would be crippled enough.

Biederman suddenly frowned as his gaze fell on the notice of another New York bank closing. He would have to send Horace to New York to retrieve the rest of his money before that bank collapsed as well.

The next morning, when Ian arrived at the People's Bank, reporters were present, and there was already a sizable crowd gathered out front.

"There he is," yelled out a man. "There's Douglas." Others shouted: "We want our money."

A pale-faced Asherton stood guard at the doors, refusing to open them. Ian walked up the steps and faced the angry depositors. Parker arrived then and went to stand beside him.

"Ye have nae need to fear for your money," said Ian.

"Is the story true that you don't have enough cash in the bank to cover our deposits?" cried out a woman.

"Your money is safe as long as you keep it in the bank," explained Ian.

"What's that supposed to mean? Do you have the funds or not?" she demanded to know.

"Not if ye all withdraw your deposits today. A bank carries a certain amount in cash reserves and other amounts in securities in the form of nonmonetary collateral. Joe Martin, you put up your barn for collateral in exchange for a loan for seed money. Sykes, you put up your home in exchange for a mortgage. The bank would have to recall your loans or liquidate the collateral. By that I mean the bank would have to sell the barn and sell the house if neither of ye can repay the loans this day."

"You can't do that," shouted Martin and Sykes.

"I don't want to do that, but the bank may be forced to it if common sense does nae prevail," warned Ian. "You people have three choices: one, ye can leave your money in the back, and it will be there when ye need it as it always has been; two, if you have loans, ye can pay them off and collect your collateral; three, ye can take your business to the Rossburg National and see if it will refinance your loans. Now, those of you who wish to make withdrawals, line up here."

Parker nudged him. Ian nodded when he saw George and Horace Biederman sitting in a motorcar observing the scene.

"Those accounts of longest duration holdin' no loans will be permitted to withdraw first," continued Ian. "Newer deposits of over $100,000 shall have to wait for collateral to be liquidated."

At this, Parker leaned over and whispered to Ian, "George's cigar just dropped out of his mouth. Wait until he finds out that his account is frozen."

Ian smiled. "To be a spider on the wall, ay?"

Many of the people lined up to withdraw funds. By the end of the day, most of the cash reserves—Biederman's money aside—were gone, and he gave Parker the order to begin liquidating some of his personal holdings.

When he arrived home, Eleanor met him at the door. He looked tired, and she put her arms around him. Neither said a word. They would not be destitute, but she knew the bank had been a great source of pride to him. He had already had to close the sawmill. The empire was crumbling.

Two days later, the other shoe dropped. A letter arrived from the president of the Board of Trade. In view of the fact that the People's Bank of Rossburg was too important to the Rossburg economy to fail, a special meeting of the membership was being called to vote on a proposal that would permit the association to petition the bankruptcy court for guardianship of the bank and its current assets.

"Can this be done, Parker?" asked Ian, pacing the floor of his attorney's office.

Stanton leaned back in his chair and sighed heavily. "Yes. If you remember, the association took over the guardianship of a machine company in 1888 for the same reason. When it was sound again, the association sold it. It is the company that Mrs. Curtis now owns. You know Biederman is behind this."

"Aye, but what is his game besides ruining me?"

Parker thought for a moment. "George could offer to buy your bank from the association, which would give him all the collateral, or under the guise of bolstering the reserves, he could buy some of the bank's collateral assets."

"Like the electric company," murmured Ian. "Parker, he wants the electric company." Ian laughed humorlessly. "I should have seen it comin'."

"Why? What?" asked Parker in confusion.

"Gas is bein' threatened by the wider use of electricity. Gas prices are down. Gas stocks are down, and George is part of the consortium that bought the gas company. With the electric company, he curbs the energy market," explained Ian. "We have to hold off the association's petition to take over the bank until I am able to liquidate enough holdings to satisfy the loan on the electric company."

"The country is in a deep recession now, Ian. Money is scarce. It could take a couple of years for you to liquidate enough property. George may have the cash now. When the association takes over the bank, he will have access to the money you froze." Parker shook his head. "The man planned this well."

"Plannin' had nothing to do with it," said Ian. "The panic caused by the Trusts in New York presented him with an opportunity that he was smart enough to exploit. I underestimated him. I should have listened to you and had more cash reserves on hand at the first sign of trouble."

"No one believed it was going to be this bad." Parker pulled out a bottle of whiskey from his desk. "You need a drink."

"No thanks. I'm goin' home."

As he walked to the door, Parker called out to him. "Ian, you know that I'm going to find a way out of this."

Ian turned and smiled. "Never doubted it for a moment."

After Ian left, Parker picked up the file again. He took off his coat and tie and loosened his shirt collar. "Damn heartburn," he murmured and shoved aside his drink.

Ian had been home only a few hours when Morgan came tearing into the house, his face ashen. "Papa, Mama, come quick," he shouted.

Ian and Eleanor rushed out of the parlor.

"What is it? What's wrong?" asked Eleanor, alarmed by the look on her son's face.

Ian took Morgan by the shoulders. "What has happened?"

"Papa, it's Mr. Stanton. He had a heart attack at the office. He's at the hospital now. I was at the school when Mrs. Stanton got the call. I took her and Annie to the hospital and came straight to tell you."

The blood drained from Ian's face. "How bad is it?"

Morgan shook his head. "I don't know."

"Ian, go," said Eleanor. "Go now! I'll call Patrick. Morgan will bring me to the hospital when he calms down."

Ian ran out of the house to his car, not bothering to collect his coat. When he arrived at the hospital, he was immediately shown to a private room. Parker lay still, his eyes closed, his face the pallor of death. Maven sat beside the bed holding his hand. She didn't look up when Ian entered. She hardly seemed to be aware that he was there. Annie stood next to her, quietly crying. When Ian looked questioningly at the doctor, the doctor shook his head and left the room.

Ian moved to the other side of the bed and put a hand on his old friend's shoulder. Parker's eyes fluttered open.

"Bloody hell, what be ye doin' in the hospital?" Ian chastised softly. "We have a battle to fight...just like the old days."

Parker smiled weakly. "Sorry, my friend, you will have to go forward without me." His breathing was labored, and his voice dropped to a whisper. "I found it...told you I would...day passed..." His voice trailed off, and he was gone.

Ian went stock still in disbelief as that all too familiar ice cold wave of shock swept through him.

"I think he was waitin' for ye to be here," said Maven, blinking back tears.

She and Ian looked at each other, both frozen in the moment, linked in time by the thread of yet another devastating loss of a husband...of a good friend and colleague.

CHAPTER FORTY-SIX

Circling the Wagons

Many people turned out for the funeral. Mary Kate and Andrew were there. Patrick stood with Maven and Annie. His wife and child were coming later.

After the ceremony, Ian stayed behind for a long time, oblivious to the cold. He still couldn't believe his old friend was gone. The pain knifed through him and desolation held him firmly in its grips. He didn't remember moving, much less driving, and was surprised to find himself at Tommy O'Brien's gravesite at the Catholic cemetery.

He kneeled down and reached out a hand to touch the headstone, the distant past flooding over him. "Parker will have your back," he murmured.

When Ian arrived home, he went straight to his study and sat down beside the fire with a decanter of Scotch. Over the course of the next several days, he hardly left the room, barely ate, and slept less. He neither sought nor wanted company.

Out of respect for Parker, the Board of Trade had postponed the vote to apply for guardianship of the People's Bank for two weeks. The end of the moratorium was fast approaching, but Ian didn't seem to care.

* * * * *

Uptown, Patrick O'Brien was in Parker's office sorting through papers. The outer office was empty and eerily quiet. He heard the front door open and looked out to see a man entering. He recognized him as Mary Kate's husband.

"Your mother said I would find you here," said Andrew, walking over to Patrick. "I hope you don't mind the intrusion. We didn't get a chance to talk at the funeral and other opportunities seem to evade us."

"It is no intrusion, Doctor. I'm afraid I haven't made myself very available," admitted Patrick. "Truth is I don't deal very well with this sort of thing...death and funerals. I find that burying myself in work helps. Please relay my apologies to Mary Kate."

"No apologies needed. She understands. I only knew Mr. Stanton for a short while, but I liked him very much."

"He thought highly of you as well, Dr. Stoddert. And may I say that it is a pleasure to meet the man who can handle Mary Kate."

Andrew laughed. "That is sometimes a matter for debate."

"I understand that congratulations are in order," said Patrick. "Mother tells me that Mary Kate is expecting a baby. You had better hope for a son, Doctor. The women in this family can be quite a handful."

"Yes, I have a sister just as determined," replied Andrew dryly.

Patrick chuckled. "My condolences, sir." A long pause ensued. His visitor appeared to be lingering. "Is there something I can do for you, Dr. Stoddert?" he asked.

"Please call me Drew. May I call you Patrick?"

"Certainly."

"If I may, Patrick, I would like to discuss the state of affairs in which Mr. Douglas finds himself. Are you aware of the situation with the Board of Trade and Mr. Douglas' bank?"

"I'm still going through Parker's files, but I am getting the picture," replied Patrick. He paused. "I don't see how does this concern us?"

"When Mr. Stanton died, Mr. Douglas not only lost his long-time friend, he also lost his trusted ally at a crucial time. He's alone in this fight with the Board of Trade, and he has lost the will to continue it," explained Andrew. "I spent a couple of years in the world of big business before going into medicine. I know the game. You know the law."

Patrick regarded him warily. "What is your point, Drew?"

"Mr. Douglas needs new partners."

"You are suggesting that we step in to take Parker's place?"

"Yes."

Patrick looked away for a minute as he struggled with the idea. "It's not my fight," he said at length.

"You are family, Patrick. It is your fight."

"I take it that Mary Kate told you about the family secret," he said, an edge to his tone.

"Yes."

"Then you know I don't wish to lay claim to anything that is Ian's, including his fight."

"That's your decision. But do you have the right to deny your son his heritage and allow the likes of the Biedermans to steal what belongs to him?" asked Andrew.

"Perhaps, I don't consider that to be part of his heritage," replied Patrick.

"Then why did you give your son the Douglas name?"

"That was Abigail's decision."

"You must not have objected too much."

Patrick had no response.

"What are you afraid of?" pressed Andrew. "That if you give Ian a chance, you might find that you like him?"

Patrick glared at him. "If it had been your mother, could you forgive Ian for what he did?"

"Your mother has. People change, Patrick. I'm older than you are. I've seen a lot of things as a doctor, and I've come to know human nature pretty well. Whoever Ian was as a young man, he is not that person now. I've talked to people around town. The good governance and prosperity of this city are due in large part to him." Andrew paused. "Did you take your stepfather to be an honorable man?"

"Yes, of course I did. I admired Parker very much."

"Then ask yourself this. Would he have stood by Ian's side for all these years if he hadn't believed him worthy?"

Patrick was silent for a long moment. "I'll consider your idea."

"The Board of Trade meeting is in four days. That isn't much time to find a needle in a haystack," warned Andrew.

After Andrew left, Patrick went into the inner office and sat down in Parker's desk chair. His stepfather's presence loomed large in the room, and Patrick felt a wrenching of his heart and conscience. So much time had been lost to him and Parker never to be recovered now. And his mother...how many more years could he afford squander with her because of his rift with Ian? If Parker's death had taught him anything, it was that time was fleeting.

He looked at the papers on the desk, then picked them up and began to read through them.

* * * * *

Without so much as a knock, Eleanor swept resolutely into the study, pulled open the drapes, and opened the window. The crisp November air immediately began to clear the stuffiness from the room.

"The association meeting is in three days, Ian. You have to fight the vote for guardianship of the bank," she declared.

Ian looked up at her expressionless and bleary-eyed. "I'm tired of wagin' battles, Eleanor. I don't have it in me anymore. What's the point?"

"The point is that you have a legacy to protect for your children and grandchildren and for the people of this town who will continue to need the help of your bank. Another owner or guardian may not have their interests at heart as you do. If you won't fight for yourself, fight for them."

"Parker is gone. I have no attorney."

The finality and sorrow in his voice tugged at her heart, and she sat down beside him and took his hand. "There are other attorneys," she said in a softer tone.

Ian shook his head. "Floyd Cross is the only one who can match Parker's wits, and he is in the employ of the Biedermans."

"Will I do?"

Eleanor and Ian looked up in surprise to see Patrick O'Brien standing in the doorway.

"Mrs. Douglas, if I may interrupt?"

"Of course, Patrick. Please come in," said Eleanor.

Patrick entered the room and looked at Ian, shocked by the disintegration of a man who had always loomed larger than life to him. "I've been reading Parker's notes and going through his files. I would like to help you with your case," he said. "I know that I'm not Parker, but I've been told that I'm a pretty good lawyer."

Ian stood up and walked over to the young man who was his son and yet a stranger. They stood head to head—the same height, the same build, the same determined manner.

"You would help me? Why?" he asked.

"Parker would want me to," replied Patrick stiffly. "And Mrs. Douglas is right. Your legacy is too important to the people of this town and to future generations to let the Biedermans destroy it."

Ian was silent as he struggled to find the will to face one more battle. He heard Parker's voice taking him to task, something Parker had never been shy about doing, reminding him that they had never backed away from a fight yet. Then, the thought of Tommy popped into his mind, and Ian scrolled through the many battles they had faced together, the last for which Tommy had forfeited his life. Parker and Tommy had believed in him enough to stand by him, to help him build his empire. This was their legacy as well.

"Ian...we are waiting for an answer," said Eleanor.

Ian looked at Patrick, a combative spark coming into his eyes. "I accept your services," he said.

He held out his hand and Patrick shook it. It was a seminal moment as father and son took each other's measure, finding common ground for the first time.

"What do ye need me to do?" asked Ian.

"I want you to get rested and nourished," said Patrick. You need to appear strong and confident." He pulled out a sheet of paper torn from a legal pad. "I found this notation in Parker's notes: *Women legal.* Do you know what it means?"

Ian explained that it probably had something to do with the pending membership applications of Eleanor, Maven, and the five other businesswomen before the Board of Trade.

"Oh, yeah, I saw the story in the *Philadelphia Inquirer*," recalled Patrick. "And Mother sent copies of the *Rossburg Gazette*."

Eleanor rose from her seat. "If the vote to apply for guardianship of the bank is close, the women could tilt it in Ian's favor."

"Not if the president and the board refuse to put their membership applications on the agenda," Ian pointed out. "And we have run out of time for that."

"But Parker told you that he had found something," persisted Eleanor.

"Parker was dying. He was probably delusional," said Ian, his voice low.

"Did he say anything else to you before he died?" asked Patrick.

"It was difficult to hear him, but he said something about the day passing. You see it makes no sense."

"Maybe, maybe not. I'll check into it," said Patrick. He pulled out some legal papers and handed them to Ian. "I'll need you to sign these forms designating me as your attorney of record."

Ian sat down and signed the papers and handed them back to Patrick. "Thank you for your help," he said.

Patrick stuffed the forms in his briefcase. "Don't thank me yet. We have an uphill battle ahead of us and not much time to make a plan. I'll keep in touch. In the meantime, don't give out any statements."

When Patrick emerged from the study, he saw Andrew coming down the stairs and hailed him. "Drew, you are just the man I want to see. I need for you to sit down with the bank president and the accountant to assess the damage of the run on the bank. I want to know how much cash is needed to adequately fund the reserves without benefit of the collateral," he urgently instructed.

Andrew smiled. "Partners?"

"Partners," replied Patrick.

Late that afternoon, Andrew's assessment of the bank's affairs was complete—and disheartening.

"What's our next move?" asked Andrew as they sat in Parker's office.

Patrick thought for a minute. "Just before my stepfather died, he indicated to Ian that he had found a way to possibly beat the vote. I have to figure out what it is he discovered. In case I don't, you need to find a way to fund the bank's reserves. If the matter goes to bankruptcy court, we must be able to show that the bank is open for business. We can't wait for Ian's assets to be liquidated."

Andrew nodded. "I guess I had better get busy then."

Andrew returned to the Douglas mansion and immediately put in a call to his father. He briefly explained the situation and asked his father to use his contacts to set up a meeting for him with a group of financiers in Philadelphia—preferably self-made men.

It was going to be a tough sell, his father warned him. Money was so scarce that the New York Clearinghouse was issuing IOUs between lending banks to free up currency for the population. The United States Treasury was down to just five million dollars in working capital after contributing close to a billion dollars to shore up the Trusts and national banks in New York. And the contagion was spreading throughout the country.

His father had no good news to report, and Andrew hung up the phone with little hope. Two hours later, his father called back to say that he was able to set up a meeting for the next day but to not expect much, if anything, to come of it.

As he was packing a bag for Philadelphia, Mary Kate came into the bedroom. "Drew, what's to happen?" she asked anxiously.

He turned and put his arms around her. "I don't know. But we're not going down without a fight." He paused. "Mary Kate, don't let your mother become too stressed by this?"

"How do you suggest I do that?" she questioned with a sardonic laugh. "The tension around here is so thick I can scarcely breathe."

"I don't know. Keep her busy...go shopping for the baby...suggest that she plan a party."

Mary Kate pulled away and looked up at him. "You're serious. What's going on, Drew?"

"Nothing. I just think that events of the last few weeks have been hard on her. Stress isn't good for anyone—including you. Go shopping," he said with a playful chuck to her chin. "I should be home by tomorrow evening." He kissed her and picked up his suitcase.

Mary Kate watched through the window as he hurried from the house to where Morgan was waiting to drive him to the train station. She had an uneasy feeling that her husband was keeping something from her.

As Andrew boarded the train, Patrick was laying out Parker's papers, notes, and files on his mother's dining room table. Before long more papers were strewn about the room, and he sat down to work, prepared to go long into the night.

The clock struck midnight when Maven entered the room carrying a tray with coffee and pie and set it on the only bare spot on the sideboard. "Patrick, it is late. Ye've been workin' for hours. You need to rest."

"I can't, Mother. The meeting is in two days. I requested a postponement, but the board refused."

"The Biedermans are behind it, no doubt," said Maven with a disdainful sniff. "They are like vultures waitin' to swoop in and pick Ian's bones."

"We are not going to let that happen," said Patrick. "Go on to bed, Mother. I'll be along." When he saw her hesitate, Patrick got up and walked over to her. "I miss Parker, too," he said, putting an arm around her.

"We cannot let them win, Patrick. This was as personal to Parker as it is to Ian," she said, wiping away a tear.

Patrick gave her a hug of reassurance. "If there is a way to beat the vote, I will find it."

Maven smiled, her eyes glistening with tears. "You sounded like Parker just then."

He gave her a look of surprise and laughed. "I did, didn't I?" He paused. "Mother, Parker wrote a note saying that women were legal. Ian believes it has something to do with the memberships that you ladies have pending before the Board of Trade. Parker's last words to Ian indicated that he had discovered something that could make a difference in this fight. You were at the bedside. You heard Parker. Do you know what he was talking about?"

Maven shook her head. "I'm sorry, Patrick. If Parker discovered anythin', it would have been after Ian had left him that day. Maybe you should talk to Parker's clerk. He might know somethin' that could help."

"You're right. I'll do that," said Patrick.

"Have ye talked with Abigail?" asked Maven. "How is the baby's cold?"

"Thomas is fine. They are coming on the train in a few days."

Maven's face lit up. "Oh, I am so happy to hear that. We could do with a little joy in this house."

"I agree." Patrick kissed his mother on the cheek. "Now, go on to bed."

The next morning, after a few hours' rest, Patrick went to see the clerk. The man had been with Parker for years and was greatly distressed by Parker's death. When Patrick explained why he had come to see him, the clerk was eager to help.

"An hour or so after Mr. Douglas left, I went in to give Mr. Stanton some papers. He was circling a date on his calendar—October 30," the clerk recalled. "He was quite excited, and he said: 'Henry, with a little luck, the association won't see this coming.'"

"Do you know what he was talking about?" asked Patrick.

"No." The clerk suddenly became saddened. "It was then that Mr. Stanton had the heart attack." He looked at Patrick. "Mr. O'Brien, if you need help closing the office—"

Patrick gave the man a comforting pat on the shoulder. "Thank you, Henry, I'll be in touch."

Patrick returned to his mother's house and sat down at the table once again. His eye fell on Parker's note—*women legal*. It made no more sense to him now that it did before. Even if it were true in the context that they thought—and there was no certainty that it was—as Ian had said, they had run out of time for it to make a difference. Parker dismissed the note as being immaterial to their defense now.

As he sifted through the papers, he came upon the calendar. Just as the clerk had said, the date was prominently circled. He picked up Parker's appointment book and looked to see what appointment he had listed. There was no entry for that date. Patrick sat back in the chair to mull over in his mind everything that the clerk had told him.

His thoughts were rudely interrupted when the calendar fell loudly on the floor, startling him. Patrick leaned over and picked it up. He was about to set the calendar aside, when he saw the note. His eyes shifted back and forth between the two items, and it suddenly hit him. Parker was a contract lawyer. He would look to the "contract."

Patrick bolted from the chair and tore through a box of his stepfather's papers. Near the bottom, he found the document that he was looking for. He leafed through it, coming to a stop at a paragraph that was underlined. He smiled. He had just found the needle in the haystack.

* * * * *

Andrew sat down at the table in a private meeting room in the Bellevue-Stratford Hotel with six notable financiers. They came in various sizes—tall and lean, short and stout, slight in build—their wealth obvious in the expensive suits they wore and in the jeweled stickpins and gold fob watches they sported. Three were clean-shaven, two had mustaches, one had a beard. All were middle-aged and all conveyed a serious manner. To another of lesser means, they would appear intimating. But Andrew met them as equals with a confidence born out of past experience in dealing with such men and out of a position of privilege.

"Thank you for coming, gentlemen," he said.

"We are here as a favor to your father, Dr. Stoddert," said a tall, thin financier with characteristic bluntness. "And I, for one, was curious to meet the man brazen enough to request capital in these difficult times."

"Your father tells us that you understand business, Dr. Stoddert," said another who was the smallest in stature and boasted a large mustache. "You must know, then, that the monetary markets are frozen."

"Yes, sir. That is why I have come to you," replied Andrew. "Men such as yourselves and my father have been through these panics before. You have learned to keep a backdoor escape."

The financiers exchanged looks of surprise. It would seem that the young doctor had more of an understanding of their affairs than they had anticipated.

A stout, balding financier motioned with his hand. "Go on, Doctor."

"Gentlemen, how many of you know Ian Douglas in Rossburg?" asked Andrew.

Four of them acknowledged that they did.

"Then you know him to be trustworthy."

"He is cunning, but he is one of the few who plays fair," said the stout financier. He took off his wire rim spectacles and began to polish them with his handkerchief. "What does Douglas have to do with this matter?"

Briefly, Andrew explained about the run on Ian's bank. "As a result, the Board of Trade is holding a vote tomorrow to petition the bankruptcy court for guardianship of Mr. Douglas' bank."

"That is rather unusual," remarked another. "Am I to assume, then, that you are here seeking capital to fund the bank's reserves?"

Andrew nodded. "If Mr. Douglas can prove the bank has adequate reserves to weather the economic constriction, the petition will stand little chance of being approved by even a judge friendly to the association," replied Andrew.

The men were silent and held their cards close to the vest.

"Gentlemen, Mr. Douglas' bank is important to the people of Rossburg," continued Andrew. "The only other bank is a national bank. It is not inclined to give loans to farmers for seed or to transport crops. It is not inclined to give mortgages to average income people to buy homes or to hardworking immigrants looking to start companies. These are the people who feed you and oil the machinery of the economy that helps to keep you rich, gentlemen."

Again, there came no readable response.

Regrouping, Andrew eyed each one of them. "Gentlemen, perhaps there was a bank like Mr. Douglas' bank that provided you with such capital at a pivotal time in your life."

The subtle reminder hit home, and they all nodded.

"But you said that the association is petitioning for guardianship, Dr. Stoddert. That would presume that the bank would continue to operate as usual, just under new ownership," the slight man with the large mustache pointed out.

"Guardianship is a loosely defined word," said Andrew. "The association intends to stabilize the bank by selling its collateral assets and, then, sell the bank."

"It sounds like a reasonable plan to me," remarked a stout man of average height, puffing on a cigar. "As long as the bank is made stable what difference does it make who owns it?"

Andrew turned his gaze on him. "Some of the collateral assets that will be sold are people's homes and farms, sir."

"My parents lost their farm that way during the Panic of 1878," interjected one of the men quietly. "They never recovered from it."

Andrew saw his opening. "Many people will endure needless losses, gentlemen, for the sake of grievance and greed."

"I see no grievance or greed here," remarked the short, stout financier. "Unfortunately, during times like this, people get hurt. It is just business."

"I stand by my statement, sir," said Andrew, taking a harder line. "The people who orchestrated the run on Mr. Douglas' bank did it to deal him a crippling financial blow and to control the energy market in Rossburg."

"How so, Dr. Stoddert?" asked another financier.

"Mr. Douglas took a loan from the bank and put up several assets for collateral," said Andrew. "One of the assets is the electric company—a competitor and a threat to the local oil industry. Mr. Douglas' chief adversary controls the oil consortium in Rossburg and, we suspect, is looking to obtain the electric company as well through the sell off of the bank's collateral assets."

One of the larger men stroked his beard thoughtfully. "Who engineered the run?" he inquired.

"George Biederman and his son Horace."

"George Biederman—he owns the Pennsylvania and Reading railroads," commented the tall, thin financier who had been silent for much of the exchange. "I had some dealings with him. Never liked him much. I can sympathize with Douglas' plight, Doctor, but though we may have resources, the nation's gold reserves are low and money is scarce."

"I can take a bank draft from a national bank," replied Andrew.

"In exchange for what?" questioned another attendee.

"Sixty percent interest on a short term loan. That's as good as the stock exchange is offering for call money and carries less risk."

"Who is guaranteeing the loan, Dr. Stoddert?"

"I am. You know my father. I am as good as his word." Andrew looked around the table. The financiers still appeared unconvinced.

"Business is business, Dr. Stoddert," the short, stout financier stated again. "It can be ruthless and is not for the faint of heart. We have all had our battles to fight. Sometimes we won; sometimes we lost. Perhaps this is a battle that is destined to be lost."

"Under normal circumstances, perhaps Mr. Douglas might agree," said Andrew. "But this is not just about business. There is a personal side to it, gentlemen. Mr. Biederman and his son have made it about family. And in their quest to destroy Ian Douglas, they will destroy the community of Rossburg as well if not stopped."

The room fell quiet. Andrew had used his trump card. All was fair in business, but there was an unspoken code that families were off limits.

The financier stubbed out his cigar. "How is this about family?" he inquired.

"Mr. Douglas refused Mr. Biederman's proposal for an arranged marriage between Mr. Douglas' daughter and Mr. Biederman's son Horace. The Biedermans have nursed a grievance ever since," replied Andrew. "This is just their latest and most damaging campaign against Mr. Douglas." He paused and looked around the table. "Gentlemen, Mr. Douglas' daughter is now my wife. This has become personal for me as well."

The tall, thin financier regarded the other men. "Well, gentlemen, I would say that this puts a different light on the matter." He looked at Andrew. "I can give you a bank draft for $50,000."

The others nodded in agreement and followed suit with the same or lesser amounts.

"Thank you, gentlemen," said Andrew.

As the financiers filed out, the tall, thin man approached Andrew. "It was a pleasure to meet you, Dr. Stoddert. Few, if any, could wring money out of us in such times. You played a good hand. I believe you have missed your calling, sir."

Andrew smiled. "Thank you, but I am happy with my calling as a doctor."

"Then you must be a very good one. I wish you and Mr. Douglas well."

When he was alone, Andrew totaled up the drafts. He had hoped for more until he could make arrangements to transfer some of his own money into the bank. Patrick would just have to work a little harder to make the case. He gathered up his papers, preparing to leave.

"Dr. Stoddert?"

Andrew turned to see a dark-haired, young woman.

"My husband said I could find you here," she said.

"I'm sorry. Do I know you?"

The woman smiled. It was a pleasant smile that lit up her face, dimpled her cheeks and crinkled her large brown eyes, trumping the plainer aspects of her appearance.

"I am Abigail O'Brien, Patrick's wife," she said.

Andrew looked at her in surprise. "Mrs. O'Brien, Patrick and Mary Kate speak of you often. I feel that I know you. It is a pleasure to finally meet you."

"Thank you. Did you collect the money you were seeking?"

"I'm afraid the investments fell a bit short," admitted Andrew.

"Perhaps this will help," she said, proffering a bank draft. "It is from the state treasury. It should carry more weight."

Andrew didn't know if he was shocked more by the amount or by the fact that it came from the state treasury. "Please forgive me, Mrs. O'Brien, but how did you come by this?"

"Simply put, my father has the governor's ear, Dr. Stoddert, and I have my father's ear."

Andrew gave a hearty laugh. "Mrs. O'Brien, you are, indeed, a good fit for this family."

Abigail smiled again, pleased with his comment. "I will see you in Rossburg, Doctor. Good luck."

CHAPTER FORTY-SEVEN

Saving a Legacy

Members of the Board of Trade pushed their way through a throng of reporters and slowly filled the hall to take their seats. Ian and Patrick sat in the front. George and Horace Biederman glanced at each other, feeling a little less smug. Douglas looked fit and confident. Their reports had been that he was a broken man.

Behind the scenes, things were moving fast. Time was of the essence, and everyone had his role to play. Eleanor, Maven and Mary Kate were charged with rounding up the businesswomen who had memberships pending before the Board of Trade. One of the women was visiting her sister in Eldridge Township, and Morgan was dispatched to drive out to the rural farm area to pick her up. Andrew and the accountant were dealing with the bank drafts.

The president of the association called the meeting to order and presented the agenda. There was just one item—the People's Bank of Rossburg. Discussion was called. George Biederman gave argument in favor of the association's guardianship; Floyd Cross presented a legal path for it.

When it came their turn, Patrick started to stand, but Ian put a hand on his arm to stay him and rose to present his own case.

Standing tall and stately, he turned and looked the members calmly in the eye. "You all know me," he said in a clear, steady voice. "Mr. Widman, I helped ye to establish your department store against the opposition of the association, and my bank gave ye a loan when

Rossburg National refused ye. Mr. Crandle, who gave ye your stake to establish your business? And what of you, Mr. Walker, when your business was in a downturn following the Panic of 1893? How many of ye are members in the association today due to my support?"

As Ian continued to go down the line of the members he had helped, many of them began to shift guiltily in their seats.

"The town requires a sound bank to serve the needs of common people," said Walker. "It's not personal, Ian."

"It is personal, Mr. Walker. The purpose of this motion for guardianship is not to save a failed bank for the sake of Rossburg," replied Ian. "The People's Bank was a healthy institution until a run was deliberately orchestrated on it. This is an attempt by someone to get ownership of certain collateral assets and to financially destroy Douglas Enterprises, and the association is being used to accomplish it."

"For what reason?" inquired a skeptical member.

"Perhaps George Biederman can best answer that," said Ian. "He is the one who engineered the run on the bank."

All attention fell on Biederman.

"What about this, George?" asked another member. "Douglas Enterprises employs most of the people in town."

"Douglas is just trying to muddy the waters," said Biederman. "There has been enough discussion. I make a motion to end discussion and take the vote." He nudged his son.

"I second that motion," Horace quickly added.

Patrick glanced anxiously at the door. Where were the women?

The president was starting to call the vote, when the door was thrown open and seven very determined ladies marched to the front of the hall.

"They cut it pretty close," remarked Patrick when Andrew sat down next to him.

Andrew grinned. "Adds drama. The funds are in place. Time to enjoy the show."

The president banged the gavel as murmurs of surprise and bewilderment sounded around the room. "Ladies, why are you here?" he demanded to know when everyone quieted down. "You are interrupting important business."

"We are here to exercise our right to vote as members of the association," said Eleanor, matter-of-factly.

"But the association hasn't voted on your memberships yet," said the president.

At this, Patrick stood up. "A vote is no longer required. These ladies became members by default when the association failed to vote on their memberships within 30 days."

"Floyd, what's he talking about?" demanded George Biederman.

Floyd Cross took out a copy of the bylaws.

"Page 45, section 10," directed Patrick.

Cross turned to the page and read through it. "He's right. It's part of the original bylaws from 1868."

It had never been an issue before, and with all the amendments that Ian had pushed through in past years making membership more inclusive, the rule had gone forgotten.

"Are you saying these women are members?" asked Crandle incredulously.

"I'm afraid so," said Cross.

The membership was stunned into silence. Sidelining the vote was supposed to keep the women out. Instead, the association's failure to act had opened the door to let them in.

"Never mind," retorted Biederman. "Even with this trickery, Douglas doesn't have enough votes to keep the motion for guardianship of the People's Bank from passing."

"The vote may be closer than you think, George," said Ian, prepared to do more member shaming.

As it turned out, he didn't need to. The door suddenly opened again, and over 100 women marched in to join their sisters at the front of the room. They were residents from all walks of life and students from Eleanor and Maven's school. Many among them were the wives of association members who stared daggers at their husbands.

Patrick grinned. "Never imagined that."

"Nor I," said Andrew, astonished. "How in the world—"

They looked at each other and uttered in unison: "Mary Kate." It had her fingerprints all over it.

Biederman was feeling less certain of himself as he took note of the ambivalence on members' faces. "Get on with it, Harvey," he shouted.

"Before you proceed, there is one other announcement we wish to make," said Patrick. "This vote is illegal."

"How so?" asked the president.

"The People's Bank of Rossburg is solvent. Anyone wishing to withdraw uncollateralized funds may do so at any time," announced Patrick. "The association has no grounds to apply for guardianship."

"That's not possible!" exclaimed Biederman, jumping up from his chair. "The bank doesn't have enough cash reserves."

Andrew rose from his seat. "Actually, it does," he said.

"Where did you get the money?"

"The state treasury for one." Andrew looked at George Biederman and smiled. "You can tell your agents that their deposits have been unfrozen. You will get your money back, Mr. Biederman, but you will be last in line."

Biederman reddened as everyone looked at him, wondering what the young man was talking about. "We don't know how well supplied the bank is," he blustered. "It could fail again in a few months. What if depositors don't return and the investors want their money back?"

Murmurs went about the room, and Andrew raised his hands to quiet concerns. "The bankruptcy court is satisfied," he assured everyone, and as soon as the transfer can be arranged, I will be making a deposit of $100,000 in the bank."

"Who are you?" asked one of the members.

"Mr. Douglas' son-in-law."

"That's good enough for me," said the man. "I am making a motion that the vote to petition for guardianship of the People's Bank of Rossburg be cancelled and the meeting adjourned."

"I second that," shouted another member.

"Wait!" blustered Biederman. "You can't do that."

"Shut up, George! The motion is carried. The matter is settled. I hereby adjourn the meeting," said the president, eager to be done with the business.

Ian turned to Patrick and Andrew. "I don't know how to thank ye," he said, shaking their hands.

"Andrew did the hard part," said Patrick. "Thanks to the capital he raised, your bank should be well protected against any other attacks. And thanks to Parker, you will have the ladies' votes to help keep the Biedermans in line."

"I can guarantee it," interjected Maven, as she and Eleanor joined the three men.

Eleanor took Ian's arm. "Let's go home."

"I second that," said Maven. She looked at Patrick with a bright smile. "Abigail and Thomas will be arrivin' soon."

As the little group emerged from the hall, they were amused to see members being besieged by reporters. While the men struggled to extricate themselves from the press, the ladies were only too happy to give reporters a full accounting. They had made history in Rossburg this day and were proud of it.

From their vantage point, Morgan, Annie, and Mary Kate laughed as they watched the Biedermans swat away reporters and run to their car.

"I'm assuming we won," quipped Morgan.

That evening after dinner, Ian, Eleanor, Mary Kate and Andrew were in the Douglas parlor still reveling in the day's events. Morgan had gone off to celebrate with Annie.

Ian was greatly moved by the efforts of Patrick and Andrew. "I'll be forever in your debt," he said to Andrew. He hoped he would have the opportunity to better express his gratitude to Patrick as well before Patrick returned to Philadelphia.

There was a knock at the door, and the maid entered the parlor to announce that they had visitors.

"Who is it?" asked Eleanor.

"Mrs. Stanton, ma'am."

Eleanor and Ian looked at each other in surprise. "Please show her in."

Everyone stood as Maven walked into the room.

"Is somethin' wrong?" asked Ian, concerned.

Maven smiled. "No. On the contrary, all is well."

Patrick walked in then with his wife and carrying their son. "Ian, this is Abigail," he said.

Ian took Abigail's hand and warmly welcomed her. "I understand that I have much to thank you for," he said. "Andrew told me of your part in securing the necessary capital."

Abigail smiled. "It was my pleasure, Mr. Douglas. Family helps family. Patrick and I thought it was time for you to meet Thomas Douglas O'Brien."

Ian regarded the baby—his grandson. The rosy-cheeked eight-month-old shyly smiled at him, and, after a few seconds, left the security of his father to go willingly into Ian's outstretched arms. Ian smiled and cuddled the little boy.

He looked at Patrick and Abigail then. "Thank you," he said, his voice catching with emotion. "'Tis an honor and a blessin'."

Mary Kate, Andrew and Eleanor came to greet Abigail and Maven. The ladies all had tears in their eyes. There was a babble of voices as everyone, in their excitement, tried to talk at once. With the baby still resting comfortable in his arms, Ian proudly surveyed his family. It was now complete, and he felt his heart swell with immeasurable peace and joy.

"He has come home, Parker," he murmured to himself. "Patrick has come home."

"How long is your stay in Rossburg?" Mary Kate asked Abigail and Patrick.

Patrick glanced over at his mother and smiled. "Abby and I have talked it over," he said. "We have decided to move back to Rossburg so I can take over Parker's law practice."

Maven let out a cry of joy. "Oh, Patrick, 'tis my prayer answered."

"Mine as well," said Ian.

"I think it is wonderful!" exclaimed Eleanor. "With the school and the dormitory, Maven and I will have need of a good attorney from time to time. Of course, we shall expect a discount."

"Of course," said Patrick with a grin. "I believe we can come to an arrangement."

Andrew went over to Patrick. "I know the legacy will be safe with you at Ian's side now. Parker would be proud."

"Thanks, Drew. You know sometimes I think Parker had a hand on my shoulder throughout this ordeal. Something tells me that he didn't miss this fight after all."

"If there was a way for him to be part of it, he would have found it," replied Andrew, paraphrasing Parker's mantra.

Patrick laughed. "No doubt." He sobered then. "I may have need of your capabilities again, Drew. There is always a Biederman lurking in the shadows."

Andrew nodded. "Any time."

"Well, I think this calls for champagne," announced Ian. "I would say that as a family we have much to celebrate."

CHAPTER FORTY-EIGHT

A New Attorney in Town

1908

Patrick's move back to Rossburg was complete by March. He, Abigail, and Thomas were staying with Maven while a grand new house was being built for them near the Douglas mansion on Grandview Place. He had rehired Parker's staff and was in the process of arranging his law books on the shelf when a woman walked into his office.

"Mr. O'Brien?"

Patrick turned. "Yes. May I help you?"

"I have need of an attorney and was directed to come to you."

Patrick tried not to show his surprise. Word was spreading fast, he thought in amazement. Already he had his first client, and the staff wasn't even in place yet. He pulled up a chair for her and took his seat behind the desk.

"How can I be of service?" he asked taking out pen and paper.

"I want to divorce my husband," she replied tersely.

Patrick looked at her struck by the lack of emotion with which she made the pronouncement. "I'm sorry, ma'am, but I don't handle divorce cases. Perhaps there is another attorney who—"

"My husband is a prominent member of the community, sir. I would not have another attorney's loyalty or discretion in Rossburg. You are new to the town, and I know how you defended Mr. Douglas against the takeover of his bank by the Board of Trade. You are the only one I feel that I can trust. I have funds, Mr. O'Brien," she assured him when he appeared to hesitate. "I have been saving for this for quite some time."

"It is not a matter of money," said Patrick. "I do not want to raise your hopes. I'm sure you are aware that a divorce is still difficult for a woman to obtain, Mrs.—"

"Biederman...Lily Biederman."

Patrick's eyes widened, and he leaned forward in his chair. "Your husband is Horace Biederman?"

She nodded. "The man disgusts me. I need to be free of him. And since I am not permitted to kill him—I'm not, am I?" she asked with a spark of interest.

"Uh, no, Mrs. Biederman, you are not," replied Patrick, not sure if she was joking.

"Then it would appear that divorce is the only option left to me, Mr. O'Brien."

"Unfortunately, Mrs. Biederman, a woman's disgust for her husband is not grounds for divorce. You must give proof of abuse, adultery, and/or abandonment, depending upon the judge's degree of sympathy. And I must tell you that sympathy doesn't often weigh on the side of the wife."

"I have proof of my husband's adultery. A maid who used to be in the employ of Mr. Douglas is willing to make a statement that my husband had an affair with her. And there is another woman who worked at the telephone company. Does that help?" she asked.

"It does as long as these women remain steadfast in their statements," said Patrick. "But I must tell you that often such witnesses recant when they find themselves at the center of the scandal, which this surely will be. Has Mr. Biederman been at all abusive to you?"

The woman looked away, and there was a long pause before she responded. "Does rape count as abuse, Mr. O'Brien?" she asked lowly. "It seems that it is the only way my husband can perform his duties."

Patrick was taken aback again. He could see the humiliation she was feeling at having to make such a disclosure.

"I'm very sorry for your trials, Mrs. Biederman," he said, sympathetic. "But there is no protection for women against marital rape in the statutes. Also, Pennsylvania does not recognize alimony or a division of assets. Should you be successful in obtaining a divorce, you would be left destitute."

"It could not compare to the hell that I am trapped in now," she responded bitterly.

"What about your parents?" asked Patrick.

"They would not be supportive. My father bartered the marriage. As you can see, I have no attractive features to recommend me...just money," she added scornfully. She looked at him. "Please help me, Mr. O'Brien. You are my only hope of escaping this nightmare."

Moved by the pleading in her eyes and the desperation in her voice, Patrick nodded. "Let me see what I can do. Have you someplace else to stay?"

"I have a cousin in upstate New York." She handed him a note card with the address. "I ask that you keep this information in the strictest of confidence. I am leaving Horace whether or not you are successful in obtaining a divorce for me, and he must not be able to find me. You have seen how vindictive Horace and his father can be."

Long after Lily Biederman had left, Patrick still couldn't shake the despair that radiated from the woman. He kept thinking about Mary Kate. That could have been her fate had Ian been a different kind of father.

* * * * *

A week later, all hell broke loose when Horace discovered that his wife was missing and he was served with divorce papers on the same day. It was difficult to determine who was the more outraged, Horace or his father. Patrick received an immediate summons to Floyd Cross' office. Patrick responded with an invitation to Floyd Cross to meet with him in his office.

Cross smiled. It would seem that Patrick O'Brien had learned something from his stepfather. He called in his secretary. "Call Mr. O'Brien and arrange a meeting at the Rossburg Men's Club," he said.

The next evening, the two men sat amicably in a private corner of the room, taking each other's measure over cigars and whiskey.

"What is it that your client wants?" asked Cross.

"As stated in the papers, Mrs. Biederman wants a divorce. She doesn't care about any other settlement. However, as her attorney, I must insist upon adequate sustenance for her, or I would not be doing my job."

Cross took a puff on his cigar. "Divorce is more common than it once was, but it is still the stuff of scandal, particularly if it involves families of prominence. What if my client says 'no' to it?"

"Mr. Biederman might find it rather embarrassing if it were made public in a court of law that he is unable to perform his marital duties without indulging in the act of rape," responded Patrick.

Cross raised a brow in surprise at the charge. He didn't like Horace, but he had never considered that the man would stoop to that.

"Nonconsensual sex in a marriage is not grounds for a divorce," the attorney pointed out. "It would not be considered, Mr. O'Brien."

"It is up to the discretion of the judge, Mr. Cross. There is always the possibility that we might get a judge that finds marital rape offensive enough to declare it abusive and worthy of consideration. With the women's movement gaining momentum, this is becoming a controversial issue. Barring that, there is also the charge of adultery," added Patrick.

"Do you have proof of it?"

"I have affidavits from two women with whom Mr. Biederman has engaged in extramarital affairs. I'm sure if I look further, I can find more. Mr. Biederman strikes me as a man who is quite taken with his prowess."

Cross saw the trap. He knew Horace well to enough to know that the man's ego would not tolerate a charge of marital rape. But if Horace brought forth women as witnesses to his prowess, he would be admitting to adultery as already evidenced by O'Brien's affidavits. The whole thing could turn into a media nightmare and a scandal of large-scale proportions.

Cross took another puff on his cigar. "It is one thing to write an affidavit, Mr. O'Brien. It is quite another to testify in open court. I would bet on those woman withdrawing their accusations with the first whiff of publicity before the case gets to court."

"Maybe, maybe not," responded Patrick, taking a sip of his drink. "You know what they say about a woman scorned. It seems Horace promised marriage to both these women."

Cross wavered a little with that disclosure. "The case will bring a lot of press, you know. Is Mrs. Biederman prepared to suffer the humiliation?"

"She is no stranger to humiliation," Patrick assured him. "She suffers it everyday in her marriage."

"Mrs. Biederman will have no support in Rossburg," warned Cross.

Patrick smiled. "Judging from the number of women who attended that special Board of Trade meeting, I believe that Lily Biederman will have more support than you may think."

The attorney sighed and sat silent for few moments. "What's your price?" he asked.

Patrick wrote out a figure on a piece of paper and passed it to him.

The attorney looked at it. "I would call that a good deal more than adequate sustenance."

Patrick shrugged. "I believe that many women would find it less than commensurate to Mrs. Biederman's pain and suffering. How much is it worth to your client to protect his vanity and reputation?"

"The Biedermans have a lot of clout in Rossburg, Mr. O'Brien. I think Horace will weather the storm better than your client. As you know, there is no alimony or sharing of assets in Pennsylvania. Whether Mrs. Biederman cares about a settlement or not, Horace will see to it that she is left with nothing. I would advise your client to reconsider her divorce action."

Patrick casually took another sip of his drink. "Mr. Cross, do you remember the case of Mrs. Laura Corey? My wife reminded me of it, actually. Mrs. Corey wanted to divorce her husband in Pittsburgh in 1906, but she faced the same threat of destitution. The story was in all the major newspapers."

"I saw something about it. It wasn't my area of interest. I didn't pay much attention to it," admitted Cross.

"Allow me to refresh your memory then. Mrs. Corey moved to Nevada where the laws for divorce are laxer. After satisfying the six-month residency requirement, she filed for the divorce in Reno."

"What is your point, Mr. O'Brien?"

"Her husband was president of the United States Steel Corporation. He had clout, too, Mr. Cross, but Mrs. Corey got her divorce and a $3,000,000 settlement," replied Patrick. "You see Nevada does allow the sharing of assets in a divorce action. Since Mrs. Corey's success, it seems that women of means seeking to escape unhappy marriages are finding Reno to be a very viable option."

The attorney eyed Patrick sharply. The message was clear, and a long silence ensued.

"My client brings the divorce action," said Cross at length.

"No. It must be mutual...neither side blaming the other," stipulated Patrick. "Or Mr. Biederman may find it exceedingly difficult to find another wealthy, young woman willing to marry him."

Cross took a healthy swig of his drink. "Mrs. Biederman appears to have left town. Should my client find it necessary to communicate with her—"

"All communication will go through me. Mr. Biederman is to have no further contact with his wife," stated Patrick.

"Horace could make a charge of abandonment that even a Reno judge might see fit to uphold," said Cross.

Patrick looked at the attorney. "Do you have a daughter, Mr. Cross?"

"Yes."

"How old?"

"Eighteen."

"Do you have her happiness at heart?" asked Patrick.

"Of course."

"Imagine her trapped in a marriage with a man like Horace Biederman."

"I would never allow it to happen," the attorney flatly stated.

"It may be out of your hands," retorted Patrick. "Men can hide their dark predilections. Sometimes we don't know someone as well as we think until it is too late."

Cross stubbed out his cigar and downed the rest of his fine whiskey. "You can tell Mrs. Biederman that Horace will agree to her terms."

Horace was furious when presented with the details of the agreement. His rage increased all the more as Cross pointed out the corner into which he had painted himself.

The next morning, the attorney wasn't surprised when George Biederman stormed into his office.

"You stop this foolishness, Floyd, and get that woman back to where she belongs before any of this gets around town."

Cross sat back in his chair and regarded his client calmly. "What do you suggest I do, George?"

"You're the lawyer, Floyd. You figure it out. That's what I pay you for."

"Mrs. Biederman has won, George. There is no getting around it. Unless you want this to become a media circus, I would advise Horace to sign the papers and come up with the money as quietly and quickly as he can and move on."

Biederman's chest heaved with anger. "What kind of attorney are you?"

"A good one, George."

"If that were the case, you wouldn't be giving in to the demands of that woman. With her looks, Lily Wadkins was damned lucky to get a man like Horace."

"She doesn't appear to agree."

Biederman glared at his lawyer and uttered an expletive.

As he started to storm out of the office, Cross called out to him: "George, when the divorce is finalized, I will no longer be the attorney of record for you or Horace."

* * * * *

It was two o'clock in the afternoon on a bright, sunny day in mid-April. But Andrew wasn't aware of much more as he paced the hall outside the hospital room, unable to focus on anything other than the fact that he would be a father in a few hours.

He had brought Mary Kate in before dawn at the first signs of labor and had anxiously hovered over her until the doctor diplomatically suggested that Andrew pursue his own medical duties for the time being. At Mary Kate's insistence, Andrew reluctantly took the doctor's suggestion and divided his time between rounds and checking on his wife. At noon, he finally gave up and set up a vigil outside the delivery room.

The nurse came out, then, and he looked at her expectantly.

"It won't be too much longer," she said. The nurse smiled. She had never seen the usually composed Dr. Stoddert in such a state before.

"Do all babies take this long?" asked Andrew.

"Some take even longer. Mrs. Stoddert is doing fine and all is progressing as it should," the nurse assured him.

An hour later, Andrew heard the first cries of his child.

The door opened and the doctor appeared. "Come in and meet your daughter, Dr. Stoddert," he said with a wide grin. "Mother and child are doing well—much better than the father, I dare say." He slapped Andrew on the back. "Don't worry. It gets easier with each time."

Andrew looked at the doctor. He didn't know if he could go through this again. He hurried into the room. From the moment he saw the baby girl with blonde fuzz and bright blue eyes nestled in her mother's arms, she had him wrapped around her tiny finger—all the anxious hours of waiting forgotten in the face of this miracle.

Mary Kate looked up at him and smiled. "Behold Ella Jane Stoddert, our future suffragette."

Andrew laughed and wondrously traced a finger along the sweet, little face. "Don't you think that battle will be won by the time she can hold a sign?"

"One can only hope," replied Mary Kate, doubtful.

CHAPTER FORTY-NINE

The Enemy We Can't See

March 1909

"Mr. O'Brien, your appointment is here," announced the secretary.

"Thank you, Henry. Please show her in."

Patrick stood as Eleanor entered the office. She sat down a chair and took off her gloves, her manner more businesslike than usual.

"Thank you for seeing me on such short notice, Patrick."

"Of course. Is there a problem at the school?" he asked, taking his seat.

"No, I am here on a personal matter," she replied.

Patrick regarded her curiously. It was clear that she had something on her mind. "How may I help you, Mrs. Douglas?"

When Eleanor explained the reason for her visit, Patrick was stunned.

"I-I don't know what to say, Mrs. Douglas."

She smiled. "There is nothing to say, Patrick."

She handed him two letters that she had written and asked him to read them. When he had finished, he laid them aside and rubbed a hand over his face, again at a loss for words.

"This is quite a selfless act," he remarked at length.

"No, Patrick, it is not. I am repaying a debt I owe. You and my children are the ones who will have to be selfless. I leave it to all of you to decide when—or if—these letters are delivered."

She dictated and signed another document, then stood up to leave. Patrick was seeing her to the door, when she stopped and turned to him. "I know what you did for Lily Biederman. I don't know all the details, of course, but I do know the Biedermans. It could not have been easy getting her out of that marriage."

"It did take some doing," admitted Patrick. "But we made Horace pay."

Eleanor smiled. "I told her you would."

Patrick looked at her in surprise. "You sent Lily Biederman to me?"

"I saw the poor woman in the park that day. She was crying and looked so forlorn I was afraid that she was on the verge of...well, doing the unthinkable," replied Eleanor. "I told her she could trust you."

"She never said that you had sent her."

"I asked her not to. I didn't want you to feel obligated. You are a good man, Patrick. I didn't know Tommy well, but I know that he and Parker must be very proud of you. For what it is worth, so is Ian."

Patrick smiled. "Thank you, Mrs. Douglas."

He had always had feelings of ambivalence toward Eleanor Douglas, but this day, he felt only admiration for her.

* * * * *

It was one o'clock in the afternoon, May 15, 1909. Andrew hung up the phone, and the bottom fell out of what had started out as a good day. He went still for a minute, then pounded his fist on the desk and let out an expletive in a rare show of unbridled anger. How, he wondered, was he going to handle this?

Bringing himself under control, he picked up the phone and called his sister to meet him at the house, then went out to find his colleague to inform him that he had to leave the hospital for the day.

When he arrived at the townhouse, Emily opened the door for him ready to leave with little Ella for a pram ride. The baby bounced in her aunt's arms excited to see her father, and Andrew took the little girl and hugged and played with her for a few minutes before handing the toddler back to his sister.

"Is it what I think it is?" Emily asked him.

Andrew nodded.

"I'm so sorry, Drew. What can I do?"

"Give me at least an hour alone with Mary Kate," he said. "And plan on spending the night."

"Of course. Ella and I will be at the park."

When the door closed on them, Andrew instructed the day maid to have his wife join him in the drawing room. He walked into the room and poured himself a drink and threw it back in one gulp.

"Andrew, what are you doing home?" asked Mary Kate, strolling into the room.

"I have something to tell you," he said. He poured another drink and held it out to her.

"No, thank you. You look so serious—Drew, you are frightening me. Is something wrong with Ella? Emily just left with her."

"No. Ella is fine. It is your mother."

"My mother? What about my mother?"

Andrew paused, searching for the right words and finding none. He was a doctor thinking like a husband. "She is sick, Mary Kate," he said softly. "Her…her cancer has returned, and the radiation treatments aren't working."

Mary Kate stared at him. "What are you talking about? What do you mean her cancer has returned?"

Andrew guided her to a chair and pulled up another to sit facing her. He took her hands in his and told her everything. As he talked, Mary Kate felt a myriad of emotions wash over her—disbelief, horror, despair, shock. She couldn't separate one feeling from the other. They all seemed to collide at once.

When Andrew had finished, Mary Kate rose from the chair in a daze. "It's not true. It can't be." She turned pleading eyes on him. "Tell me it isn't true."

"I'm sorry, Mary Kate. I wish I could."

Tears began to stream down her face, and her body shook with quiet sobs. Andrew stood up and took her in his arms.

"Is there nothing you can do?" she asked, lifting a tear-stained face to him.

Andrew shook his head regretfully. "There is a German scientist, Paul Ehrlich, who is experimenting with chemicals in a therapy called chemotherapy to kill cancer cells, but the research is still too experimental."

"How long until—until she—" Mary Kate couldn't finish the sentence.

"I'm afraid not long," said Andrew. "It could be a few weeks; it could be a few months. The cancer has spread to her lungs."

She pushed him away, suddenly filled with anger. "Why didn't you tell me when Mama first became ill? How could you keep that from me?"

"I'm sorry, Mary Kate. When the radiation therapy appeared to be successful, your mother decided against telling you and Morgan."

"Why?"

"When some people have an illness like this, they are afraid of being pitied and treated differently. A sense of normalcy is important to them. Your mother didn't want the specter of the disease to overshadow her life or the lives of you and your brother."

"You still should have told me," she retorted angrily. "You are my husband!"

"I was your mother's doctor first. I had to defer to her wishes."

Andrew moved to take her in his arms, but she forcefully resisted pounding her fists against his chest and screaming at him, feeling a sense of betrayal. He took the brunt of her anger until it was spent. When he put his arms around her this time, she gave into great wracking sobs and clung to him for support.

"I need to go home," she sobbed. "I need to spend this time with my mother."

"We are all going," said Andrew. "We will leave as soon as possible. I've asked Emily to stay the night. She can watch Ella while you pack. Mary Kate, take comfort in the fact that your mother saw her daughter married and has known her first grandchild."

Mary Kate wiped away her tears and looked up at Andrew. "But she won't know her second."

Andrew looked at her questioningly, and she nodded. He hugged her tighter, struck by the thought that as one life was ending, another was beginning.

CHAPTER FIFTY

The End of a Chapter

Mid-June

Dr. Howard emerged from the bedroom and looked at Ian. "It will be just a short time," he said solemnly. "She wants to see Mary Kate and Morgan."

Andrew squeezed Mary Kate's hand and gave her a smile of support as she struggled to compose herself. Morgan had not taken the news well about his mother's illness and was having great difficulty accepting the inevitable.

"I can't," he said, angrily backing away. "I can't go in there and say goodbye as though Mama were leaving on some damn trip for a couple of days. She's not coming back from this one, Papa." He turned and ran down the hall to the stairs.

Ian looked stricken and was about to start after him, when Andrew stayed him. "I'll talk to Morgan."

Ian nodded. He didn't want to leave his wife's side, and his own emotions were too close to the surface to be able to deal with his son's anger and denial at the moment.

Andrew looked at Mary Kate.

"I'll be fine," she said. "Go see to Morgan."

She took a deep breath and squared her shoulders, then opened the door and walked into the bedroom. Her mother lay propped up against pillows. She looked pale and fragile and her breathing was labored, but there was an aura of serenity about her.

Eleanor smiled. "Come sit."

Mary Kate sat down on the chair next to the bed and took her mother's hand.

"I am so happy that we found each other," said Eleanor, her voice weak. "I am proud that you are my daughter."

Mary Kate smiled, blinking back tears. "I am proud of you, too, Mama. Who knew you would end up being an anarchist."

"Times are changing," said Eleanor with a light laugh. "Let Ella and the child you are carrying and any other future grandchildren know that their grandmother was a modern woman."

"You may count on it, Mama."

Eleanor became solemn then. "Morgan is having a difficult time right now, but he is young and has his life ahead of him. And he has Annie and his engines and his motorbikes. He will be fine. But your father—your father has a hard time accepting the losses. He has suffered so many and each one has left its imprint on him. Promise me you that won't let him grieve too long."

"We'll take care of Papa. Don't worry," said Morgan, quietly entering the room. He walked over to the other side of the bed and kissed his mother on the cheek. "I love you, Mama," he murmured, choking back a sob.

Eleanor reached for her children's hands and closed her eyes for a moment, her strength waning. "I think it is time for your father to return," she said.

Her daughter and son hugged her and gave her one last kiss.

"Mary Kate," said Eleanor, her voice a whisper, "never doubt yourself. You are a good mother."

Mary Kate smiled. "So are you, Mama."

CHAPTER FIFTY-ONE

Lost

Ian walked slowly through the eerie quiet of the Catholic cemetery, pausing to touch the headstones of his parents and sister Katherine. Sweet and bitter memories assailed him. He moved on to Tommy's grave and was immediately engulfed in sadness and guilt that he had not had the chance to make peace with his childhood friend. Ian didn't often come here. It was a part of his life that had always been too painful to remember but, lately, he felt the need to connect more with the past.

After a half hour, he got into his car and drove to the cemetery on the hill. He walked over to where Parker was laid to rest. Ian could still hear him dispensing advice, and he smiled wistfully. His old friend and partner had been gone for nearly two years, and Ian missed him greatly. Without Parker, he felt directionless. He knew that he had the support of Andrew and Patrick, but it wasn't the same. The history wasn't there.

Twenty feet away lay Eleanor. The angel atop her stone monument stood vigilant. Ian stooped down and placed yellow roses upon the grave. He put his hand over her name that was engraved in the stone, hoping to feel her presence. Time will heal the pain everyone had told him. But he knew from experience that it didn't. Time only dulled the pain if one was lucky.

Mary Kate allowed her father to mourn for a month before stepping in to honor her mother's wishes. To accomplish her task, she enlisted Abigail, and they shamelessly conspired to use the grandchildren to draw Ian out of his grief.

On this day, Mary Kate handed little Tommy a book. "You and Ella take this to Grandpa and ask him to read you a story," she said.

"Take Ella's hand," his mother instructed him. Abigail partially opened the door to the study and quietly nudged the toddlers inside.

Tommy and Ella performed flawlessly, and their mothers exchanged pleased smiles as they watched Ian take the children on his lap and begin to read to them. Ella popped her thumb in her mouth and Tommy twirled his hair, sure signs of contentment, as they nestled against Ian's chest and listened to the story.

Twenty minutes later, Ian emerged from the study smiling and carrying a child in each arm. "Do you suppose ye can find some ice cream for these two?" he asked.

"I-cream," repeated Tommy excitedly.

"Yeah," said Ella, pulling her thumb out of her mouth.

Ian handed the children over to their mothers. "I think I'll go to the office for awhile."

It was the first time he had gone to the office since Eleanor had died, and Mary Kate and Abigail exchanged conspiratorial smiles.

"Don't think I don't know what you two were up to," Ian lightly chided them.

Mary Kate regarded him with mock surprise. "Whatever are you talking about, Papa?"

Ian shook his head. "Using your children like that…you should be ashamed."

"We admit nothing," said Abigail with a twinkle in her eye.

"You are obviously the wife of a lawyer," quipped Ian.

Mary Kate laughed and kissed her father on the cheek. "Have a good day, Papa."

Over the weeks, Mary Kate continued to see improvement in him, and she and Abigail were not above employing the children when needed. Her father's friendship with Maven also seemed to bring a level of comfort and healing, she noted, their shared experiences and losses giving them a special understanding of each other's pain.

Gradually, Ian started to take more of an interest in business affairs and the outside world again. Although, he had moved back to his own room, Mary Kate often found him sitting in her mother's bedroom with a picture of her in his hand adrift in memories. But he seemed less lost. And by September, Mary Kate felt comfortable enough to return to her home with Ella to await the birth of her second child.

CHAPTER FIFTY-TWO

Driving Miss Lizzie

1910

The year started out momentous with the birth of another little "suffragette" to Mary Kate and Andrew—Susan Elizabeth. Andrew was gratified to find that the doctor had been right. With each birth, it was a little easier, and he weathered the second event much better than he had the first.

Morgan was finishing his third year in college and proved to be a much more attentive and enthusiastic student than he had been in high school.

Ian went to the office every day, but emotionally it was still a battle for him to push past the moment when everything had turned dark for him. The evenings were the most difficult, and he found himself going more and more to the men's club. With Morgan being away at school most of the time, the house felt bigger and emptier than ever before. He usually visited Mary Kate and the grandchildren in New York once a month. Other times, he joined Maven and Annie at Patrick and Abigail's house for Sunday dinner, where he looked forward to playing with little Tommy.

It was the first week of May, and Ian was marking one more day, when a perturbed Maven marched into his office with an astonishing request.

Ian blinked in surprise. "Come again," he said. He couldn't believe that he had heard her correctly.

"I wish ye to teach me to drive," she repeated.

Ian leaned back in his chair bemused. "What occasions this? I remember the day when ye would nae ride in a motorcar."

Maven gave an indignant huff. "Horace Biederman raised the trolley rates, and I'll not give that man one penny more. I would ask Morgan to teach me, but he will not be home from college for another month. And Patrick is busy with some case. He suggested that I ask you."

"Punting the ball, ay?"

"What?"

"Nothing. I suppose I could find some time to instruct ye," replied Ian not overly enthused.

"Good. When can we start?"

"Parker's car is a sports model that will be too difficult for ye to drive. I would suggest that ye trade it in for a Ford Model T first. The Bailey brothers be expectin' a delivery of the cars in a few days. I can make the transaction for ye?"

Maven considered his suggestion for a minute and nodded. "If ye think it best."

"I'll call and reserve a car," said Ian. "Once word gets out that the shipment is here, the motorcars will sell out quickly."

* * * * *

Saturday morning, Ian rose and quickly dressed. Maven's new car had arrived and had been delivered to her. Today was to be her first driving lesson. He looked at his pocket watch. With Maven, being late wasn't an option.

When he pulled up in front of the neat two-story house, he saw that she was already sitting in her car impatiently awaiting him. He got out of his vehicle and walked up to her.

"Ye're late, Ian Douglas," she greeted him.

"Sorry. I got a bit of a late start. Ye bein' look as fresh as the mornin' dew."

"And ye be full of blarney. Now, how does this contraption work?"

Ian smiled. That was Maven—ever practical and to the point.

"Well, there be a few things ye need to learn before ye can take to the streets," he said. "The first thing is to get Lizzie started."

"Lizzie—for heaven's sake, Ian, you named this machine?"

"Not me. She has come to be called the Tin Lizzie or just plain Lizzie. And, as Morgan is always tellin' me, even machines deserve respect."

"Then why has she not been given a nicer color than black?" questioned Maven.

"It keeps the price lower," he started to explain, then stopped. "Let's stay focused on the important things," he said, beginning to see that this was not going to be easy. "Now to start, ye have to crank her. The crank be in the front just below the radiator—"

"Yes, I know. 'Tis that thing hangin' down. I saw Parker crank his car many times," she interjected impatiently. "What else?"

"Well, ye must remember that all the levers must be in their proper positions before crankin', that is in the retard position," Ian went on, "or ye could be seriously injured. Carelessness has resulted in broken arms."

"So, our Tin Lizzie is cranky," quipped Maven.

Ian glanced at her. "Those three pedals and these levers all have a purpose. Pay attention. 'Tis important."

Maven sighed and became more attentive. But, as he painstakingly described the use of every component and its interaction, she was getting fidgety.

"Can we go now, Ian? I know all about the pedals and levers. The rest I can learn as we go."

Ian snorted. Women had no appreciation for the beauty of a machine. He cranked the car and climbed into the passenger side. Trying to remember all of his many instructions, Maven jerkily pulled onto the road.

"Turn right at the next street," he said. "We'll travel the less congested streets until ye have a better feel for the car."

"Really, Ian, ye worry too much."

The car jerked and sputtered along for several feet before Maven got the hang of it. She turned right onto the street as Ian had instructed and picked up speed. When she narrowly missed a tree, Ian was beginning to question his judgment in letting her behind the wheel.

He suddenly gripped his seat tighter and turned pale when he spied an older man slowly starting across the street. "Maven, slow down...SLOW DOWN! You are goin' to hit Mr. Ertel!"

"I cannot remember which pedal to press," she cried, flustered.

"Never mind! Use the horn!" shouted Ian.

Maven squeezed the bulb horn that made a loud aahhoogaa sound, and the pedestrian looked up at the commotion. He stopped in the middle of the street when he saw the car barreling toward him at 20 miles an hour. Maven sounded the horn again, and the man sprinted back to the side as they sailed past.

Ian looked back to see Mr. Ertel shouting at them, angrily waving his cane in the air, and made a mental note to send a gift of penitence. The old man was known to like his whiskey and cigars.

"Do ye suppose we could avoid hittin' pedestrians?" Ian asked facetiously.

"Well, he should have looked before crossin' the road," retorted Maven.

Ian was about to debate the matter further but decided it was better not to distract her, and he struggled to calm himself. As they drove on a few more miles without incident, moving along at a slow, even pace, he relaxed more.

"We are comin' up on Shepherd's Hill," he said "'Tis nae steep, but apply the brakes when ye start down."

"I have everythin' under control," she assured him.

She mistakenly pushed the throttle lever, and Lizzie leaped forward with more speed.

"Maven, slow down!" shouted Ian as they started down the hill. "Press the brake!" The clanging of the trolley suddenly penetrated the air. "Speed up! Push the throttle!"

"Make up your mind. Speed up, slow down. Slow down, speed up. Which is it?" she yelled back.

"We are comin' to the tracks at the bottom. The trolley car will be upon us."

Grasping the gravity of the situation, Maven shoved the throttle full tilt, and they cleared the track with just minutes to spare. Ian let out a gasp of relief, his heart pounding, as the trolley rattled past behind them. His first thought was that Horace had come close to getting his revenge after all.

"Well, that was...invigoratin'," remarked Maven, taking a deep breath to catch her breath.

"Invigoratin'!" exclaimed Ian. "Ye almost got us killed!"

"How can ye be expectin' me to think when ye're barkin' orders?" she retorted.

Ian glared at her and declared the lesson over.

But Maven stood firm. "Would ye be sayin' the same to Morgan?" she questioned stoutly.

"Men understand machines," he retorted. "Women don't and should nae be operatin' one."

Maven bristled. "Perhaps it is the fault of the instructor."

Ian glared at her again. "I do nae think so."

"Well then, Mr. Douglas, do ye know how best to use a washin' machine or a sewin' machine?"

"A washin' machine and a sewin' machine do nae kill due to the incompetence of the operator."

"Tell that to the women and children workin' in the factories. Competence comes with learnin', Ian. And the best way to learn is through practice."

Ian had no counter to that, and he heaved a sigh of exasperation. He should know better than to argue with her. Grudgingly, he relented, but, for the rest of the lesson, he steered Maven onto a country road where, aside from her nearly hitting a cow, the drive was uneventful.

When they returned to the house, Maven hopped spritely out of the car. "Well, I believe that went well."

Ian stepped out of the car with a slower, stiffer gait. "Aye—if one does nae count nearly runnin' down an old man and a cow and almost bein' hit by a trolley car," he grumbled to himself.

"When is the next lesson?" asked Maven.

She gazed up at him. Her green eyes glowed with excitement, her cheeks were rosy, her hat was askew, and her auburn hair had come loose from its pins. In that moment, he was harkened back to the Basin and the memory of a 16-year-old Maven.

"Ian?"

He snapped himself back to the present. "What?"

"When is our next lesson?" Maven asked again. "How about tomorrow?"

"Tomorrow?" He took a deep breath. It didn't leave him much time to recover from this lesson.

"We will meet after church," she decided. "Would you like to come in for a cup of tea?"

Ian declined. He needed something stronger than tea.

"All right, then. I'll be seein' ye tomorrow," she said.

He nodded and gave her a fixed smile. "God help Rossburg," he murmured.

CHAPTER FIFTY-THREE

Just a Matter of Business

"Mr. Douglas, Mr. O'Brien is asking to see you. He doesn't have an appointment."

Ian looked up at his secretary. "Mr. Struthers, place this reminder in your notes—Mr. O'Brien never needs an appointment. I regard him as family."

"But, sir, the mayor will be here soon."

"The mayor can wait a few minutes. Please show Mr. O'Brien in."

Patrick entered the office. "Thank you for seeing me, Ian. I know you are a busy man."

"I always have time for family, Patrick. Have a seat. Judgin' by the expression on your face, this nae be a social visit. Are Abigail and Tommy all right?"

"Yes, they're fine. It's Mother," said Patrick, sitting down in a chair. "She won't listen to me. Maybe she'll listen to you."

Ian's brow furrowed in concern. "What is the problem?"

"The school is running out of capital."

"'Tis impossible. With the money Eleanor left, the school should be well funded."

"Normally it would be. But you know these are not normal times. Because of the financial panic of '07 and the resulting recession that has gripped the country for the past two and a half years, fewer students are able to pay. And you know Mother. She can't turn anyone away. She's the only one who stands between these young women and the streets. More and more show up at the school every day."

"What about the reserves?"

"She ran through that money and is well into the money Parker left her. I tried to give her funds, but she won't hear of it. I'm hoping you can talk some sense into her. She's thinking about selling her house and moving into a rental lodging."

"I'll talk to her," said Ian. "Perhaps I can convince her to sell her car instead," he added with a wry smile. "Agreein' to teach your mother to drive was not one of my best decisions. Every time she takes the wheel, the residents of Rossburg have cause to fear for their lives. Maybe they should know they have Horace Biederman to blame for it."

Patrick chuckled. "Mother is not shy about using her horn."

"Hopefully, I can make her see reason in garagin' the car for the winter."

"Hope springs eternal," said Patrick. "You know Mother. She is not easily convinced about anything."

After his meeting with the mayor, Ian drove to the school. He walked purposefully into Maven's office at the school and shut the door.

Maven looked up from the ledger into which she had been entering expenses. "Ian, what are you doing here?" she asked in surprise.

"I understand the school is short of capital. Why did ye nae tell me that you needed money?"

Maven frowned. "Patrick told you. He shouldn't have. 'Tis just temporary."

"This recession could go on for another year. How much do ye need?"

"I'll not take your money, Ian," she said, her tone resolute.

"Now is nae the time to let your pride get in the way, Maven. Patrick said ye have run through the reserves and the money Eleanor left the school and that ye now be into the money Parker left ye."

"Patrick should mind his own business."

Ian pulled up a chair and sat down. "This school was important to Eleanor, and she was proud of it. Ye both worked too hard to bring it about only to lose it now. It matters what ye do here, Maven."

"I cannot take money from you or Patrick, Ian. I will find a way," she replied, her features set in a stubborn line.

Ian let out a sigh of exasperation. "What choice do ye have? Houses are nae sellin' in this economy. Of course, ye could sell your car," he slipped in casually. "Even in these times, the Model Ts are sellin' as they come off the line."

Maven's eyes widened with alarm at the suggestion. "Well, I am sure there be somethin' else I can do."

"Perhaps there is. Ye can hold a fundraiser."

"Oh, I don't know about that, Ian. That was Eleanor's area of expertise. I'm not very good at askin' people for contributions. Besides, as ye said, no one has any money."

"There are a few who still do, and I know who they are. We can arrange a two-day Christmas gala event. People are usually more charitable at that time of the year. I can talk to the manager of the theater about offerin' a benefit presentation of Charles Dickens' story, *A Christmas Carol*, and then we can follow up with a ball at the house the next evenin'. There are so few balls given these days that people will be scramblin' to attend."

"Ian, I cannot ask ye to do that."

"You are nae askin'. I am offerin'. Eleanor believed very much in this school. Ye've already given many women the chance to have a say in their lives, but there be many more in need of it. Ye can nae stop now."

Maven looked at him. "You are right," she said with a spark of determination. "We shall hold a fundraisin' event. But, Ian, is four months enough time to plan?"

Ian shrugged. "You and Eleanor managed to put together Mary Katherine's wedding in seven months. I'm sure you and I can pull off a fundraiser in four."

Maven laughed. "Well, the fundraiser would be a good deal less challengin'."

"How about lunch at the Carleton House to discuss the details?"

Again, Maven hesitated. "What will people think?"

"'Tis business. Besides, since when do you care about what people think?"

She stood up and reached for her hat. "I'll drive," she said.

"No, I will drive—in the interest of keepin' the people of Rossburg safe," said Ian.

Maven let out a huff of annoyance. "Ye sound like Patrick."

She was still registering her indignation as he firmly guided her to his car and handed her in.

CHAPTER FIFTY-FOUR

A Clean Slate

As Ian had predicted, the elite who still had resources in place were eager to attend the two-day fundraising event being held a week from Christmas. It had never been done before, but Ian brazenly decided to charge prospective donors a fee just to register for the gala. A few had grumbled, but all had rushed to secure a spot on the invitation list.

The theater presentation of *A Christmas Carol* was a huge success. And now this night, the Douglas mansion was once again alive with the sights and sounds and the energy and excitement of a grand ball. And flush with holiday cheer and fine champagne, guests were proving to be generous without too much encouragement.

Maven gazed about her in amazement.

"Might I have this dance, Mrs. Stanton?" asked Ian. He didn't wait for her to answer before sweeping her onto the dance floor and leading her into a waltz.

Maven looked at him in surprise. "Parker said you didn't know how to dance."

Ian laughed. "I do nae prefer it, and, as usual, Parker made his own assumptions. But as this is for the benefit of the school, I am making an exception. You look beautiful tonight by the way." When Maven blushed and looked away, he smiled. He was happy to see that she hadn't changed much over the years. With Maven there would always be continuity.

She gazed up at him, her green eyes sparkling. "It has been a wonderful gala—both events so well attended. Even the Biedermans are in attendance," she added amusedly. "Horace is here with his new wife."

"Poor woman. Someone should warn her what she has gotten herself into," said Ian. "Ye might be interested to know that Horace and George were among the first to apply for places on the guest list. I made sure they paid double the fee."

Maven laughed merrily. "Eleanor would be pleased. Thank you, Ian. I could not have done this without ye."

"I beg to differ, but it was my pleasure. Mary Katherine has been pesterin' me to socialize more anyway."

"How are Mary Katherine, Andrew, and the children?"

"They be doin' well." Ian chuckled. "I gather Andrew has his hands full. His sister has practically moved in with them. I believe he'll be lookin' for a larger home soon to accommodate all his girls. I hope for his sake the next child is a boy." He glanced over to see Morgan and Annie hiding away in a quiet corner. "What do ye think?" he asked with a nod in their direction. "Might there be an announcement soon to come?"

Maven smiled. "Time will tell." She paused. "You were right, you know."

"About what?"

"Do ye remember the arguments we used to have years ago about acceptin' one's lot in life?"

"Yes. It created quite a divide between us then," recalled Ian. "You said that it was the will of God…that we should accept the hand we were dealt and do the best with it we can."

"And you said that man made his own fate, that God would not have given us brains to think, reasons to dream, or the need to achieve if we were not meant to do so," said Maven. "What ye said at the school that day about how the school was givin' these girls a chance to choose their futures made me realize that perhaps you were the one who was right."

"For what it is worth, you were right as well," said Ian.

Maven looked up at him in surprise. "How so?"

"You once told me that life should nae be about the pursuit of wealth and power...that it can blacken the soul."

Maven was silent for a moment. "I was angry. 'Tis not you, Ian."

"I've done things that I nae be proud of, Maven."

"We all have," she replied.

The music stopped. Ian led her over to a tray of champagne and handed her a glass, reluctant to let the moment end. It felt comfortable being with her.

"I never told you how much I admired how you and Eleanor created this school and challenged the Board of Trade for membership," he said. "There was a time when I worried that you...well that you might end up like the other women in the Basin...the light and life drained out of ye. I should have known ye would find your way."

"I have been very lucky," she said.

"I thought we had just established that luck has nothin' to do with it," responded Ian.

"Perhaps, I should say, then, that good fortune provides one with opportunity," she rephrased.

"That only works if the person is smart enough to recognize opportunity and has the courage and will to act upon it."

Maven burst into the light musical laughter he had always found so enchanting. It had been a long time since he had heard her laugh like that. "Okay, you win," she said. "I should have remembered that few people win arguments with you."

"Look at the pot calling the kettle black," said Ian. "A more stubborn woman I have yet to know. The difference between you and me is that I am usually right."

"Ian Douglas," she sputtered, "the years have not tamed your arrogance one bit it would seem."

"Nor your temper," he shot back. "And I remember many a time when it got ye into trouble." He smiled. "There were a few good times we had back then, ay?"

Maven nodded. "Aye...more than a few."

Ian became pensive. "There was a time I could nae bear to think about them. Now, I take some comfort in them." He looked at her. "Ye once told me that I had pushed ye away. You were right. I was afraid that ye would pull me back to the Basin, and I could nae go back there. I had to be as far away from it as I could. All that I saw in that place was death and sorrow."

"I know," she replied softly. "I came to understand that."

He gave a humorless laugh. "The irony of it was that, with all the turmoil between Eleanor and me at the time, I could nae let go of it...of you...until ye forced me to see the truth of things and how much pain I was causin' ye." Ian looked into her eyes. "I'm so sorry that I hurt ye, Maven. I shall always bear the shame and guilt of that."

"No, Ian, I do not want you to. Life is about makin' mistakes, learnin' from them, and movin' on. I've moved past that point a long time ago, and so have our children. There is no reason for you not to as well. This is a new time, a new age, and we are wiser people. Clean slate?"

Ian nodded. "Clean slate."

She pretended to spit on her hand and extended it, as they had done when they were kids to seal a pact.

Ian grinned and followed suit, joining his hand with hers. "As I remember it, the spit is supposed to be real."

"My pact, my rules," she said. "Oh, I see Mrs. Grayson. Please excuse me, Ian. I must have a word with her."

"Of course. Another dance later?"

"Perhaps."

As she crossed the room, Ian watched the statuesque figure stroll gracefully, confidently across the floor.

CHAPTER FIFTY-FIVE

The Tapestry of Life

The Christmas holidays had come and gone, and, since the ball, Ian found himself becoming more and more introspective. He hadn't seen much of Maven. They both seemed to be going in opposite directions.

This day, he was feeling more introspective than usual, and he found himself wandering by Maven's dress shop. He stopped. It had changed little over the years. Sandwiched between larger, more modern buildings, the shop retained the charm of yesterday while still fitting into its more contemporary surroundings. That was the wonder of Maven. She had a way of marrying the past with the present and making it feel comfortable. He opened the door and walked inside. There were two young women straightening up the store.

"May I help you?" asked one.

"Is Mrs. Stanton here?"

"I'm sorry, sir," responded the other. "She is gone for a little while. You might find her at the school. Do you wish to leave a message for her?"

Ian smiled, hard pressed to hide his disappointment. He knew she spent most of her time at the school and hadn't really expected her to be here. He had just hoped. "Tell her that—never mind," he said. "I will see her at another time. Thank you."

A short while after Ian had left, Maven returned to the shop.

"Mrs. Stanton, a gentleman was just here to see you," said one of her assistants.

"A gentleman...who?" asked Maven. She couldn't imagine any man walking into a woman's dress shop.

"He was an older gentleman...quite dashing...with a Scottish accent."

Maven looked at her assistant in surprise. "Mr. Douglas?"

"He didn't say his name."

"Did he say what he wanted?"

"No, ma'am, but he said he would see you at another time."

"Oh," said Maven, a bit perplexed. "Well, you girls may leave now. I'll close up."

Her assistants left, and Maven tied up a few loose ends and closed the shop. When she opened the door to leave, she ran into Ian.

"I missed you earlier," he said. "Your assistant told me ye would be comin' back. I took a chance that ye might have returned."

"Aye, the girls told me that you were here. Is somethin' wrong?"

"Not unless you say 'no.'"

Maven looked at him in bewilderment. "I beg your pardon?"

"It has come to me that the money raised at the Christmas gala will nae sustain ye forever, now that ye be expandin' your services. We need to discuss more fundraisin' events—over dinner."

Maven was taken aback. "Tonight?"

"Aye, I believe that was my intent."

"Oh. Well, I don't know. 'Tis awfully short notice. Annie is—"

"Out with Morgan. It is his last night before he returns to school. And if ye would put in a telephone, I could have called to give ye more notice."

"As well as everyone else in town," she retorted. "All right, since it is for the school, I suppose I cannot refuse. But I need to freshen up."

"I'll pick you up in one hour at your house. I'll drive," said Ian, reading her next thought.

She gave a sigh of exasperation. "Honestly, I fail to understand why men always think they should be the ones to do the drivin'."

Ian refrained from remarking that men generally preferred to arrive at their destinations in one piece.

When Ian arrived at seven o'clock to pick her up, Maven was ready and waiting. Ian had to smile. Eleanor had rarely been on time for anything. Fashionably late, she had called it. As he handed Maven into the car, she was already laying out some ideas she had for the fundraising—as always, to the point.

At the restaurant, they slipped easily into conversation. They talked, they debated, they reminisced, and they laughed as the years fell away and the sorrows and difficult times faded far into the background of comfortable memories.

"Papa?"

"Mother?"

Maven and Ian looked up to see Morgan and Annie staring down at them in surprise.

"Oh, Annie…and Morgan. I didna expect to see you here," said Maven. "Mr. Douglas and I are discussin' fundraisin' events for the school."

Morgan looked at his father. He was more relaxed and engaged than Morgan had seen him since his mother had died. In fact, he hadn't seen his father smile and laugh like that for a long time. Mrs. Stanton and his father didn't look like they were discussing fundraising events.

"Why don't ye join us?" offered Ian.

"No, thank you," said Morgan. "We were just leaving when we noticed you. We're joining some friends at the theater."

"Have a nice evening," said Maven.

Morgan and Annie glanced quizzically at each other as they left the restaurant, then shrugged off the encounter as their thoughts turned to the evening ahead of them.

* * * * *

As the weeks passed, Ian found reasons to stop by the school more often—to check the electricity hookups or the telephone station or to help with maintenance on the building. Sometimes he succeeded in talking Maven into lunch or a late dinner. Maven welcomed his help and looked forward to his visits. She didn't find anything strange in them. The school was Eleanor's legacy, and Ian was helping to preserve it.

In March, Morgan and Annie announced their engagement. Patrick and Abigail held a reception for the young couple in their home on Grandview Place. It was a lively time with plenty of food and dancing. The older folks weighed in with the occasional waltz that was mixed in with quick time mazurkas and cake walks for the young people.

As nightfall descended, Maven slipped outside to get some air and catch a moment to herself.

"It would seem that we think alike," said Ian, joining her.

Maven smiled. "It is a bit loud in there. I don't know how little Tommy can sleep."

"I hope ye nae be plannin' to drive home after the party. Shall I give ye a lift?"

"No, thank you. Annie and I be spendin' the night here. Patrick insisted. He threatened to disable the car if I didn't."

Ian chuckled. "Smart lad. Ye be menacin' enough in the daylight hours. Ye'd be downright dangerous at night. Did you ever figure out how to turn on the running lights?"

"I did," replied Maven indignantly. She turned and looked down over the valley at the twinkling city lights. "It is beautiful up here. And quiet."

"I still have a few choice lots that I control," said Ian, coming to stand beside her. "Ye could have a nice little house up here nearby to Patrick."

"I'll admit the offer is tempting," replied Maven. "But I need to stay close to the shop and the school."

"How are things at the school? Do we need to be plannin' another fundraisin' event?"

Maven laughed. "I think we have picked all the pockets clean. Another fundraiser may see us run out of town on a rail."

"If I've learned anythin' about the rich, they always have another pocket to pick in spite of their protests," said Ian.

"I think we can give their pockets a rest for now," Maven assured him. "The recession is windin' down, and there be more payin' students. But perhaps later. Those seekin' to escape the factories continue to increase in number. That is such a horrible life." She turned and looked up at him. "It must have been terrible for you and Tommy workin' in the sawmill."

"Poor workin' conditions give one a strong incentive to strive for somethin' better," replied Ian.

They fell silent for a few minutes, each preoccupied with his own thoughts.

Maven was the first to stir. "The air is turnin' colder," she said with a shiver. "I should go back inside now."

Ian put a hand on her arm. "Wait…please. Do nae go in yet. I want to talk with ye about a matter." He took off his coat and placed it around her shoulders and led her to the settee. "Maven, I've been doin' a lot of thinkin' lately," he said, as they seated themselves.

"About what?" she asked.

"Us…what happened in the past."

"Ian, I thought we had agreed to lay that to rest and move on. Clean slate, remember?"

"I am movin' on," he replied. Maven looked at him in puzzlement, and he struggled to explain. "When Parker died and then Eleanor, everythin' changed for me. That world was gone. I did nae feel that I belonged in it anymore. Everythin' I had built no longer had meanin' for me without them. I was goin' through the motions for the sake of Mary Katherine and Morgan."

Ian stopped for a moment to organize his thoughts. "Then you and I began to work together on fundraisers for the school, and my life started to have purpose again. I realized that it was because of you, Maven. The hours we have spent together these past months have been the happiest I've known in a long time. I feel alive again. And I think that it has been the same for you."

"What are ye tryin' to say, Ian?" she asked guardedly.

He took hold of her hand. "I want us to be more than friends."

Maven pulled her hand away. "Ian, don't. We had this conversation before years ago. I cannot have it again."

"It is different this time, Maven. Our paths have intersected. We are both in the same place now. We want the same things. I'm not that young, insecure man anymore tryin' to escape the Basin. I know the difference between needin' ye for selfish reasons and lovin' ye with my whole heart."

Maven angrily jumped to her feet. "We cannot be together, Ian. We can only be friends." She threw off his coat and fled into the house.

She quickly crossed the foyer and was starting up the stairs, when Annie stopped her. "Mother, are you all right?" she asked, concerned. "You look upset."

Maven forced a smile. "It has been a long day. Tell Abigail and Patrick that I have retired for the night."

Shortly after Annie relayed Maven's message, Ian made his farewells. "I seem to have upset your mother," he said to Patrick, his manner stiff and troubled. "Please convey to her my regrets and apology."

As he departed, Abigail looked questioningly at her husband. "What do you suppose that was about?"

"I'm not sure," said Patrick. "But if I had to guess, I would say that Ian and Mother's past is catching up with them."

CHAPTER FIFTY-SIX

More Than Friendship

Children scampered about the Douglas estate looking for hidden treasures at the annual Easter egg hunt for the families of Ian's employees. Mary Kate and Abigail supervised the event, while Annie and Morgan supervised the kids. Andrew stood on the sidelines talking with Patrick and encouraging 15-month-old Susan. Three-year-old Ella and four-year-old Tommy didn't need any encouragement. Ian hadn't felt much like holding the holiday event this year. But as he watched the excitement of the children and heard their laughter, he was glad that Mary Kate had pushed him into it.

His eyes searched the grounds for Maven. At one point, he found her helping Annie and Morgan corral the kids for the egg hunt and tried to talk with her then, but she said she was needed elsewhere and hurried off.

He hadn't seen her since Annie and Morgan's engagement party the previous month. She would send word through Annie that she was too busy to meet with him whenever he dropped by the school, and she was never at home to him when he came by her house. It was clear that she was avoiding him.

Maven was furious with Ian for acknowledging his feelings for her. Until then, she could tell herself that what they felt for each other was nothing more than a friendship that had become closer with the death of their spouses. Now that he had spoken those words, it unleashed a torrent of emotions in her that she had thought she had buried a long time ago. How dare he resurrect them now that she had made peace with herself, with her life!

She tried to beg off the event today, but Annie and Abigail refused to let her. The more distance she tried to put between her and Ian, the more events conspired to draw them together. Now, Annie and Morgan were going to be married. How was she ever going to distance herself from Ian as their families became more interlinked?

Ian came upon her sitting on a secluded bench under a shade tree and quietly sat down beside her. She didn't move or say anything, and she trained her eyes on a distant point.

"Remember when we sat on this very bench over 20 years ago?" he asked.

"Aye. I told ye then there could never be another time for us."

"And I told you that life is unpredictable."

"Ian, please—"

"Let me finish, Maven. When ye found new love with Parker and I found love with Eleanor and we both found new purpose, I thought that this...this connection between us had been severed. But when we started to work together on the fundraisers, I felt it again...pulling us back together. I think ye have felt it, too."

"We have drawn closer together in friendship, Ian. That is all. Our day was done a long time ago. We found love and happiness with other people. Eleanor was my friend, and Parker and Tommy were yours. We must respect that. And we have children to consider. We lost Mary Katherine and Patrick once. I'll not chance losin' them again." She stood up, tears welling in her eyes. "There can be nothin' more than friendship between us, Ian. Please, let us not talk of this again, or we may not be able to claim even that."

As she walked away, Ian felt the weight of yet another loss. But Maven was right. They couldn't risk losing their children again, and how could he betray the memory of people so close to his heart?

* * * * *

Mary Kate and the children had remained in Rossburg for another three weeks for the dedication. At Maven's suggestion, the school was being renamed the Eleanor Douglas Institute for Women, and much of the town turned out for the event. Maven gave the dedication address—a beautiful memorial from the heart. No one could guess that she was fighting a tumult of emotions.

When she finished, Mary Kate took her place at the podium to pay tribute to her mother and to Maven for their efforts to better the lives of women. It was at times a humorous remembrance as she recalled her mother's visit to the New York City police headquarters to secure the release of jailed suffragettes, as well as other incidences. And it served to keep the mood light.

It was afterwards at the reception that Mary Kate first noticed the strange interaction between her father and Maven. They were cordial, but their conversation was strained, and they clearly weren't comfortable in each other's company. She wondered if it had anything to do with the noticeable change in his demeanor at home.

Morgan had said that their father had found new life in assuming their mother's fundraising role for the school. But when she, Andrew, and the children had arrived for the Easter holiday, she didn't see that spark of enthusiasm in him. Ian had put on a good face and denied that anything was wrong, and Mary Kate had attributed his solemn manner to the approaching anniversary of her mother's death.

But after the Easter egg hunt, it had become obvious to Mary Kate that there was something more. Her father had played and joked with the children, but he was absent from the moments, and there was an air of sad resignation about him. He was going through the motions again. She had questioned Morgan about it, but he was oblivious to anything other than Annie and his motors. Andrew had said that she was over-thinking things.

Now, as she watched her father and Maven at the school dedication reception, she knew that she wasn't over-thinking anything. They didn't even act like the old friends that they were. After considering the matter for a few days, she left the children in Abigail's care and went into town.

The flustered secretary entered Patrick's office. "Mr. O'Brien, there is a very determined young woman demanding to see you, and she doesn't have an appointment."

Patrick laughed. He knew who it was without even asking. "Show her in. She's family," he explained. "Her brother is marrying Annie."

"Oh," said the secretary. He turned and nearly crashed into Mary Kate who had become too impatient to wait any longer. "Pardon me, madam," he said, quickly sidestepping her.

Patrick stood up and closed the door. "Home for a month and already intimidating my staff."

Mary Kate made a face at him and dropped into a chair. "When are you going to hire a female secretary?"

"When Henry retires. He served Parker for over 20 years. I can't just boot him out. Besides that, he is valuable to me as a researcher. Now, what has you in such a good mood?"

"There is something wrong between your mother and my father," she said. "It seems to have started a month ago."

"I know," responded Patrick retaking his seat. "And it didn't just start last month. What you are seeing is the latest reaction to a chain of events that started when I told your father that the school was in financial trouble."

"Is the school still in trouble?" she asked, concerned.

"No. And the truth of it is that it wasn't quite the emergency I represented then either."

Mary Kate looked at him in bewilderment. "I don't understand."

"I wanted to see if your mother was right."

"About what? Patrick, you are not in a courtroom. Just give it to me plain. Morgan said that when Papa took over my mother's fundraising role, he hadn't been so happy or engaged since Mama died. Now, all of a sudden he isn't. He's miserable. What happened?"

"Two many ghosts," replied Patrick.

"You are talking gibberish again. What's that supposed to mean?"

Patrick took out the bottle of whiskey and glasses and poured drinks for them.

"Isn't it a little early in the day?" she questioned with an arched brow.

"Trust me. You are going to want it," he said, handing a glass to her.

She looked at him in sudden alarm. "This is how Andrew began when he told me that my mother was dying. Is something wrong with my father?"

"No, nothing like that."

Mary Kate relaxed. "What is it then?"

Patrick told her about Eleanor's visit to him before her death, then showed Mary Kate the letters her mother had left behind.

When Mary Kate had finished reading them, she took a healthy swig of her drink and sat in silence for a few minutes, dazed. "Mama knew she was dying then," she murmured aloud.

Patrick nodded. "She left it to the three of us to decide when or if these letters are delivered. I think you know my decision."

Mary Kate nodded. "I'll speak with Morgan. He still hasn't been told about you and Papa. How do you want to handle that?"

"Our families have seen enough drama," replied Patrick. "Let's leave things the way they are."

"If you think it best." Mary Kate became pensive then. "I think Mama always knew," she said at length.

"Knew what?" asked Patrick.

"That the story had to end this way."

CHAPTER FIFTY-SEVEN

Full Circle

Ian descended the stairs and was about to go into the study when the housekeeper approached him.

"This letter just come for you, sir."

Ian took the letter, surprised. "Who is it from? The postman does nae deliver on Saturdays."

"Mr. O'Brien brought it by, sir."

"Patrick? Is he here?"

"No, sir. He said he would see you later."

"Thank you, Mrs. Hardesty." Ian walked into the study, perplexed, and opened the envelope. When he unfolded the letter, he was shocked to see that it was in Eleanor's handwriting and even more shocked when he read it.

My dearest, darling Husband,

We traveled a long and wondrous journey together. We had our ups and downs, the trials mostly due to our own faults. We had lessons to learn. Thanks to Maven, we learned them in time to find the love and happiness with each other that neither of us had thought possible. Though my journey there has come to an end, yours yet continues. I have come to believe that for a moment to be right in life, it must be right in time. The time is right now for you and Maven to be together, and I encourage you with a glad heart to finish your journey with her. It is meant to be.

Eternally,
Eleanor

Ian sat down in a chair and reread the letter, his hands shaking. He had no idea how or what to feel.

"Papa."

He looked up to see that Morgan and Mary Kate had entered the room.

"Papa, we want to speak with you," said Mary Kate.

* * * * *

Maven hurried into the parlor and picked up her hat, ready to leave for the market, when she saw the letter on the table. Funny, she hadn't noticed it there before. She opened the envelope and unfolded the letter, slowly sinking into a chair in disbelief as she read it.

My dear Maven,

I have come to believe that we get who and what we deserve in life. Years ago, Ian and I were angry, selfish people. We deserved each other then, and we suffered those years for our shortcomings. Unfortunately, regrettably, so were you hurt.

Still, when Ian and I thought that all was lost between us, you showed us the way to a new beginning, a second chance that resulted in a full, rich, and immeasurably happy life for us. Words cannot express my gratitude to you. But that life is done now. The Bible tells us that to everything there is a season and a time to every purpose. This season, this time belongs to you and Ian, and I give you both my blessing to embrace it.

Your good friend,
Eleanor

Maven looked up stunned and overwhelmed with feelings that she couldn't begin to describe. She noticed Patrick standing in the doorway.

"Did you know about this?" she asked in a tremulous voice.

Patrick nodded. "A few months before her death, Mrs. Douglas came to my office to take care of her legal affairs. She gave me this letter, asked me to read it, and, with Mary Kate and Morgan's approval, to deliver it to you at our discretion. I just delivered a similar letter to Ian."

Maven put a hand to her mouth, fighting back tears and struggling to compose herself as every emotion she had fought so long and hard to bury burst through to the surface.

She looked so conflicted Patrick walked over to her. He stooped down in front of her and took her hands in his. "Mother, it is all right if you and Ian want to be together," he said. "Mrs. Douglas is right. This is your moment, if you want it. And you have the blessings of Mary Kate, Morgan, and me as well. It is up to you and Ian now."

"But Parker—"

"Parker loved you and Ian best of everyone. He would want you both to be happy. You are always preaching to your students a clean slate, a new chapter, a new life. Take some of your own advice." Patrick stood up and smiled. "If you are ready, there is someone outside waiting for you."

Maven laughed and cried at the same time, wiping tears from her eyes as she hurried to the door.

Outside, Ian nervously paced, wondering what her answer would be. He stopped in his tracks when she appeared on the porch, and he looked questioningly at her, his heart pounding. When Maven smiled and nodded, relief flooded his features and his mouth curved up in a boyish smile. Mary Kate and Morgan stepped forward to give her words of encouragement to dispel any doubts she may have about their support.

Then, Ian came up to her and held out his hand. "Let's take a stroll," he said.

Maven gazed up at him and placed her hand in his without fear, without reservation, their lives at last aligned. As they walked down the street together, their happiness filled the air, and the sun shone a little brighter over the last of the Pine Street Warriors.

Afterword

Ian and Maven married and enjoyed 25 years together. They died within a month of each other.

Mary Kate continued to fight for women's rights after the 19th Amendment was passed until her death at the age of 86. She and Andrew had two daughters and two sons. Due to his experiments with radiation, Andrew died at the age of 56 of cancer. Their daughters were active in the women's movement. Their oldest son took over the reins of the Stoddert shipping line from his paternal grandfather. Their youngest son continued his father's work in the advancement of medical research and technology.

Emily Stoddert remained active in the women's movement until her death at the age of 82. She happily never married.

Morgan Douglas guided Douglas Enterprises into the aeronautical age, becoming an important supplier of engines for fighter planes during the Second World War, and the company continues to this day. He married Annie, and they had three sons who carried on the legacies of their father and grandfather.

Patrick O'Brien went on to become a federal judge. He and Abigail had two sons who became prominent attorney's. The Stanton-O'Brien firm continues to represent Douglas Enterprises. Patrick and Ian enjoyed a close relationship, but the true nature of their bond was never disclosed to anyone outside the circle of Maven, Ian, Patrick, Abigail, Mary Kate and Andrew.

Lily Biederman joined a more radical group of suffragettes in upstate New York after her divorce from Horace. She never remarried.

The *Eleanor Douglas Institute for Women* became incorporated into a liberal arts college. Abigail was the first dean of women's studies and Annie served as chief administrator.

About the Authors

A. J. Billman is a resident of Florida and taught creative writing for several years. She is an award-winning author of short stories.

Kathy Keller is also a resident of Florida and a published author of several fiction novels that encompass the genres of historical romance, historic fiction, and time travel. She has a degree in journalism from The American University, Washington, D.C.

The authors are mother and daughter who grew up in the Williamsport, Pennsylvania area. They teamed up to write the fictional Douglas Saga, which is based on the colorful history of Williamsport spanning the years from the Golden Age of the Lumber Barons to the turn of the 20th Century.

Connect with the authors at http://www.KathyKeller.com

Books by Kathy Keller

The Homeward Heart
A Love Too Proud
Destiny's Shadow
Millionaires' Row (co-author A. J. Billman)
Millionaires' Row: The Legacy (co-author A. J. Billman)
The Paradox
A Little Gentle Persuasion
Lady of the Sea

www.ingramcontent.com/pod-product-compliance
Lightning Source LLC
LaVergne TN
LVHW091528060526
838200LV00036B/525